D1461410

GROWLING
OVER THE
OCEANS

GROWLING OVER THE OCEANS

The Avro Shackleton,
The Men and The Missions
1951-1991

Deborah Lake

Souvenir Press

Dedicated to the men and women of the
world's flying services.
And particularly to Kevin Byron, better known as
'Scrote', once flying on the Old Lady.
As well as the Shackleton teams, air and ground,
who now drink at the great bar in the sky while
other poor souls do Stand-by Crew.

ACKNOWLEDGEMENTS

My thanks also go to the many people who sent photographs; sadly, not all could be used but my gratitude is there for everybody who helped in the creation of this book.

By the same token, I acknowledge the invaluable assistance provided by copies of the Berwickshire News, Flight, the London Times, the New York Times, Sunday Dispatch, Aeroplane, and the official publications, the London Gazette, Hansard and the files of the Associated Press.

CONTENTS

INTRODUCTION

**Group Captain D H A Greenway OBE RAF (Ret'd)
formerly Officer Commanding 8 Squadron and
Deputy Captain of the Queen's Flight**

There were several different marks of Shackleton over the years. Flying in them, we were all involved in a classic anachronism – or a series of anachronisms – that culminated in the Airborne Early Warning version which became the province of Number 8 Squadron.

2009 was the year that marked the sixtieth anniversary of the Shackleton prototype's first flight. I find it amazing but totally understandable that we still remember the beast and continue to reminisce about how wonderful it was. It remained operational for forty years.

Those of us who operated the Shackleton all over the world can be proud of our association with it. We flogged off, often into awful weather, doing ridiculous things, while we were all shaken to death by the vibration and the noise. And remember, we got all this free!

Personally, I was always delighted that I had an excellent bunch of mates in the aircraft with me who all shared the same experiences. Afterwards we could go to the pub or bar and lie about the wonderful time we had gone through. Despite the somewhat 'gung-ho' attitude we must have displayed, we could have done none of it without the wonderful work of our ground crews. They did a fantastic job. Nobody who flew the Shackleton can thank them enough for the outstanding contribution that they made to the Old Lady's success in all the tasks she undertook.

Throughout the Shack years, the rest of the world whizzed around in jet aircraft with no idea of the benefits of a vibrating airframe, leather upholstery or, indeed, of the advantages of self-catering. People fail to realise that the beast was actually designed to fly slowly and for long periods to allow loitering at low level in an operational area so that the crew could monitor submarine, surface vessel and later, air traffic.

Shack flying was about people. My theory is that, because it was so awful, it forced us all to get on as a team and make the thing work. Thus we all got on like a house on fire – and that was why it was really special.

The Shackleton filled my essential pilot's criteria. First, I had no wish to fly an aeroplane you had to climb into through the top. Secondly, I liked to look out of the window and see the things going round. And thirdly, and most important too, I insisted that I flew with a competent NCO – and in the Shack we had an abundance of the latter. They used to refer to their pilots as 'Chauffeurs Electronic', which I suspect we were, especially in the Airborne Early Warning version.

There are many stories about Shackleton people, often amusing, sometimes painful, for military flying often combines the two emotions. You will find some of them in the pages that follow.

PREFACE

This book, a determinedly non-technical volume, deals with the men who flew and serviced the Avro Shackleton, the last aircraft to serve operationally with Coastal Command or, as it was widely known, the Kipper Fleet. Of the 188 aircraft built, a mere eight went for export.

The aeroplane discharged its duties during the Cold War period between the Western Powers and the Eastern Bloc. Much of this book is simply the recollections of those who served, no more, no less. I have written a few sentences but the words really come from those who dedicated their lives to serving their country. A few of the pieces have appeared in low circulation magazines, mainly those published by RAF units, but they bear their repetition very well.

The Shackleton lasted for forty years in the Royal Air Force, finishing in 1991. It visited many countries. Place names used are those current at the time; the modern equivalent is mentioned once only for those that are now different.

The Royal Air Force has much restyled since the Shackleton joined its first squadron in 1951. Coastal Command who ran the Kipper Fleet, those aircraft dedicated to the task of maritime air action, is now a handful of paragraphs in the history books. The Kipper Fleet still exists although it is essentially confined to a single airfield with a scattering of Nimrods.

The men who flew and serviced the Shackleton are no longer young bloods. I simply urge the reader to remember that old men, with the grey thick in their hair, once did quite remarkable actions. This book touches on their story.

CHAPTER ONE

Flight magazine was justifiably proud of its hard-earned reputation as the journal of record for all that mattered in flying. Its journalists sometimes claimed to be on the mailing list of practically any organisation that had any dealings with aviation. In its issue of 17 March 1949, readers of the Service Aviation page found the following:

> The Avro Shackleton, a maritime reconnaissance bomber powered by four Rolls-Royce Griffons made its first flight at Woodford on Wednesday of last week. Mr 'Jimmy' Orrell, Avro's chief test pilot, flew the aircraft, which was in the air for thirty-three minutes.

The magazine sold for one shilling, twelve times more than the price of its first issue in January 1909. It was no stranger either to the Avro Company or its founder, Edwin Alliott Verdon Roe. Both appeared in its columns from its early days as a penny weekly with remarkable frequency. Roe himself, born near Manchester in 1877, had left London's St Paul's School at the age of fifteen. An interest in matters mechanical eventually led him to an early career as a marine engineer. At sea, the rolling waves made way for white clouds for the junior engineer became totally entranced by watching soaring sea birds. When

Roe learned that the Wright Brothers had flown in December 1903, his own thoughts turned towards powered aviation.

After successful experiments with models, one of which collected a whole £75 in a competition, Roe built a full-sized machine. It failed initially but finally flew, much helped by a more powerful engine. Following several self-piloted successful excursions at Brooklands, the inventor claimed, reasonably enough, to be the first Englishman to fly in Britain. Sadly, his claim failed for his efforts were not officially recorded by the Royal Aero Club. The honour went instead to a gentleman aviator, John Theodore Cuthbert Moore-Brabazon. He embraced a successful flying and political career to end his days as Lord Brabazon of Tara.

Edwin Alliott Verdon Roe thoughtfully dumped his first name. This move helpfully produced the immediately recognisable commercial identity of Avro. He founded in 1910 the first British aircraft manufacturing company, with the invaluable aid of his brother Humphrey, and went, profitably, into business himself. Manchester's new company, Avro Aviation, grew rapidly. Soaring fortunes came with Roe's own designs. Mechanics, draughtsmen, designers, men of varied skills besieged his premises in the hope of working in aviation. A local brewing company coughed up sufficient cash for Avro, now a limited company, to move to new premises at Miles Platting, west of the centre of Manchester. A young draughtsman, Roy Chadwick, just eighteen years of age, joined the company as Alliott's personal helper and associate designer for a weekly salary of one pound. Many early aircraft artificers used any scrap of paper to hand, from old envelopes to the margins of newspapers for sketches and abstruse calculations. Chadwick was no exception.

Roe struck aviation gold in 1913 with his Avro 504. The aeroplane, with input from the young Chadwick, was designed in excellent time for immediate service when the First World War began. With a firm nose-mounted engine, the two-seater attacked soldiers on the ground as well as making bombing raids on their positions. Such aggressive behaviour by the men who flew it swiftly earned the 504 a melancholy distinction. It became, within days, the very first British aeroplane to be shot down by enemy forces. After this dismal moment, the 504 slowly retired from active fighting on the Western Front.

Zeppelin attacks on Britain subsequently persuaded anxious authorities to equip it with a machine gun to confront enemy airships. Encounters between the two seem, sadly, to have been non-existent.

The Avro 504 had a main role that it filled admirably. It served as the basic training machine for the new waves of military pilots. It was not, as its admirers proclaimed, tricky to fly but it did take skill to handle it well.

Avro expanded. Roy Chadwick and a design team moved to Hamble. Amongst their aircraft came the Avro Baby at a staggering 870 lbs total weight.

After politicians scrawled signatures on the treaty that brought the fighting to an end, Avro Aviation entered a gentle, barely discernible decline. The demand for aeroplanes peacefully withered. Amongst varied efforts was the Avro Atlantic, a folding wing variant of the lightweight Baby, to go with Sir Edward Shackleton and his planned 1921 South Pole Expedition. This tiny machine contrasted with the Aldershot, a biplane bomber with a wingspan only twenty feet less than the Lancaster of the Second World War.

Ten years of slower trade saw Alliott Verdon Roe sell control of his company to Armstrong Siddeley. Roe himself moved to an original first love, the marine world. He bought an interest in a boat-building firm, Saunders, at Cowes in the Isle of Wight. Saunders Roe produced another useful combination of letters from each name. As Saro they unsurprisingly turned their attention to flying boats.

Despite the grievous departure of its founder and superlative creator of aircraft, Avro carried on. Roy Chadwick moved house from Hamble to Manchester to become Chief Designer. Amongst other aircraft, his team produced the Avro 652, the basis for the Anson.

One month after it published the first report of the Shackleton, on 21 April 1949, *Flight* produced a more informative piece. The coverage looked at the obvious resemblance between the Shackleton and other beasts from the Avro stable. Described as having an air of 'sturdy efficiency', the new machine was 'manifestly a descendant of the Lincoln bomber'. This, as the readers well knew, was developed from the wartime

Lancaster which itself still operated in Coastal Command. *Flight* mentioned that 'the Shackleton is evidently equipped with elaborate search radar' before it drew attention to the 'unusual twin-cannon installation in the nose', a reference to the neat barbettes or mounds on each side of the front fuselage.

Chadwick himself, now Technical Director of the company but retaining much interest in designing aeroplanes, had preserved the habit of using any scrap of paper for his purposes. His wife and daughters were accustomed to newspapers and empty cigarette packets with incomprehensible pencilled scribbles on them.

The original concept of the Shackleton is customarily dated to mid-1945 when the Air Ministry issued Operational Requirement 320 for a maritime reconnaissance aircraft. Avro alone, for various reasons, were very much the favoured company to tackle the design and production work. By the time the official specification, R5/46, appeared, Roy Chadwick and Avro were ready. Their drawings showed a well-designed aeroplane that would use runways. The Ministry emphasised that the 'Air Staff require an aircraft for general and reconnaissance and anti-submarine duties.' It was to be based on the Lincoln design, which rather ruled out the idea of a flying boat, and be able to operate anywhere in the world. Avro further needed to ensure that the aircraft provided a first-rate view for search from all crew stations. Fatigue had to be reduced to the absolute minimum, a stipulation that clearly demanded comfortable work-stations and unrivalled soundproofing allied to ease of movement within the whole aeroplane.

The Ministry further demanded truly superior handling characteristics, as the planned operational flights would require low-level action. Furthermore, the aircraft needed good ditching properties coupled with an ability to float if forced down on to the water. This need held a faint echo of the thoughts of an early air officer in Coastal Command. He believed that aircraft designed to fly long distances over the ocean should be made of linen and wood. Wreckage floating on the waves gave the crew more chance of survival. Chadwick and his acolytes began work.

The Second World War remained fresh in the collective memory in 1949. Military aviation had significance. An erstwhile ally, the Soviet Union had infuriated many of the former Allies by its trespass on the national integrity of some weaker countries in Eastern Europe. In consequence, few in Britain objected to the conscription of young men. Large armed forces assisted by numerous aircraft were widely believed to be the ultimate defence against unfriendly powers. The previous war had proved that air power was an unrivalled bargaining weapon.

When the Royal Air Force formed on 1 April 1918, the concept was simple enough. All flying machines, whether equipping the Royal Flying Corps or the Royal Naval Air Service, would be operated by the new organisation. The war against a brave and determined enemy ensured that squabbles about who operated what, where and how were shelved until the task was done. Phraseology often owed much to the original parent service but the common desire to defeat the enemy took care of many operational problems. Aeroplanes worked no matter which uniform the crew wore. The new organisation hardly ruffled the system. It was not until the conflict ended that old rivalries came forward to occupy sharp minds with matters less urgent than the salvation of the nation.

Spats with members of the new service were not simply muttered words between men with stripes on their arms in back street bars in Plymouth. More important differences stalked the panelled corridors of Whitehall. If air marshals truly considered that everything military that flew was their particular province, admirals had the right to argue that all grey-painted British ships that floated on the sea were their especial responsibility. This was a convincing argument until applied to the aircraft carrier.

That knotty problem – a ship with aeroplanes – was eventually solved by an uneasy compromise. Sailors operated the ship. Men from both services and the Royal Marines coped with the aeroplanes in the air or on the vessel. No party was happy. Minor irritations abounded. RAF officers, themselves often former British army men, found it weird that naval officers remained seated during the Loyal Toast on dinner nights. Explanations that wooden sailing ships had little headroom thus ensuring that loyal subjects who stood without great care in confined dining rooms could fall stunned to the ground met with sparse enthusiasm from the objectors.

Admirals believed the purpose of aeroplanes was to see 'over the horizon and beyond' where an enemy surface fleet or hostile submarine lurked. The new RAF considered aircraft to be worthy of more wide-ranging tasks. Information from much further afield was essential. The nation was habitually involved in exciting affairs in far distant lands. Observation of a potential enemy demanded eyes over the land as well as the ocean. Both sides believed their cause had substantial merit. Admirals and air marshals continued to bicker.

Inter service squabbling took a back seat in 1936. The Air Council prepared for war. Its solution was functional commands, a suggestion that delighted the Navy Board. *The Times* reported the development in its customary dignified manner:

> A reorganisation of RAF commands which will be carried out next month, will arrange the Air Force on the lines which would be required in time of war. For defensive purposes there will be three commands – bomber, fighter and coast defence – all under the ultimate control of the Air Ministry through the Chief of Air Staff. A fourth command will undertake practically the whole of the training work. An important part of the scheme will relieve the commanders-in-chief of a large amount of administrative work and enable them to concentrate on the strategical, operational, and training work.

The Admiralty thankfully waved farewell to the task of defending British coasts from air attack for they had gained precisely what they wanted. They returned to the heady days of 1918 with their own flying service. The Royal Air Force retained a minimal authority over any shore training that involved aeroplanes but for all practical purposes the Royal Navy flew and serviced their flying machines entirely by themselves. They knew, as did many others, that another war steadily approached.

The RAF had used the name 'Fleet Air Arm' for naval aviation as early as 1924. Somehow it stuck. The Admiralty appropriated it. In 1939, the Air Ministry formally returned complete control of the Fleet Air Arm to the Admiralty. Sailors became even happier.

The new Coastal Command's task was primarily long-range reconnaissance together with a nod in the direction of anti-submarine warfare. By 1939, the Command, with nineteen squadrons, boasted a strength of about 220 aircraft. It had already gained the reputation of being a separate air force with an interesting collection of water-borne and land-based aeroplanes. The Avro Anson was one of the latter, although an import from the USA, the Lockheed Hudson, was scheduled to replace it. Amongst the aircraft that landed on water, the Saro London and the Supermarine Stranraer were both biplane flying boats.

The more modern Short Sunderland had arrived in response to a 1933 Air Ministry specification. Developed from the stunningly successful 'Empire' class monoplane civil flying boat, the Sunderland turned into a pure military machine. Intended initially for coastal reconnaissance, they took on a fierce fighting ability. An Air Ministry Directive of 1 December 1937 declared the primary role of Coastal Command was reconnaissance in home waters and co-operation with the Royal Navy to protect shipping. The Sunderland filled the role admirably.

Offensive strikes were the province of the Vickers Vildebeest biplane, the final refinement of a design that first flew in April 1928. The aeroplane was Coastal Command's aggressive might against enemy shipping. It could carry a lone 2,000 lb torpedo, although it rarely did so for few were available. The Admiralty had first claim on them for their Fairey Swordfish machines. The single-engined Vildebeest thus scarcely rated as a fearsome creature.

The arrival of hostilities forced some immediate changes. There were not sufficient eyes in the sky either to spot or deter a determined U-boat from the Kriegsmarine. Within weeks, single-engined Tiger Moth and Hornet Moth aeroplanes, the majority impressed from civilian owners, arrived on active service as Coastal Patrol Flights. Their schedule usually called for them to scout the waves at dawn and dusk. Sanguine thinkers trusted that a sleepy look-out in a U-boat conning tower would mistake the distant shape for a torpedo-armed Vildebeest or Swordfish. Sadly, the puttering biplanes enjoyed no such weaponry although both Moth types acquired a wicker basket in which rode two carrier pigeons. They possibly enjoyed riding along with one flare pistol and a partially inflated car wheel inner tube. If the worst happened and the aircraft splashed into the sea, the optimists among their pilots believed they would survive. On limited occasions, a real twenty-five-pound bomb was available although there are no records of one ever being used.

Naval slang soon gave Coastal Command a nickname. Aside from the universally recognised 'tinfish', seamen casually referred to the torpedo as a 'kipper'. The Swordfish, a collection of wires, double wings and fixed undercarriage armed with the weapon became known as the 'kipper kite'. It was a short hop to refer to all aircraft involved in the U-boat war as kipper kites or a collection of the same lined up in proximity as the Kipper Fleet. Whatever the origin, the name stuck. It remains in use despite monumental changes in the organisation of British forces.

When the war in Europe ground at long last to a German defeat, the three operational Commands of 1939 could all claim they had fought a valuable war. Coastal Command had reason to feel slightly aggrieved for many of their big aircraft, with the notable exception of the Sunderland, had been short-term borrowing. Coastal Command had operated several four-engined types – the Flying Fortress, the Liberator, even the Lancaster – to the chagrin of Bomber Command who eventually managed to acquire many of them on the plausible grounds that if Berlin collapsed, the U-boats would surrender.

The need for a new maritime reconnaissance and attack aircraft was seriously important by the end of the war. Coastal Command finished the conflict with 511 anti-submarine aircraft. This Kipper Fleet included Sunderlands which had destroyed, as the Germans admitted, twenty-seven U-boats. The flying boats were aided by an assortment of long-range four-engined aircraft plus a miscellany of types originally destined for other tasks.

The reliable Sunderland clearly would not last for ever. Fingers scratched heads in the Air Ministry and Coastal Command Headquarters to produce a comprehensive specification. Four engines were deemed essential along with the fundamental requirement for the aeroplane to fly and fight at long range. The Sunderland had not been able to cover the middle of the Atlantic during the war, a weakness hard-pressed U-boat commanders had welcomed. It took land-based aircraft, operating from Iceland, to turn the tide. Many senior officers, influenced by the remarkable success of the Sunderland as well as nostalgia, believed that maritime reconnaissance demanded an aircraft that operated from harbours, lakes and even the open sea.

The less sentimental supported a land plane. A multitude of operating bases with support and supply staff were already scattered across much of the world. The astronomical cost of establishing similar facilities for flying boats would add untold noughts to the defence bill. Longer-range aircraft, able to operate far across the Atlantic, would need more fuel, even crew, and there was a limit to how large a flying boat could be. Despite talk of depot ships roaming the seven seas, as well as docking facilities on every friendly coast, the practical choice was for land-based aeroplanes.

So came Chadwick's offering, the Avro 696. This was the single serious contender from the British aviation industry. It also proved to be the only aircraft designed specifically for maritime reconnaissance to serve in the British forces. The need for it had become more pressing. With the firm nod of interest from Whitehall, which included a provisional order for the production version, Avro's designers began serious work. They used a variant of Chadwick's much used mainplane wing that had first appeared on the prewar Manchester and was subsequently found in various guises on several multi-engined Avro aircraft. The team set aside space at the factory and made a full-sized mock-up of their design able to carry the multitude of equipment and the crew to use it.

Contract 6/ACFT.1077/(CB6(a) was issued to Avro for three prototypes on 28 May 1947. Specification R.5/46 had become reality. Avro were required to build three prototype aeroplanes for long-range maritime reconnaissance. To prevent any future confusion, they were to carry serial numbers, VW126, VW131 and VW135.

Roy Chadwick did not lead the Shackleton team for very long. On 23 August 1947 he died when a passenger in one of his own designs, the Avro Tudor which was, incidentally, Britain's first pressurised airliner. In an example of one of the classic problems with aviation, the aircraft had been serviced the previous day. Aileron cables were disconnected and reassembled with no helpful diagram. They were inadvertently crossed. On take-off, the aircraft banked sharply to the right and smacked into the ground. Both test pilots and the designer died. Chadwick was just fifty-four years of age.

In 1948, Great Britain joined with France and the Benelux countries to deter Soviet aggression. The grouping was less than fearsome but the following year, the United States and Canada joined their wartime companions in an enlarged alliance of twelve nations – the North Atlantic Treaty Organisation. NATO's task was to counter the post-war Communist expansion in Europe. The aim was to preserve the safety and freedom of the North Atlantic area. Each original member agreed to be responsible for a specific military task. Britain, regarded as both a maritime and airborne power, accepted a role that required patrols of vast tracts of the waters around Europe, both by sea and air.

Avro's design was ideal. Chadwick had pushed through its name, the Shackleton, as a tribute to his wife's ancestor. Early opposition faded away. It was no secret that the aircraft was at least two years away from delivery, a factor that exercised the collective minds of Whitehall. Britain lacked not only maritime reconnaissance but a range of front-line types. As long as peace prevailed, Whitehall could afford to wait for new aeroplanes. More important needs crowded the political agenda.

The second aircraft flew on 2 September 1949, a few days before the Society of British Aircraft Constructors Flying Display at Farnborough. *Flight* noted that the aeroplane was the largest aircraft on show. Its pilot, John Baker, made a memorable event of what could have been an ordinary display by flying at very low level with two engines intentionally shut down. Few doubted that it was a serious warplane although the front gun barbettes had vanished for ever. Even so, the tail guns with a further turret midway along the upper fuselage clearly belonged to a weapon of war.

The Shackleton delighted both experts and amateur enthusiasts alike but their real awe was reserved for another Avro arrival, flown by Eric Esler, Avro's deputy chief test pilot. *The Times* of September 7th 1949 told its readers:

A surprise last-minute entry was the Avro 707, the first aircraft in this country to have wings shaped like an equilateral

10

triangle. It is believed to be only the third aircraft in the world to have the delta wing . . . The authorities are understandably reticent . . . and it is described merely as a research aircraft.

Few people knew that the 'single-seat machine powered by a Rolls-Royce turbo-jet' was close to Roy Chadwick's heart, a one-third size miniature of an aircraft very much in his thoughts at the time he died and for which he had sketched preliminary designs. Avro had submitted their tender for a four-engined delta-wing bomber to the Air Ministry in May 1947. 'Much of the delta development to date,' the company told Chadwick's widow in 1952, 'is due to him.'

At the end of the month, on 30 September 1949, another edition of the newspaper reported the fatal crash of the Avro 707, an incident which caused the death of its gallant pilot, Eric Esler. A spokesman for Avro voiced their profound regret. He finished by saying:

> The cause is unknown. Although the accident is bound to be a setback to the plans which are afoot, the research work will continue.

Nobody mentioned the Avro Vulcan.

The third Shackleton prototype rose up over Woodford for the first time on 29 March 1950. With four engines, triple tail fins and general appearance to mislead them, a few non-expert onlookers assumed it was an updated Lancaster or Lincoln heavy bomber. They were not totally mistaken. Aside from its proven heritage, the role requested by the Air Ministry had grown. It had swollen from simple maritime operations to include tactical bombing and transporting troops if necessary. Politicians and civil servants in both the Ministry of Supply and Air Ministry had no qualms about ordering aircraft 'straight from the drawing board'. They much preferred, though, if the drawing board covered a stunning range of alternatives. A few days after the flight, Avro received the specification for the Mark Two Shackleton before the Mark One had even joined Coastal Command.

The third prototype was almost identical to the production air-craft, the first of which had made its maiden flight the previous day. That machine's immediate destiny was not squadron service despite the pressing need to replace the ageing Lancasters in Coastal Command. It went straight to manufacturer's trials.

Construction had become far more complicated since the days of creating flying machines from wood, linen and piano wires with converted car engines to give power. Manufacturing had moved on. It is one thing to design an aeroplane and build it carefully and deliberately, from the blueprints. It is quite another for everything to work as planned. Add the multitude of modifications already thrown up by the flight trials together with demands for further equipment tests and the long delay between an order from the drawing board and squadron service becomes a touch more intelligible.

In the next few months, the four Shackletons went through a stunning array of trials. They were joined in June by the second production aircraft. A Coastal Command crew had already tasted the delights to come during a visit to the Avro works at Woodford. They were probably the first uniformed personnel to register unhappy comments about the noise level from the four heavy Rolls-Royce engines that powered the aeroplane.

Charles Stuart Rolls, born in 1877 and an old Etonian, met Frederick Henry Royce, once a newspaper boy and then a Post Office telegraph boy, in 1904. Both had made their own way in life since their widely disparate schooldays. They joined together in the business of making and selling motorcars. By the time the Kaiser's armies marched into Belgium, they had become famous for their expertise exemplified by the elegantly long 40/50hp-engined Silver Ghost of 1907, which remained in production until 1925.

Rolls was a fervent balloonist who made more than 170 ascents. Captivated further by the aeroplane, he met the Wright Brothers when they visited Europe. He bought one of their machines. He subsequently died on 12 July 1910 during a flying meeting at Bournemouth.

Royce had already suffered ill health. Unceasing design work laid him low in September 1908. The death of Rolls caused a collapse in his precarious well-being, serious enough to demand an operation in 1911. His determined recovery benefited by a move to Le Canadel in southern France. His choice of villa had a drawing office and he acquired eight staff. Royce continued to control the main schemes of the firm until his death in 1933.

Frederick Royce had never responded to pleas by Charles Rolls to evolve an engine for aerial use alone. The First World War changed his mind. He turned the smooth engine from the Silver Ghost into the much more powerful 200 horsepower Eagle. Better than six thousand were built, the final version offering over 350 horsepower. The Falcon, designed for fighter aircraft, later joined the Eagle. The family finally included the Hawk, created especially for non-rigid airships, while the Condor appeared after the war was won.

After the Armistice, Rolls-Royce went back to building the world's finest motorcars. Their scorning of continued work on aviation engines did not last. When Sir Richard Fairey, a formidable builder of aeroplanes, produced an outstanding light bomber, the Fox, his original choice of engine came from the United States. He decided that the Curtiss D-12, a powerful 500 horsepower piece of engineering that replaced gearing to the airscrew crankshaft with a direct-drive connection was ideal. With a new propeller designed to operate at a higher speed added to the mixture, the D-12 was hailed as the most technologically advanced engine in the world.

Fairey had agreed to make the engine under licence in Britain. This did not please the authorities. British-designed aeroplanes should have British-designed engines. Rolls-Royce duly received a Curtiss D-12 engine along with a demand that they produce a better version. The Kestrel series emerged from this activity, the most powerful of which gave a comforting 750 horsepower. This engine re-established Rolls-Royce in the flying business.

They were soon needed. The Schneider Trophy contest spurred the development of racing seaplanes which cried out for abundant horsepower. The only saving grace was that the engine need operate only long enough to finish the race. Britain duly won the event in 1927, 1929 and 1931, thus keeping the trophy for all time. The final triumph in 1931 used a Supermarine S6B which set a world air speed record of 407 mph with its special Rolls-Royce engine. The aeroplane came from the drawing board of Reginald Joseph Mitchell, appointed as the company's chief designer in 1919 at the young age of twenty-four. As every British schoolboy subsequently learned from his weekly comic paper, both Mitchell and Rolls-Royce were to be inextricably linked for all time by the Spitfire fighter and its fabled Merlin engine.

Like every other maker of engines, Rolls-Royce wanted more power to provide even better performance for aircraft. Although the Merlin had many fine points, their Griffon – named after the European vulture species – showed exceptional promise. Given that producers of everything from kitchen furniture to aeroplane engines develop their designs, it is hardly amazing that the first Griffon was based upon the 1928 Buzzard, in itself scaled up and developed into the 'R' engine that powered the Schneider Trophy victor. That version needed highly specialised and expensive fuel which gave it a desperately short working life. Work on a derated or reduced performance engine that used ordinary aviation fuel slipped away once the trophy had a permanent London home. A sombre 1939 thrust further development of the engine back into contention.

The first production Griffons had single-stage superchargers. They went into the Spitfire XII to give fearsome low-level achievement that successfully took on German Focke-Wulf 190 hit-and-run fighter bombers along the English south coast. With a two-stage supercharger, the Griffon bestowed quality high-level capability on the Spitfire XIV and XVIII.

Roy Chadwick and the Avro design squad were well acquainted with the Merlin engine. Four went as a staple ingredient into the Lancaster bomber, its civil version, the Lancastrian, the Tudor transport, the Lincoln bomber and the York freighter. The team swiftly discarded any thoughts that Merlins could further serve their duty in the new Shackleton. Whether calculated in the drawing office or in the margins of the evening newspaper, it became clear that the new aircraft needed an abundance of power. Four Merlins would not lift the aeroplane with all its planned equipment, a ten-man crew and much else beside.

The Griffon 57 would. Tests showed that the Griffon was ideal for the new project. Rolls-Royce had produced a truly serious engine. It had acquired a two-stage supercharger with an aftercooler. Twelve cylinders, forty-eight valves gave better than 2000 horsepower, which was supplemented when essential at take-off by water methanol injection. This gave chemical inter-cooling so that more power was available when needed. Water cooled the intake charge and combustion. The methanol additionally acted as extremely high-octane fuel as well as adding more oxygen to combustion. Although the performance usually created ear-splitting bangs and apparent bursts of flame from the engine, the procedure was invaluable to get the aircraft flying.

Additionally, the Griffon 57 boasted a rare feature, a genius design, for it had the remarkable property of a contra-rotating drive. This turned two thirteen-foot three-bladed airscrews in opposite directions. Engineers induced glazed looks in non-technical listeners by explaining how the Griffon worked a six-bladed propeller.

The drive from the crankshaft, they pointed out, had a coupling drive to a double pinion. The rear pinion drove a gearwheel bolted to the inner airscrew shaft which was therefore driven in the opposite direction to that of the crankshaft. The front pinion operated an idler wheel, which in its turn drove a gear wheel bolted to the outer airscrew shaft.

Taking any nod of faint understanding as acquiescence to continue, the engineer could then add that the two shafts had a common axis. Reversing thrust loads were absorbed by bearings mounted between the two shafts. The reason for this arrangement, he would glibly explain, was to increase the airscrew blade area, thus absorbing more engine power, within a diameter limited by the height of the aeroplane's undercarriage.

This interesting arrangement of contra-rotating blades required a gadget cheerfully called a translation unit, or TU, which had nothing to do with altering the pilot's occasionally colourful language into an unknown tongue. In essence, the TU ensured that the pitch of both sets of blades were in step, one with the other. An alteration in the angle at which the blades met the airflow changed the rate of rotation or revolutions per minute. Piston-powered aircraft need a high RPM for taking off and landing but can manage the cruise with a more sedate RPM. To make life simple on the Shackleton, the pilot had a pitch lever to alter the RPM. This dealt with the front set of blades alone. The TU then arranged that the rear blades conformed.

In practice the first aircraft carried the Griffon 57 as the outer engines and a more powerful Griffon 57A with longer endurance inboard. This arrangement soon died. The outer engine nacelles were widened so that all Shackletons could wear the Griffon 57A inboard and outboard. This useful alteration changed the aircraft's official designation. An MR1 thus treated rejoiced in the name of MR1A.

The Shackleton's four engines battered the ears of incautious hearers with a noise that attracted the alliterative and onomatopoeic name of the Griffon Growl. Inevitably, the Shackleton acquired the name of Growler although there were many who maintained that any multi-engine piston aeroplane was a noisy brute.

Production aircraft from the original 1946 order began to arrive in 1950. The wings, fuselage and tail came from the Chadderton factory in the north of Manchester before vehicles took them to Woodford for assembly, engine installation and flight-testing. The Air Ministry dusted off its plans to allocate the arrivals. In February 1951, Coastal Command's Operational Conversion Unit at Kinloss in Scotland received its initial aircraft. On the same airfield, with hard-worked Lancasters, was Number 120 (properly pronounced One Twenty, its members insisted) Squadron. They would be the maiden squadron to operate the post-war's final word in maritime reconnaissance aircraft.

Kinloss was not alone as the weeks went by. Two new Shackleton centres emerged at St Eval in Cornwall and Ballykelly in Northern Ireland. The other Cornish post, St Mawgan also received the new aircraft, as did Gibraltar together with Northern Ireland's Aldergrove. Many other airfields accepted Shackletons for a day or a night or even longer as the years went by. Most pieces of hard standing and tarmac received a near permanent reminder of the visitor. The Griffon engine took any opportunity to haemorrhage oil through any convenient joint which cheerfully soaked into the surface below.

No single person seems to have guessed back in 1951 that the

Shackleton, the Growler, further known variously as the White Whale or the Old Grey Lady according to the fuselage colour scheme applied, was to remain in service use for a further forty years. Including the three prototype aircraft, a total of 188 Shackletons emerged from the Avro factory. Of these, eight served with the South African Air Force from 1957 to 1984. For the Royal Air Force, sixteen squadrons operated Shackletons, as did half a dozen miscellaneous units concerned with specialist trials and training.

With an operational air crew consisting normally of ten men – two pilots, a flight engineer, two navigators and five other categories to work the signals, radio and radar, sonobuoy and other equipment as well the armament, plus an encyclopedic range of ground technicians, the Shackleton on call enjoyed considerable attention as long as it was operational.

Their stories follow.

CHAPTER TWO

Military aviation rarely has a recruiting problem. A long, long queue of potential pilots normally keeps recruiters occupied while a formidable list of candidates applies for every other available aircrew category.

In 1951, the British armed forces enjoyed the benefit of peace-time conscription, generally referred to as National Service. Wartime necessity had become a peace-time obligation. Every able-bodied male Briton approaching the age of eighteen had to register for military employ. Residents of Northern Ireland avoided the obligation for fear of promoting civil unrest. Further, although no official ban existed, very few black conscripts were recruited and there were, as far as can be ascertained, no non-European officers.

Conscripts could apply for aircrew positions. If successful, they gained rank and a gratifying rise in their pay. At a daily rate of four shillings, the ordinary national serviceman's weekly wage was a stark contrast to the money that even moderately skilled civilian workers commanded. As aircrew, the conscript could feel relatively affluent in comparison to his earth-bound colleagues. The Royal Air Force, not with complete innocence, often persuaded applicants to extend their service term. From time to time, the Air Ministry tossed out tempting statements along the lines of this effort in 1950:

Opportunities of obtaining commissions or of training as pilots in the Royal Air Force are open to many of the young men who will be registering for National Service on March 4th. There are 700 vacancies for commissions in the RAF and 300 places for training as pilots open to National Service men this year.

Of the 300 places for pilot training, 100 are reserved for ATC cadets. National Service pilots are trained up to full 'wings' standard and have officer cadet status during the greater part of their training. All those who are suitable are commissioned into the Reserve on finishing their whole-time National Service, and it is a condition of their acceptance that at the conclusion of their whole-time National Service they will join the RAFVR or the Royal Auxiliary Air Force.

The post-war Royal Air Force had plenty of jobs to offer. A whole variety of skills were needed to run the service efficiently. Officers in the service were organised into specialist branches. Aircrew were General Duties officers while those whose work intimately connected them with operating aeroplanes, such as air traffic controllers, joined the GD Ground Section. Administrators went to the Secretarial Branch, engineers lived in the Technical Branch and a host of others belonged to a specific professional branch. For the aircraftmen, a similar arrangement applied. They divided into trade groups. These, in turn, had basic trades and advanced trades when appropriate. A worker on engines, for instance, could be either a basic mechanic or a higher grade fitter. A plethora of clerks specialised in everything from keeping accounts, taking shorthand, typing or producing charts that showed just how much time the engine fitters had to wait for spares to arrive.

Coastal Command took its fair share of signallers and air gunners for the newly arriving Shackletons. The gunners in particular, often designated as Radar Gunners, found themselves doing much of an air signaller's work as well as their own. They also learned how to become general hands, labourers and all-round dogsbodies as well as putative chefs in the Shackleton galley.

The vast majority of conscripts accepted their fate with

reasonable equanimity. A good number further decided that the 'call-up' was their ticket to a near lifetime-long job with a pension at the end of their service. Conscription only applied to males. Female volunteers could join one of the three auxiliary services which were designed to assist the fighting arms. Women who joined the WRNS were forbidden to serve at sea while those in the army had no hope of firing a weapon in the frontline. In the WRAF, women did not serve in any capacity on board aircraft. Gender equality lived far away in the future. Some firmly believed the uniformed military would never see women as equals to the men.

Since the end of the Second World War, Great Britain had involved itself in a series of military endeavours. Troops had been needed for occupation duties in Germany and Japan. Trouble occupied military thinking in Palestine, in the Indian sub-continent, in Africa and various other patches of land that were once part of the British Empire. Uniformed personnel were well aware that they had a better than evens chance of performing in a battle zone at some time during their service life. Even relishing the comparative luxury of occupied Germany and the British Army of the Rhine could come to an abrupt end if Ivan's tanks squealed over the borders.

Nerves had been frayed by the eleven vital months of the Berlin Airlift that began in June 1948. The Soviet Union ideologically distrusted plans suggested by their wartime Western allies for German currency reform, unification and reparations. As Berlin sat in the middle of their Zone of Occupation, the Kremlin thought they could simply isolate the city. They need only close the rail, water and road routes into their region from the West. This unilateral decision almost sparked new bloodshed. Fortunately, an alternative supply system was just available. The Soviet Union refrained from closing the three air corridors. These were protected by a written agreement and their closure would be cause for war. Named Operation Vittles by the United States and Operation Plain Fare by the British, the two air forces took on the enormous task. They had to move more than food. Berlin needed coal and heating oil particularly as the power came from Russian-occupied territory. The Airlift saw one aircraft landing in Berlin every two minutes throughout the day and night. The Kipper Fleet became part of the effort. Sunderlands flew in salt, sanitary towels and other essentials, landing on Lake Havel in the middle of the city.

By Easter 1949, the daily tonnage delivered to Berlin was all but 9,000 tons. The Soviets reopened the land links although air supplies continued for four months to build up reserves. 101 airmen died in total in crashes as they faced down the threat. This encounter led directly to the formation of the North Atlantic Treaty Organisation.

One of the fiercest combats came in 1950 when the Cold War turned uncomfortably hot. The Communist regime in North Korea and the US-supported government in South Korea escalated border clashes into full fighting. Western influence at the United Nations Security Council quickly produced a resolution that not only condemned the North Korean action but authorised military intervention. All told, twenty-three countries supplied fighting troops and ships or provided medical support. In the West, several governments feared that the bloody scuffle in the East would somehow spread to Europe.

This conflict in the Far East put an enormous burden on Britain not only in terms of new and modern equipment along with personnel but also as a drain on cash. The country had debts from two world wars which it had to pay as well as meeting the expensive introduction of the welfare state. The Royal Air Force needed considerably more strength to meet its new commitments as part of NATO and in Korea. Modern designs, mostly ordered 'direct from the drawing board' were far from full production. As a stopgap, the United States offered aircraft on loan. Bomber Command received the Boeing B29, promptly named the Washington by London, Fighter Command collected North American F-86 Sabres while Coastal Command became home to the Lockheed Neptune. Finished in a workmanlike dark blue, its long range made it an ideal candidate for maritime patrol work.

As 120 Squadron steadily converted its air and ground crews to the Shackleton, the Aeroplane and Armament Experimental Establishment at Boscombe Down tested selected production aircraft. Avro were making twenty-nine production aeroplanes with serial numbers running from VP254 to VP268 and VP281 to VP294. In July 1951, the Ministry of Supply in the guise of the AAEE took control of VP263. This aeroplane had made its initial flight in March and had gone to the RAF in April. With the knowledge that three prototypes had been tested by the maker in addition to further assessments by AAEE and the Royal Aircraft Establishment, a reasonable onlooker could assume that very little of great import would be noted in the AAEE Official Report.

The first Boscombe Down trial took the aircraft to Gibraltar. Adverse weather diverted the Shackleton to Lisbon where it landed after eight hours in the air. It took a further fourteen-hour sortie to complete the trial and return to the United Kingdom. With little exception, all flying was between 1,500 and 2,500 feet with an indicated airspeed that began at 145 knots at each stage and reached 155 knots towards the end. Some seventeen airborne hours were spent in darkness and cloud with moderate turbulence.

The evaluations produced some sharp criticism. The emergency lights at the first pilot's position were mounted under the highest point of the cockpit coaming. Wiring and a hot air pipe entirely obstructed their illumination. This fault utterly obscured the air speed indicator and partly hid the artificial horizon instrument, a combination which hardly assisted flying on instruments alone.

The flight engineer's position also suffered from some poor lighting. Both he and the radar operator had to endure uncomfortable seating positions. The galley, noted by AAEE as 'of the type designed for the Tudor aircraft', was mounted across the fuselage on a bulkhead by the rear mainplane spar. The angle adopted refused to let the sink drain properly. Objects slid out of compartments when the doors were opened and the draining board needed a rim to stop crockery sliding to its doom. With neither refuse bin nor plate rack, the chances of damage were high.

Noise and vibration, the report's authors sniffed, had hardly improved. As for sanitary arrangements, they were grossly inadequate. One Elsan and one relief tube were hopeless for a ten-man crew on a fourteen-hour flight. The arrangements were, they believed, just suitable for a three-hour journey. On a brighter note, the AAEE considered that the detailed improvements needed would be met by modifications already scheduled for subsequent aircraft.

The men of 120 Squadron, preparing for the arrival of the Shackleton, suffered a bad day on 15 March when one of their old Lancasters did not return from a navigation exercise. It crashed, with no survivors, in appalling weather near Garve village about twenty miles north-west of Inverness. It took three days to find the wreckage.

By the end of May, familiarisation and conversion to the new type was sufficiently advanced for Intensive Flying Trials to begin. These were planned to last three months and designed to assess the strengths and weaknesses of the aeroplane and its systems. The squadron's eight aircraft were to complete one thousand hours of flying time between them each month. Only two machines would operate at the same time. The concentrated flying would aid the preparation of servicing schedules and identify spares provisions. It would further ensure that the Pilot's Notes were accurate as well as give an indication of any modifications needed for the future.

The squadron drew up sixteen-day schedules to give crews firm data of the planned programme and indications of sortie length, rest days and time off. In the north of Scotland during the summer, daylight persists so the crews had no need to worry their heads about night flying rules and procedures. The only requirement in practice was four serviceable Griffons, a functional airframe and a working radio. In actual fact the aircraft were rarely operationally fully serviceable. Amongst minor niggles that did not affect the actual Trials, the heaters either failed to work or became white hot. Sonics and some navigation aids sulked while the ASV13 search radar, designed to seek out surface vessels, often disappointed. The scanner jammed distressingly often while power supplies were a further problem.

The flights included navigation exercises. These usually went over the Atlantic. Many were well in excess of ten hours' endurance to include night flying in empty skies over vast waters. Others involved practice bombing-missions, homing to base using radar and other aids only. Additionally, all crews endured routine local flying with a set quota of take-offs and landings, or, in everyday parlance, 'circuits and bumps.'

For many, the biggest disappointment by far was the much-trumpeted 'super galley'. The floor covering was linoleum with a cross-hatch pattern that stood proud from its surface. Publicity in the press suggested it was affiliated to a hotel kitchen. In practice, cooking a modest bacon and eggs meal for ten crew members proved to be a wearing and sometimes daunting task, especially in turbulent conditions. Meals often regressed to a lone sandwich or soup accompanied by coffee. When a fried egg did make an appearance, a few more cautious crew members would peruse their food for faint imprints of cross-hatched floor covering.

The Intensive Flying Trials were an open invitation for all varieties of experts to express opinions, not necessarily connected to the handling aspects of the aeroplane. Aviation medicine pundits declared that the contra-rotating airscrews made too much noise. Hearing had to be protected, claimed the experts. Halfway through the Trials every crew member received a specially padded helmet. New versions of the aircraft would, it was assumed, be made with extra fuselage sound-proofing.

The hard-worked Shackleton was clearly still some distance from being the perfect aeroplane with which to find and destroy hostile submarines or ships. The radar and sonic systems on which success depended were often unreliable and technically inadequate. The Griffon also proved to have a few problems. Pilots and flight engineers saw the appropriate engine gauge show a loss of oil pressure. Remedial action was clear. The guilty engine was shut down and the aircraft returned to base or diverted to a suitable close airfield. Investigation after investigation showed that the problem was no more than the fracture of a capillary tube. This relayed the oil pressure reading to the dial. It took the experts some long while to come up with the solution.

The Trials crews learned swiftly about their aircraft. Lessons that would have taken many months in normal squadron flying were quickly absorbed. The knowledge helped integrate the aircraft more swiftly into Coastal Command. Aircrew were not over-impressed by a subsequent advertisement from Avro that acknowledged that flying over vast areas of ocean caused both mental and physical strain on the aircrew. After which, the makers, aided by carefully drawn artwork of a returned Shackleton, claimed that:

> The confidence inspired by the four Rolls-Royce Griffon engines, and the degree of crew comfort achieved by the spacious layout and galley facilities of the Avro Shackleton are such that returning crews of Royal Air Force Coastal Command disembark, unwearied by their long patrol – almost as fresh as the crew now setting course.

By July 1951 enough production Shackletons had passed through 38 Maintenance Unit to allow the next unit, 224 Squadron, to start business. They had the misfortune to collect an unlucky duckling at an early stage. Numbered VP283, the MR1 Shackleton had already suffered a Category 3 scrape at 38 Maintenance Unit at Llandow where aircraft were prepared for squadron use. The repair took a while but the 'as good as new' machine arrived at its Gibraltar home on 25 July. It did not last long.

On 12 August 1951, operating on a conversion flight, the Shackleton was on a final approach to Gibraltar North Front when the undercarriage hit the runway with some force. Both of the main landing gear legs broke away. The pilot, sensibly enough, abandoned the approach. With no wheels, pilots do have problems in landing without casualties. No serious injuries resulted when the aircraft ditched some six miles out to sea.

For the ground crew of 120 Squadron, the three months of the flying trials had also been rigorous. As Jack Wilson, an airframe technician, recalls:

> Over a period of three months, intensive flying trials were carried out. Being ground crew we worked shifts to keep the aircraft flying as much as possible. Ground crew were on twelve-hour shifts with a crew manning the squadron for twenty-four hours each day. Spare parts did not exist so we had to use one aircraft as a 'Christmas Tree' in order to keep the others serviceable.

The sheer size of the Shackleton posed problems for the servicing teams:

We did not have the luxury of hangars, we had to do all our day to day servicing on the dispersal area, rain, hail or shine. I remember being the NCO on duty over Christmas 1951 when we had severe gales, with the aircraft turning themselves into wind and concrete picket blocks being attached, trying to keep them from moving too much. We did not have it too cushy.

Once the Intensive Flying Trials finished, 120 Squadron turned its attention to becoming a top grade maritime reconnaissance squadron. The role included search and rescue flights for the equipment that located dubious vessels and worked equally well when searching for a drifting rowing boat. The squadron began a series of flying exercises designed to bring everyone to maximum efficiency. Many of the procedures had already been a feature of the Trials but the squadron now moved to its main purpose of ferreting out enemy shipping and submarines.

A navigation exercise at night, known not unreasonably as a Night Navex, usually created an operational task rooted in reality. Briefing included a general scrutiny of the weather charts often hand-drawn by the duty meteorological officer. They showed not only current weather but that anticipated during the flight. Frequently the task for the crew was to find a real ship, usually a passenger liner, known to be in the Atlantic and report its position. Once found, the crew went on to seek submarines. This generally involved a flight to the north of Iceland, a happy route for Soviet underwater boats. To add to the excitement, a collection of practice bombs usually sat in the bomb bay for later use.

A bus, fitted with no more than basic seats, took the aircrew to their Shackleton. Before the first Griffon growled into action, every crew member made his particular pre-flight checks for the long airborne hours ahead. Finally, a grunting cough and an instantly vanishing lick of flame told the waiting ground crew that number three engine, the starboard inner, was alive. More coughs, more moments of bright flame as numbers four, two and one followed. The weighted aircraft made its cautious way along the narrow perimeter track. Turning was a delayed action as power, brake and rudder pedals were used to inch the nose in the right direction. Shackletons were not like motor vehicles. They had no steering wheel.

Cleared for take-off, the Shackleton lined up on the runway. The Griffons roared to reach full power. The machine edged forward, steadily picking up speed. The long parallel lines of the runway lights flashed by each side of the cockpit. The under-carriage, once heavy with laden weight, handed over the job to the wings which bit into the air as the aircraft lifted into the night sky.

The Shackleton's patrol height over the Atlantic was no more than 800 feet. With careful judgement, all four Griffons were synchronised to at least make their discordant roar less intrusive. With the auto-pilot engaged, the aeroplane rumbled onward, untroubled by the occasional turbulent air current.

As the aircraft neared the search area, the two navigators requested a three drift wind. The flame float dropped down to the sea. Finally, a minuscule light appeared on the black surface of the water below. It is now that the pilot earned a few coins from his wages. He had to hold a rigid course to make it easier to track the flame float through the drift sight. This allowed determination of the wind speed and direction. Any turbulence could be a disaster.

Although every spare eye on the Shackleton looked out for the target, it was usually the radar operator who picked up the intercept with his box of tricks. Once they identified their ship, the Shackleton crew turned on to the homeward leg. They still had to drop their practice bombs and keep alive to the chance of finding a tiny submarine in the vast expanse of ocean. As dawn slid over the horizon, the time came to use a target smoke float and drop the practice bombs. Once that was over, the crew could anticipate going home.

Coastal Command was no exception to the general rule that new faces kept squadrons fresh. Novices to maritime reconnais-sance discovered that complicated procedures lurked in wait for them. Amongst the more thankless jobs on long patrols was the task of the flight engineer. A long-standing directive ensured that operational piston aircraft with more than a single engine had an engineer. Put at its simplest, his job was to monitor, before the arrival of computerised black boxes with their built-in wizardry, everything mechanical on the aeroplane. On the Shackleton he supervised the Griffon's fuel gauges and flows as well as engine starting. Griffons were almost entirely automatically regulated. This left the pilot with just basic engine instruments to indicate the RPM and boost.

Although the Griffons were expected to roar dutifully for long hours, the flight engineer could do very little about the engine's prodigious appetite for fuel and lubricants. It gulped Avgas, or high-octane aviation petrol, rather as an alcoholic is deemed to swallow booze. There were some who darkly suspected that its designers had a significant stake in desert oil wells. Additionally, replacing weary Griffons became a regular practice for the hard-working ground crews.

Flight engineers had the reputation of being a special breed. They often seemed to be older, grizzled, rough and ready types, able to do virtually any job in the aeroplane – as well as flying it in an emergency – and instantly ready to crush any other aircrew immediately to hand including, so legend claimed, young newly-qualified pilots. They developed, most crews believed, a sixth sense about their aircraft, a nose for trouble allied with an exact knowledge of what was or was not acceptable in the arcane realm of unserviceability of equipment. Above all, they were always able to offer unfailingly sound advice to the captain concerning the engines and aircraft systems. Custom further dictated that they took charge of the flare pistol.

The introduction of the Shackleton, combined with retirement from the service of many wartime aircrew, created an urgent need for flight engineers. As Jim Humphrey remembered:

I joined the Royal Air Force at the end of 1948. My rank was Cadet Aircrew (Air or Flight Engineer). After six months at Kirton-in-Lindsey to brush up my general education, I was posted to St Athan's East Camp for my Flight Engineer training and was presented with my brevet at Christmas 1950. I had managed a total of five hours flying time in Lincolns.

Leconfield, Yorkshire was my next posting for an air

gunner's course. Total flying time in a Vickers Wellington was 20 hours15minutes.

From Leconfield I was posted to Kinloss to 236 Operational Conversion Unit and completed ground and flying training for the Avro Lancaster. Total flying time was 49 hours 5 minutes.

Many flight engineers anticipated a posting to the Lancaster's successor, the Avro Lincoln. Jim Humphrey was considered good enough to join the newest piston aeroplane on the inventory if he managed to pass the training.

I was informed at the end of this course that I would be flying Shackletons. The ground and air training for that was successful and I was posted to 120 Squadron based at Kinloss.

The Shackleton had a huge bomb bay. There was a story, true or not, that Avro wanted to build stronger bomb bay doors in case of ditching but the Air Ministry said 'no need'.

The aircraft had three fitted heaters which used Avgas for fuel. There were two types. One was an American-made heater which worked perfectly – the other was British, a kind of copy of the American one. The difference was the American one worked, for it was not restricted by too many safety devices. The British one had too many fitted which caused the heaters to switch off. To get round this problem I used shorting-out devices, which helped to keep them working. You could say that it was slightly illegal.

Other flight engineers adopted the same remedy. Most took it as their duty to keep the aircraft as comfortable as possible. A sharp eye on the heaters ensured that the chances of them catching fire and destroying the aircraft were much reduced.

Another difficulty was prop noise/vibration especially in the Flight Engineer's and Wireless Operator's (Signaller) position. To help eliminate this, the contra-rotating prop blades cross-over point was altered so that when the aircraft was stationary and the props were lined up in the usual position, say for exhibition purposes, the props took on a different angle to the usual 'Y'. The props lined up like a tilted 'Y', only by a few degrees.

Hydraulic failure was another difficulty. The original pipes fractured due to vibration. Emergency air had to be used to lower the undercarriage. Eventually the hydraulic lines were modified to help to prevent this problem.

A safety modification was carried out on the front hatch in the nose compartment. This was after an accident over Lough Neagh during a night bombing practice. The navigator stepped on the hatch, the hatch went out from under him. The Range Launch picked him up but he died before reaching the shore. A good man was lost.

The Air Ministry decided that Kinloss would be ideal for the new Neptune which was to equip 217 Squadron. This created headaches for Kinloss which had insufficient accommodation to permanently host two fully equipped operational maritime squadrons. A new Shackleton squadron, Number 220, formed on 24 September 1951 thus had only a brief stay there. It transferred to St Eval on 14 November with the MR1A which boasted modest improvements on its predecessor.

Maritime warfare was a specialised business. Each of the ten crew members needed specific skills. Gordon Marsden arrived at 120 Squadron as a brand-new navigator after some taxing flying training. He suffered the fate of most men who hail from Northumberland. Dubbed Geordie by his comrades, his assertion that the nickname only applied to people from Newcastle-upon-Tyne achieved no mileage. Geordie he became and to Geordie he answered throughout his service career and beyond.

He completed his original studies at Number 3 Air Navigation School at Thornhill in Southern Rhodesia, now Zimbabwe. On returning to Britain in 1951, Geordie found himself at Swinderby as a pupil at 204 Advanced Flying School on de Havilland Mosquito aircraft. In the normal course of events, he would have gone to Malaya where active service beckoned. A colonial insurgency seeking independence, a struggle that started in 1948, evolved into a communist terror campaign.

Geordie did not, though, serve over the green dark jungle:

The Russian submarine threat intervened. I was sent with five or six others to No 1 School of Maritime Reconnaissance at St Mawgan in Cornwall where Lancaster ASR 3s were flying the course students to prepare them for all forms of dealing with the Russians. After another three months training there, the whole course moved to the other end of the country on to 236 Operational Conversion Unit at Kinloss in Morayshire. And what did we find here? Number 120 Squadron just completing the assessment trials on the Shackleton and 236 OCU already using the Shack Mark One for the conversion of these new crews. What a change from the St Mawgan Lancasters. There was room to move about inside and a six feet long (at least) table for the nav to spread out his maps and charts, and the rest of the ten crew seemed perfectly satisfied with their accommodation.

Potential maritime crews had a taxing time. They bombed skids towed by fast boats in the Moray Firth, used radar to bomb markers, did radar homings, dropped sonobuoys as well as operational flying exercises. There were compensations. The nearby Forres pub known to all and sundry as the 'Red Beastie' was one. It became host to parties to celebrate successful passing-out of courses at Kinloss. Not that alcohol was the only refreshment at Kinloss as Geordie recalls:

The Morayshire coast at this time was not the most hospitable but we were adequately catered for at coffee time by the ladies of the 'Church of Jocks' providing coffee and rolls for those who had missed breakfast. After another three months on this conversion course we were despatched to the various squadrons operating in Cornwall and from 1 April (seriously) Northern Ireland. My lot was with 120 Squadron who moved on 1 April 1952 from Kinloss to RAF Aldergrove and I was in fact transported across in the move.

The Shackleton, designed for long patrols across oceans which are usually devoid of outstanding characteristics, demanded a pair of excellent navigators. One was the routine navigator, the other the tactical navigator. Both were ideally fully conversant with the available radio aids. Navigators who popped out near the top of their course in Southern Rhodesia were particularly useful. They had polished their knowledge above countryside that generally lacked striking aspects. They knew how to coax information from erratic radio aids and were generally regarded as people who could navigate a warplane around the world almost by instinct.

The routine navigator maintained the Air Plot, which was the position where the aircraft would be in still air. Once this was established, he would find wind speed and direction by using a variety of radio and radar aids to establish the aircraft's true location. His responsibility, in the maritime world, was essentially to get the aircraft to the search area. As Geordie Marsden recalled, the available aids were:

First, the Shackleton's own radar – a scanner known as ASV13 which could pick up land points on coasts and so on up to about fifty or sixty miles if lucky.

Second came a radar lattice system called Gee, developed during the Second World War mainly for Bomber Command. This needed special charts, mainly the North Sea and English Channel areas.

Third, a similar American system called Loran which operated on different frequencies and covered a large area of the North Atlantic and there were other Loran chains in other parts of the world. They all needed special charts.

Fourth was a radio system working in the medium frequency range about 250 kcs (the frequency of 247 kilocycles) called Consol which was a Second World War German system that both sides employed. Fortunately their transmission stations were not put out of use at the end of the war. There were three stations for Consol – one in Northern Ireland, callsign MWN, one in northwest France with the callsign TRQ and a Norwegian one, identified by the signal LEC. Using any two stations would give a quite accurate 'fix' or ground position. In the Mk1 Shack this had to be obtained by the radio operator but I think the nav had his own radio receiver in the Mk2.

Relating the air position to any fix position at the same

time gave the wind effect and could be used as the wind velocity for any future Dalton Computer calculations. We could also use a '3 drift wind' on the computer because the wind at one thousand feet was not normally significantly different from that on the surface.

Consol had its origins in pre-war Germany. Dr Ernst Kramer, a devotee of composer Richard Strauss's music, developed an improved version of an American system. He called it Sonne after a Strauss opera character. It served as a navigation aid for Luftwaffe aircraft flying over Atlantic waters between France and Norway and for the U-boats of the Kriegsmarine.

Sonne charts fell into British hands. Its effectiveness proved, the British developed it as Consol, dog Latin which can mean 'by the sun', a neat nod to the German name. A Consol site used three aerials in a straight line with an aerial spacing of a few wavelengths.

The navigator, or an unwary signaller asked by a polite navigator, heard a series of dots merge slowly into a steady tone which then turned into dashes or, indeed, dashes that became dots. He need only count the number of each transmitted in one minute. The total was always sixty. A special Consol chart gave him the bearing of the transmitting station.

The Dalton Computer, known unkindly as the Prayer Wheel or the Whizz Wheel, was not a sophisticated electronic device but a manual method to ascertain wind velocity and drift. A rotating bearing disc covered a grid-piece with marked rectangular graduated lines. On the reverse sat a circular slide rule. The computer allowed the navigator to convert indicated air speed to true and determine ground speed to ascertain progress and calculate arrival times. Along with the square Douglas protractor that gave full 360 degree usage for plotting routes, the Dalton was probably the most important item in the navigator's flight bag.

The tactical navigator took over when action could be imminent. He also had equipment designed to make life easier. He controlled the Air Position Indicator or API and the Ground Position Indicator, usually referred to as GPI. Without them, the tactical navigator would have had a difficult time. The API was an early electrical/mechanical computer which gave the navigator a continual latitude and longitude read-out of the air position. This saved a massive amount of plotting. The GPI was fed by the API but also required the most reliable wind information for the area put into it by the navigator. The GPI shone a small cross on to a special chart below. As the aircraft moved, so did the cross. The tactical navigator marked the centre of the cross about every two minutes to give an accurate record of activities including dropping sonobuoys to detect submarines or bombs even if they were merely practice versions.

The first Shackletons carried little more than the armament of the Second World War. By about 1955, though, new developments increased the effectiveness of the Growler. Directional sonobuoys arrived. These transmitted a signal which gave the direction of the enemy submarine's cavitation or propeller noise. Allied with a well maintained GPI, this gave the aircraft considerable help. If the activity happened on convoy protection with a naval escort close by, it was simplicity itself to tell the surface guardians what was happening.

All maritime aircrews practised this technique. Every year they went to HMS *Sea Eagle* at Londonderry, the home of the Joint Anti Submarine School, obviously known as JASS, to mariners and airmen alike. With a stunning collection of realistic training aids, the unofficial motto of 'There's many a true word spoken in JASS' imprinted itself especially on the minds of tactical navigators.

Some considered that the most dismal aircrew work on the first Shackletons in service was done by the signallers. John Perigo, a one-time signaller who eventually wore an Air Electronic Officer brevet, recalls the early fifties:

The emphasis was on Morse code and the workings of a high-frequency radio equipment that appeared to have been designed for the flight of Icarus. Signallers then proceeded to the School of Air Gunnery at Leconfield to add Air Gunner to their qualification. Those destined for the Kipper Fleet then proceeded to the Maritime Reconnaissance School to learn radar operation and sonics – a system of dropping listening buoys into the ocean for detecting and tracking submerged submarines. Then it was off to the Operational Conversion Unit for a first date with the Grey Lady.

Signallers usually had a busy time of it when they were airborne. A main concern was high-frequency radio operated mainly with Morse code although some voice was used. The signallers needed to use radar for surface contacts and, when close enough to land, assisting the navigator with radar fixes. Sonics came into their own to track a submarine that had the temerity to submerge after sighting. The signaller was also expected to use the Mark One Eyeball as a visual look-out, usually from the nose turret and beam windows. He was also the man with the job if any gunnery was needed, be it air-to-air or air-to-sea.

John Perigo also noted the most important aspect of the signaller's work as far as most of the crew were concerned:

> By virtue of numbers and availability the signallers also did most of the in-flight catering, mainly tea, coffee, sandwiches, greasy fry-ups and of course the infamous Honkers' Stew, a noxious brew of just about anything available in the ration pack. No two stews were ever the same but the legend lived on throughout the maritime career of the Shackleton. Why do we remember those days with affection? Must have been the company of friends because the job was dire!

The fourth Shackleton unit, Number 269 Squadron, came into existence almost a year after the aeroplane joined the Royal Air Force. On 1 January 1952, 224 Squadron, then at Gibraltar, graciously passed over the weariest Shackletons in their charge. This included one aircraft that was under repair after hitting a sea wall. 269 Squadron officially set up in business at Ballykelly on 10 March 1952.

With four Shackleton squadrons already flying, with the US Neptune arriving to equip other maritime reconnaissance units, Coastal Command concentrated on its front-line tasks. Low-level sorties to hunt submarines were a high training priority but the Command also had search and rescue responsibilities. Training, training, and more training would bring the Command to greater wartime readiness. The next years would test the system and the men who worked it.

CHAPTER THREE

The statement from Buckingham Palace was stark:

> It was announced from Sandringham at 10.45 am today, February 6, 1952, that the King who retired to rest last night in his usual health, passed peacefully away in his sleep early this morning.

The new Queen was on holiday in Kenya. Her husband, the Duke of Edinburgh broke the news to her. They flew from Nyeri to Entebbe in Uganda. A storm delayed their departure for Britain but they were in the air shortly before midnight, British time. During the next hours, the machinery of the nation ran through everything that the sovereign's death entailed. The Accession Council held a short meeting to sign the Proclamation of Queen Elizabeth II. Parliament was suspended. The Members took oaths of allegiance to the new sovereign. The British military in its turn adapted quickly to the thought that they were now the Queen's Men.

Sir George Bellew, himself a former squadron leader in the wartime Volunteer Reserve, and holder of the challenging post of Garter Principal King of Arms, grasped the chance to persuade the appropriate bodies that it was a befitting moment to change the Tudor Crown – which did not actually exist –

depicted above the Royal Cipher to a more realistic interpretation of the actual Crown of England.

Queen Elizabeth agreed. A subsequent Sovereign's Declaration announced that:

> The Queen wishes the St Edward's Crown to take the place of the Tudor Crown in all future designs embodying a representation of the crown.

Existing schemes were not to be changed until required nor unnecessary expense incurred. In the Royal Air Force the detail of buttons and badges changed only slowly. Popular legend quickly claimed that the new distinction was the 'Queen's Crown' as opposed to the 'King's Crown'. The unspoken implication was that the former system would return in the distant future if a king came to the throne. It is a virtual certainty that St Edward's Crown will remain in use irrespective of the gender of the monarch.

The men of 120 Squadron knew they would be amongst the first to take part in exercises with the Royal Navy. Exercise Castanets was already scheduled. The first phase was devoted to convoy attacks by surface ships, submarines and aircraft. Later came the technique of aircraft harassing enemy submarines as they moved to and from their patrol positions. Although the RAF would only pretend to attack, a self-respecting RN skipper and his crew would be anxious to avoid any theoretical damage from the crabs in their shiny new 'hostile' aircraft. To the Royal Navy, wearers of light blue uniforms were trespassers of the worst sort. Royal Air Force crews, both ground and air, similarly concluded that the fish-heads simply wanted to keep all action on the oceans in the hands of those in dark blue outfits.

Nine nations were scheduled to take a role in the exercise. On the water, 150 warships with a myriad of motor launches and other small craft, along with some four hundred aircraft, would take part in mock warfare. Over one hundred fleet auxiliary vessels would represent merchant ships, either in convoy or as individual targets for submarines or aircraft.

On 8 April, a Shackleton set off for the United States. It had an important passenger. Air Marshal Sir Alick Stevens, the Air Officer

Commanding in Chief of Coastal Command would not only discuss NATO matters and maritime fighting but show off the newest British weapon. The Shackleton's appearance convinced a number of American onlookers that it was a Lancaster, a belief that remained predominant throughout the following years.

120 Squadron spent its time preparing for Castanets. Jim Humphrey noted that on the 16 April he flew in Shackleton WG511 for a Navigation Exercise combined with an Endurance Trial. The crew each put twenty hours in their flying logbooks. Fifteen hours were spent on the navigation phase while the remainder was devoted to circling Lough Neath at the minimum propeller RPM, not a feature of normal flights. The prudent limit of endurance, abbreviated to PLE, was to have 400 gallons of fuel remaining in the tanks at the end of the flight. WG511 landed with less than 100 gallons available for use.

The next Shackleton squadron appeared on 1 May 1952. Based on paper at St Eval, 240 Squadron moved to Ballykelly in Ulster the following month. Once there, with few enough aircraft, the aircrew learned about their new aeroplane from 120 Squadron. Joint flights became common.

Flight had its reporter on hand for an important occasion as its issue of 13 June 1952 recorded. Headlined 'Happy Returns to Her Majesty' the article described how:

> Coastal Command sent eighteen new Avro Shackletons to London on June 5th for the ceremonial fly-past in honour of the Queen's birthday, Their arrival over the city centre, just before 1300 hr, was heralded by the low-pitched roar of seventy-two Rolls-Royce Griffons – an impressive sound, matching the splendid sight of eighteen gleaming white aircraft spread out in three flights of six. Despite slipstream and thermal turbulence, station-keeping was excellent during the run-in to Buckingham Palace; then, having saluted the Sovereign on behalf of the RAF, the Shackletons turned away to the south-west and headed for St Eval.

The weekly had used its helpful contacts at the Air Ministry to put its own reporter on board. After describing the route taken, the article continued:

At 1,000ft, over the City conditions were difficult; station keeping was obviously hard work, but a gentle turn to port brought the formation into line with The Mall – which runs at about 235 deg – and over the Palace exactly at 1300 hr.

From each aircraft anything up to ten pairs of eyes peered at the Royal balcony for an instant; then, with a notable easing of the tension, the Shackletons were pointed south across Kingston-on-Thames and the formation opened out slightly . . . the homeward route roughly followed the coast, diversions to seaward being made past the major towns. St Eval was reached at about 1500 hr; the crews felt rather tired by now, and very deafened – but proud that they had represented their service in its salute to Her Majesty.

Prior to 'the day' much practice flying had been done off the Cornish coast. Formation flying, especially with eighteen aircraft, is far from an everyday job for Coastal Command and the polished formation seen over London reflects credit on all concerned.

The Queen was joined on the Buckingham Palace balcony by the Duke of Edinburgh, Queen Elizabeth the Queen Mother and Princess Margaret. Squadron Leader Laband, known generally as Bill in 220 Squadron, which he commanded, and the crews who flew the aeroplanes so well, had made the Shackleton almost a household word.

Twelve days later, on 17 June, the MR2 prototype, adapted from an MR1 taken off the production line, made its first flight. The Shackleton was clearly destined for a long career, apparently not having the luxury of a 'best before' date stamped anywhere on it.

With Exercise Castanets yawning closer, much of 120 Squadron, both men and aircraft, set off to Scampton in Lincolnshire. A substantial number of 240 Squadron went with them. Exercise flying was excellent practice for the future.

By 23 June, the work-out was close to a new phase. Land-based aircraft of Coastal Command and the Royal Canadian Air Force along with carrier-borne aeroplanes from HMS *Indomitable* and HMCS *Magnificent*, all serving in Blue Force, were to search the seas and harass any Red Force submarines they found in the Atlantic approaches.

On the afternoon of 25 June 1952, a mixed crew from 120 Squadron and 240 Squadron took off from Scampton in VP261 with thirteen men, two of them supernumerary passengers, on board. The majority came from 240 Squadron, happy to gain experience of their new aircraft. The captain, Wing Commander Wilfred Montague Bisdee, was normally OC Flying at Ballykelly. The regular captain, Flying Officer Robert Owen Blackall came from 120 Squadron.

After lifting from the runway, the Shackleton ground its way eastward towards the sea. Then it turned north, hunting at low level some twelve miles out to sea as the afternoon turned into a clear sunset.

Crowds along the coast, enjoying the evening on Holy Island and at Berwick upon Tweed, heard an explosion. To the east, they watched the sombre signal of a black smoke cloud rise emphatically into the air.

HMS *Sirdar* saw the result. Lieutenant Humphrey Michael Woolrych, the First Lieutenant of the submarine was awarded the George Medal. His citation read:

At 1934 hours on the 25th June 1952 HM Submarine *Sirdar* sighted a large curtain of flames about one mile away. She surfaced and found this to be the wreckage of a Shackleton aircraft which had burst into flames on hitting the sea. As the submarine approached the flames, one of the crew was seen to be waving from a position close to the northern end of the burning wreckage. No boat was carried on the submarine and Lieutenant Woolrych volunteered to swim to the survivor. At 1940 he swam to the man and brought him safely back to the submarine. A second member of the crew was then sighted to the south of the flames and about five yards from the most intense area of the fire. At 1954 Lieutenant Woolrych again dived overboard and disregarding his own safety swam to this survivor. Owing to the proximity of the flames it was necessary to tow Lieutenant Woolrych and the airman from the vicinity. The airman, who was suffering from severe burns to the face and hands, was most skilfully brought on board the submarine by Lieutenant Woolrych. The airmen undoubtedly owed their lives to the speed and skill with which Lieutenant Woolrych recovered them from the sea.

When it comes to danger, to saving life, neither crabs nor fish-heads argue about details.

The Berwick harbourmaster, Captain Tom Richardson, in an interview with the *Berwickshire News* recalled:

It was low tide at the time and I knew it was impossible for her to come in. I was at the dock and had just piloted a ship in, when I saw the puff of smoke out at sea and I knew something was in trouble. I then went over to my home, which overlooks the harbour, and kept my eyes on the sea. Through the binoculars, I saw a naval craft, which I did not immediately identify as a submarine, coming in and I thought she would have survivors on board so I dashed down to the shipyard on my bicycle. I said to George Hepburn and Edward Brown, who were there, 'Have you got a boat handy? There's a naval craft coming in and I think she has survivors on board.'

We got the first boat we saw and went out to this submarine. We were preparing to take the two airmen off and bring them in on the launch when the submarine captain saw the lifeboat heading towards us.

The two rescued men, one a navigator, the other a signaller, were swiftly transferred to the lifeboat that had hurried from Holy Island. Crowds lined the jetty to stare as rescue craft reached the long Berwick jetty. Local fishermen arrived in their small cobles, clinker-built boats similar to that rowed by Grace Darling to the *Forfarshire* a century earlier. Rather than carry the two men on stretchers to the distant waiting ambulance, the fishermen rowed in excess of one hundred yards to deliver the pair. Once stretchered on to the vehicle, the survivors were rushed to hospital.

One body arrived later at Berwick. A local fishing vessel, the *Elizabeth Crawford* reached the quay with the corpse of nineteen-year-old Leading Aircraftman Peter Reginald Wadsworth, one of the two supernumeraries.

Subsequent enquiries were hampered by the simple fact that it proved impossible to collect meaningful wreckage. No recordings of the flight, now so common with 'black boxes', existed. The only evidence came from onlookers on boats. Their recollections varied. Some claimed the aircraft suddenly exploded although memories could well have been confused by dummy attack manoeuvres.

The Shackleton crew had undoubtedly seen HMS *Sirdar*. In an apparently disciplined display, the aircraft dropped two smoke bombs on the half-submerged shape. VP261 then turned steeply at low level to start a second attack run. The aircraft possibly stalled in the turn. An aircraft's lower wing moves through the air more slowly than its companion when banking. Alternatively, the Shackleton suffered a catastrophic loss of power. Either a Griffon misbehaved or a flight deck occupant accidentally closed the master fuel cocks, possibly by using them as a grab handle or, unharnessed, falling on them as the aircraft turned. In due course, a general warning went to Shackleton crews. The fuel cocks also received a protective cover.

Jim Humphrey was at Scampton with the 120 Squadron detachment. He recalled:

After returning from an anti-submarine patrol who was waiting for me but my former crew. I told the flight engineer, an old and true mate, that all the aircraft needed was refuelling.

As I reported to Exercise Headquarters I was informed to report back to RAF Aldergrove. At Liverpool whilst waiting to board the ferry to Belfast, I purchased a newspaper and read that a Shackleton had crashed into the North Sea.

When I got back to Aldergrove I was told it was my old crew. They had apparently spotted a periscope of a sub which turned out to be HMS *Sirdar*, dived towards the sub but unfortunately things went wrong and they hit the sea.

Immediately the sub surfaced and, disregarding the burning fuel, managed to rescue two of the crew, one was the sergeant navigator and the other was the signaller, who had incidentally got through the Second World War without a scratch. The navigator was saved but the signaller died.

The remainder of the incident is somewhat surprising. A

rating who dived into the sea was the brother of my future sister-in-law.

I did not fly for two months because of a suspect appendix problem and had to travel to RAF Cosford near Wolverhampton. I had a lift from Aldergrove in a Met Flight Hastings to Bovingdon, at that time an American base on the A41.

I decided to hitch a lift into the centre of London. A car stopped and the driver asked me where I was going. I told him and he offered to take me to the railway station in London. I was in uniform and during the journey the driver asked me what aircraft I was flying. I replied, 'a Shackleton, sir'.

He told me that his son used to fly Shackletons. He told me his surname and I am convinced there were tears in his eyes (and mine) when I told him I used to be in his crew at RAF Aldergrove.

It took me quite a time to get over the incident.

Although the Griffon was expected to give trouble-free service for long hours at a time, it had problems that caused hearts to thump and mouths to dry. The translation units in particular had a less than endearing occasional trick. If they failed when the aircraft was cruising the only immediate indication was a slight drop in the airspeed of between five and ten knots. When determined eyes did a visual check of the four engines, it was possible to see a shadow out of synchronisation on one engine as the rear propellers rotated at a different pitch to their fellows. The only solution was to close down the affected engine, which often meant a termination of the flight.

The experts thought through the problem and duly produced an answer. In simple terms, the translation unit needed regular oiling. A two hour interval was deemed proper. Flight engineers, who promptly received the responsibility for 'lubricating the TUs', would occasionally beckon a newly qualified crew member to tell them they had to do the job. After joyfully watching the panic spread across the victim's face at the thought of clambering out on to the wing clutching an oil can, the flight engineer would simply tell the captain on the intercom. He in turn warned the crew. They all had to acknowledge the warning for it was well known that sudden alien and unexpected noises in aeroplanes cause alarm. At this point, the captain exercised the propellers of all four engines in turn. One by one, the revolutions were reduced and restored, reduced and restored and then returned to the cruise position. Roaring noises echoed through the whole length of the Shackleton as the Griffons responded. This simple activity recharged the oil in the translation unit and, the boffins believed, essentially reduced the risk of breakdown.

Less common was a collapse of a translation unit when a Shackleton took off using water methanol injection to supercharge the Griffons. The affected engine would jump up and down, so much so that the engine spinner seemed to rapidly bounce some two or three feet in both directions.

Enough Shackletons from Avro's factory floor arrived in sufficient time for the next unit, Number 42 Squadron, to join yet another NATO exercise, Mainbrace, scheduled to last from 13 to 25 September. On 28 June 1952, the squadron took on maritime reconnaissance with the Shackleton. They had a temporary move from St Eval to Kinloss to carry out their quota of exercise patrols. They enjoyed, as did the other RAF maritime squadrons in the Shetlands, Northern Scotland and Norway, regular duty flights of mail and supplies from a Dakota of Coastal Command's 18 Group Communications Flight.

Their permanent home at St Eval was not one of the finer examples of RAF accommodation. The squadron and its Mk1 aircraft endured a dismal and distant side of the airfield. They had a shed, one leaky hangar and three caravans. The shed provided a home for the engine and airframe crews. One caravan went to the electronic tradesmen. Of the others, one protected the squadron stores while the third belonged to the ground engineers. The flight sergeant and his minions used steel cabinets to safely hold their Forms 700, the aircraft maintenance records.

Coastal Command's squadrons, both those equipped with the Shackleton and those adapting to the Neptune, had a fill of exercises designed to improve their efficiency. The NATO intention with Mainbrace was largely a naval matter although it called on the land, sea and air forces of eight nations. The high-minded purpose was to develop the organisation for mutual defence in the alliance countries of the eastern Atlantic and northern

Europe. Essentially a maritime exercise, the Allied Forces, named as usual Blue, would come under attack by Orange sea and air forces. In essence, the Orange enemy, assisted by strong air and submarine elements, were to invade Norway from the north and attack Denmark from the south.

Coastal Command squadrons scattered across northern Europe from Topcliffe in Yorkshire to Norway for the exercise. Not everything went absolutely to plan. Ballykelly deployed six Shackletons to Topcliffe along with eight crews, for spare hands would be necessary. On the appointed day, each Shackleton took off with its aircrew and ground crew on board. That left two crews, all of whom were sergeants, to move to Topcliffe under less glamorous arrangements than flying.

The men departed Ballykelly at 1500 hours after the Shackletons left. A three-ton truck, a standard vehicle for the three British services of the time, took them and their luggage to the local railway station at Limavady Junction. From there, they took the train to Belfast where they changed trains, riding one that took them to Larne. From that port, they boarded a ferry that took them across the Irish Sea to Stranraer. After an apparently unending voyage, the men took a train from Stranraer to Glasgow where they changed again. This time they boarded a train bound for Newcastle-upon-Tyne. From there they took yet another train to Thirsk which greeted them a full twenty-four hours after setting out.

The ubiquitous three-ton lorry collected them all to take everyone to Topcliffe. The airfield was, the signallers of the group repeatedly reminded the more doubtful, a modern station with brick buildings. Built shortly before the Second World War under the Expansion Plan, the accommodation enjoyed proper heating as well as commodious single bedrooms. They would not have to endure metal Nissen huts or cramped wooden huts that apparently dated from the days of the First World War. The signallers knew these things for they had trained at Swanton Morley, a most congenial station of identical vintage.

The truck arrived at Topcliffe. It lumbered along smooth roads towards the airfield where it finally ground to a halt in the shadow of the air traffic control tower. Close by were the aircraft hangars. Alongside them was a row of tents. Inside each of these were canvas camp beds with detachable thin metal legs. Each tent, the new arrivals learned, would accommodate a complete crew. It never serves well to be the last to arrive.

Some newspaper editors turned Mainbrace into rather more than simply 'another NATO exercise'. After one week of activity, the *Yorkshire Evening Press* of Saturday 20 September carried the Great Flying Saucer story, based on the eye-witness account of a Shackleton captain. The next day, the *Sunday Dispatch* produced a similar version. Under a black, glaring headline 'SAUCER' CHASED RAF JET PLANE, its reporter wrote that the Royal Air Force was investigating a strange object that followed a fighter aircraft:

It was seen by two RAF officers and three aircrew as they stood near Coastal Command Shackleton Squadron HQ at Topcliffe.

They had just landed after a flight and were watching a Meteor coming into land at the neighbouring Dishforth RAF station.

One of them, Flight Lieutenant John W Kilburn, 31, of Egremont, Cumberland then spotted 'something different from anything I have ever seen in 3,700 hours flying in a variety of conditions.'

He told me last night:

'It was 10.53 am on Friday. The Meteor was coming down from about 5,000ft. The sky was clear. There was sunshine and unlimited visibility.

'The Meteor was crossing from east to west when I noticed the white object in the sky.

'This object was silver and circular in shape, about 10,000ft up some five miles astern of the aircraft. It appeared to be travelling at a lower speed than the Meteor but was on the same course.'

John Kilburn also allegedly mentioned, during interview, that the object 'maintained its forward speed for several seconds before it started to descend, then began swinging with a pendulum action, something 'similar to a falling sycamore leaf.'

After dismissing his own thought that the mysterious body

46

could have been a parachute or an engine cowling, he added that the thing followed the Meteor when the fighter turned towards Dishforth. He then delivered the coup de grace:

> After a few seconds, it stopped its pendulum motion and started to rotate about its own axis. It then made off at an incredible speed towards the west turning south-east before disappearing.

The *Sunday Dispatch* had been an enthusiastic participant in recounting flying saucer stories in what was generally accepted to be a circulation battle with its rivals. Several books on the subject had recently appeared. The British press had competed fiercely to serialise them for their readers.

Although the usual conspiracy theorists fell upon the information with pleasure, believing that it proved that beings from alien worlds were gazing upon the planet, *Flight* failed to join in the frenetic excitement. The magazine concluded its report of the exercise with a simple observation:

> An unscheduled entrant in the exercise was the 'flying saucer', reported to have been seen by Coastal Command personnel at Topcliffe, Yorkshire on September 20th. In the 'saucer sightings and movements' file at Maritime Headquarters, Pitreavie, the object was described as 'silvery white,' making identification with either Blue or Orange forces difficult.

For Geordie Marsden, Mainbrace was a symptom of things to come:

> 120 Squadron from Aldergrove and 240 Squadron from Ballykelly were both despatched to Sola airfield near Stavanger in Norway. There were about five crews from each so it meant that around sixty NCO aircrew had to be accommodated.
>
> When we got there we found that our dwelling was to be a large L-shaped room on a hillside which had previously been used by the Luftwaffe. This room had sufficient two-bunk beds, each with a hessian mattress cover. Next door, in

another room, was a quantity of hay which was meant for stuffing the hessian to provide a mattress. There were also blankets for each bed but the whole set-up was a bit rough for the RAF who were used to sheets and proper mattresses.

Anyway we were all accommodated in this room but once the exercise started there were crews moving in and out the whole time of the day and night so that no one was able to get any proper sleep. The exercise lasted about fifteen days so by the end of this time everybody was ready to strangle the man in the next bed or the one above because it was virtually impossible to get a full night's sleep. At the end of the fortnight we were all relieved to fly back to the home bases and get some comfortable kip in our own comfortable billets.

The next Shackleton operator came into existence on 25 September 1952 when 206 Squadron began maritime operations at St Eval. Like the other units based there, they had an ongoing task, flying out over the Atlantic in a round of exercise and training flights.

The ground crew from 236 Operational Conversion Unit who despatched Shackleton VP286 from Kinloss on a gunnery exercise on 8 October 1952 waited in vain for its return. The captain, Flight Sergeant John Claude Western aged thirty, and the other thirteen men on board died when the aircraft crashed in the Moray Firth waters off Tarbat Ness. Two were supernumerary passengers, both aged nineteen.

The Times carried a succinct account:

Fourteen airmen in a Shackleton aircraft from Kinloss Airfield, Morayshire, which yesterday fell into the sea off Tarbat Ness in the north of Scotland, were last night posted as 'Missing believed killed.'

The Shackleton, a Coastal Command aircraft, was on a local air-sea firing practice. The pilot of another aircraft reported seeing the Shackleton dive into the water. The missing men were all from Kinloss Airfield.

The crew of the Lossiemouth fishing boat *Vervena*, returning home from the fishing ground, saw the flash and smoke of an explosion, and immediately went back to the spot. 'When we arrived,' said Skipper J. Crockett, 'we found ourselves amid wreckage strewn over a wide area. We searched but could find only three bodies.'

Until dusk a search for survivors was made over a wide area by other aircraft, a launch, a lifeboat and other vessels and a helicopter.

With little evidence available, no definite cause for the crash could be determined. Some believed that the aeroplane simply exploded. Echoing thoughts about the VP261 accident, a belief took hold that the aircraft stalled in a steep turn at low level.

The Royal Aircraft Establishment had investigated ditching a Shackleton in experiments with specially constructed models. They produced a Test Report in 1953 with carefully phrased conclusions. Both were apparently written to reduce any fears about ditching amongst maritime reconnaissance aircrew. The front page summary which most recipients would read in preference to wading through pages of prose said:

> The model tests indicate the ditching behaviour of the full scale aircraft will be satisfactory provided that the bomb doors do not collapse.

Within the Report proper, the same conclusion was phrased differently:

> The model tests indicated that the ditching behaviour of the full scale aircraft will be unsatisfactory unless the bomb doors can be prevented from collapsing . . .

This splendid effort, illustrated with fifty-four photographs of models breaking up when they hit the water, would not actually add very much to the already existing conclusions made by most aircrew. In general, not many of them expected the Shackleton to survive landing on the ocean unless the conditions were absolutely favourable. As full rehearsals were impracticable, surviving a ditching was no more than a matter of chance.

Logic told members of the Royal Air Force, both aircrew and ground crew, that the accident was one of those things that happened from time to time. The many surviving wartime personnel had all grown accustomed to sudden departures by friends. Even young conscripts had grown up in a world at war where death was not uncommon.

For the Shackleton crews, trips that lasted anything from one hour to sixteen hours were all part of the job. They had a fulfilling role which paid money, admittedly not as much as civilian jobs paid, on a regular basis. The aircraft may have had a few drawbacks but they were easily shrugged off. There were tailwheel shimmy problems and signallers lost radar contacts when the fixed rear fitting blotted out their radar signal. Some further regarded the radios as a joke. Neither did the aircraft heaters invariably work properly. The Griffon engines threw off their exhaust stubs with wearisome regularity, continually deafened the crew and produced a debilitating vibration. It was no rare occurrence for a Shackleton to return with one engine out of commission. Add in the smell that was the aeroplane's personal signature, a combination aroma of hydraulic oil, damp tea towels, personal crew boxes with often grubby contents, sweat, fried bacon and the inevitable honkers stew plus the constant reminder of the Elsan toilet and, as the wearers of the uniform cheerfully agreed, it was great to be alive and flying in the RAF. Volunteers who offered to fly as supernumerary passengers were not dismayed by statistics that revealed some 605 RAF service personnel had lost their lives in 1952. Air accidents were not the sole dangers that lurked in the shadows.

It was not a life that spent days, weeks, months and years doing the same repetitive job day after day. Squadrons moved away on Exercise detachments. November 1952 saw four Shackletons from 120 Squadron fly to Keflavik in Iceland for another NATO exercise, this one named Autumn Bear. The aim of the exercise was to test the available ASW weaponry under Arctic operating conditions. This would, of necessity, include the performance of ships, aircraft and men in extremely cold weather. The Shackletons made anti-submarine patrols and gave close support to Royal Navy ships in the exercise. One crewman never forgot the sight of the Northern Lights at 73 degrees North. 'Sitting in the mid upper gun turret gave the best view', he noted but 'the static around the aircraft props, aerials and gun turret was out of this world.'

It was long rumoured that a Land Rover, allegedly the first to reach the country, was provided by the RAF for use as a crew coach. It was further alleged that a sergeant with an eye to the future sold the vehicle to a local citizen. Like most Shackleton crew stories, anonymity reigns.

In September 1952, the Aeroplane and Armament Experimental Establishment at Boscombe Down laid their hands on the first Mk2 Shackletons. One immediate concern and thus the subject of tests flights was crew well-being during long flights. This was simple realism. Uncomfortable crew members could fail during action against an enemy.

The assessment took all of October. In the Report Summary, published the following year, the authors noted that recommendations in the first reports on the Mark One were strongly reinforced. Their main criticisms again 'concerned the high levels of vibration and noise and the grossly inadequate sanitary arrangements'.

The AAEE team spent some fifty hours in flight on the aircraft. On a flight to Gibraltar, the aileron control on the automatic pilot gave up at an early stage in the flight. For the next eleven hours, lateral control was maintained manually, a task made no simpler by air turbulence. Constant supervision was needed to stop the aircraft wandering off course.

The report produced an eight-item list of major detailed criticisms accompanied by the observation that 'omission from the above list of other criticisms . . . is not intended to imply that modification action, where possible is not necessary.'

A short appendix included extracts from the Shackleton modification index supplied by the manufacturers yet to be incorporated. Of the six entries concerning crew comfort, modification 370 introduced a new seat pan for the flight engineer and rear observer's seat. In the report on that position, AAEE had noted that 'the location of the slow running cut out switches was such that they were liable to be knocked by the flight engineer.' To emphasise the seriousness, AAEE noted that, during a flight, one engine stopped when the engineer brushed his shoulder against the switches while turning in his seat.

It was not the AAEE's task to decide either the cost of modifications or how they should be met. That went higher up the line, eventually ending with the politicians. In real terms they had insufficient money on which to call. Not many things could be cut. The defence budget had problems because of the increasing costs in maintaining the British Empire. With the birth of the welfare state, many observers believed that the demands on the national exchequer would continue to grow. How this would affect the services was hardly mentioned. The Shackleton still had plenty of service ahead. Whether the finances were available to look after it was another matter.

CHAPTER FOUR

After the revival of Number 206 Squadron, the formation of new Shackleton squadrons dropped. The generally accepted explanation put the blame for the delay on the production of the new MR2, which was to prove a modest variation on a familiar theme.

The MR2 was clearly not a spanking new type but a modified version of the first Shackletons with a completely redesigned and lengthened nose. The rear fuselage became a cone shape and twin retractable tail wheels made an appearance. A radome was fitted on the bottom of the fuselage just aft of the wing. This withdrew into the body of the aircraft when not in use.

Braking and taxiing problems, especially in cross winds, had caused MR1 pilots to mutter dark imprecations. Their difficulties eased with the installation of toe brakes and lockable rudders. The new nose acquired a turret with two remotely controlled guns while the bomb aimer took to the comfort of a prone arrangement. Two clear look-out positions, one above and one below, improved his view of the world outside. The redesigned tail cone also incorporated a transparent viewing post to evaluate attacks that used bombs or depth charges. The improvements were much welcomed by the men who flew in the Shackleton although noise levels showed no obvious amelioration.

Nearly one hundred NATO exercises were scheduled for 1953. They ranged across the whole gamut of armed forces and the territory of the Treaty. When normal training was added to the mix, it became clear that military flying was not always a matter of cakes and ale.

Britain had a full menu when it came to possible military endeavours aside from the ever-present threat of a full shooting war with the Soviet Empire. An Avro Lincoln strayed into the Soviet Zone of Germany in March. On a training flight from Leconfield, it ended up as a victim of the Soviet Air Force. Seven men died when MiG-15 fighters shot down the bomber.

Although Britain had tried to divest itself of the remnants of Empire once the Second World War ended, the granting of self-rule to India and Pakistan had, it seemed, simply encouraged the growth of nationalist movements in a dozen other territories that had once been Whitehall's province.

One problem that lurked in the darker recesses of Government policy was Egypt and the Suez Canal Zone. Britain had bought most of the Suez Canal shares in 1869. British administrators ensured that the ruling Khedive acted in British interests as far as the Canal was concerned, a policy that resulted in occupation by the British military in 1882. The country subsequently became a British Protectorate when the First World War started. Egypt received independence in 1922 but British forces remained to guard the Canal. The 1936 Anglo-Egyptian Treaty gave Britain an eternal right to keep troops in the Suez Canal Zone. German attempts to seize the country in the Second World War were effectively ended at the Battle of El Alamein.

In 1952, the dissolute King Farouk found himself unemployed when Egyptian Army officers took control of the country. All three British armed forces were soon fighting a minor guerrilla war in the Canal Zone which joined Kenya and Malaya as a further location in which anti-terrorist operations were the order of the day.

Murmurs of discontent were lost in the preparations for the Coronation of the new monarch. There would obviously be a fly-past over London but great brains decided that this should be limited to jet fighter aircraft, 144 Meteors from the RAF and 24

RCAF Sabres. The fly-past would use a formation of two broad arrowheads of 72 Meteors each linked by the Sabres in six boxes of four aircraft. They were all, so the press report stated, to fly over the Mall at a speed of 345 mph, which was a precise enough calculation of the 300 knot flying speed. Not even Griffons at full power would persuade a Shackleton to reach that pace.

Maritime aircraft would nonetheless have their chance to shine. The Air Ministry proclaimed in January that a Royal Review to salute the Coronation would take place on 15 July at Odiham in Hampshire. The planned fly-past of thirty types of aircraft, designed as a meticulous tribute to the new sovereign, would include the Shackleton.

Number 120 Squadron, slogging away at Aldergrove, achieved a minor unwelcome record with a modernised Mk2 Shackleton, WL749, it received on 20 April 1953. Twenty-four days later, it failed to meet the runway precisely. It landed short. This caused substantial damage to the left main undercarriage which collapsed in protest. The aeroplane swiftly changed direction as it ran along the ground. It eventually nosed its way into the runway controller's caravan. By good fortune, nobody suffered anything worse than fright and bruises. Technical officers had no hesitation in classing WL749 as beyond economical repair. As an airframe filled with spare parts it promptly became an extremely fruitful addition to the squadron's assortment of helpful stores.

Shackleton squadrons generally had nine aircraft. Squadron personnel were split into two Flights, 'A' and 'B'. The system was simplicity personified. 'A' Flight consisted of the aircrew, irrespective of rank while 'B' Flight was home to all the specialist ground crew who maintained the aircraft readiness.

On 2 June 1953 more than eight thousand people in Westminster Abbey witnessed the crowning of Elizabeth II as Queen. Under the inspired name of Operation Pony Express, RAF Canberras flew television film of the Coronation across the Atlantic for evening transmission in Canada and the United States. For many people, the Queen's standing was enhanced by news that reached London on the evening of her Coronation. Mount Everest, its 29,035 feet for so long a symbol untouched by human feet, finally succumbed to Edmund Hillary, a New Zealander, and Tenzing Norgay, his Sherpa companion, members of a British expedition to the top of the world.

The Coronation Review of the Royal Air Force was widely billed as 'the greatest display of air power ever mounted by the service in its thirty-five years' history'. The Shackletons were a tiny part of a fly-past that mustered 641 aircraft of thirty different types. A further 318 aircraft sat on the ground. A single Mk2 resplendent in a shiny white and grey finish kept station with three other Shackletons to do the honours for Coastal Command. All the static aircraft were accompanied by other equipment that represented all branches of the Royal Air Force.

A Shackleton crew member, part of two nine-aircraft formations, tersely noted:

17.7.53 – VP259 – duration 6 hours 10 mins. Coronation Fly-past for HM Queen over RAF Odiham. The runways at Odiham were full of neatly parked aircraft.

His description contains a later comment – 'there were probably more aircraft in the fly-past than the RAF have today.'

One reporter summed up the fly-past succinctly as:

. . . a remarkable achievement of organisation and timing. The forty-nine formations, groups and individual aircraft had taken off from widely scattered bases, and because of the differences in distances from Odiham and the wide disparity in their speeds they had to keep to a rigid schedule in order to take their appointed place in the groups as they began to form up near Leavesden, Hertfordshire, from which they flew in a straight 'corridor' to Odiham. In spite of a gusty wind and some cloud, the formation flying and the spacing between the groups were excellent. The stream of aircraft took approximately twenty-seven minutes to fly past.

Some minor cheer ran through the politicians when the Korean War reached its effective end. An Armistice was signed at Panmunjon on 27 July 1953. The talks had dragged on for two years and it was, both sides agreed, merely a temporary measure 'until a final peaceful settlement is achieved.' That conclusion never came. The treaty became the only surety for peace in Korea.

Ceremonial fly-pasts were not the main function of Coastal Command although none could deny the expertise of the Shackleton squadrons when it came to keeping large aeroplanes in formation. They had a serious and more important reason in their lives, a purpose which more often than not involved time away from home.

In August 1953, 206 Squadron set off from St Eval on a round tour that would eat up some forty thousand miles and involve the squadron in exercises over the Indian Ocean alongside training and goodwill visits to Ceylon (now Sri Lanka), New Zealand, Australia and Fiji. As was normal, the squadron needed to take ground crew and spares for virtually any problem that might befall the aircraft. Some sixty servicing personnel flew in the Shackletons with a further bevy, complete with spare parts, joining them by courtesy of Hastings aircraft from Transport Command.

The first two Shackletons left on the evening of 12 August and went to Ceylon by way of staging posts at El Adem and Khormaksar. Two other aircraft left the next day, nosing their way to Ceylon by way of Habbaniya, Iraq. All four aircraft met over Ceylon and duly landed at Negombo. After ten days of exercises, 206 went to Fiji via Singapore, Australia and New Zealand for a further exercise with Royal New Zealand Air Force maritime squadron Sunderlands.

Trips to distant locations, some pleasant, a few undesirable, consistently featured in the lives of Coastal Command air and ground crew. The Shackletons in particular habitually undertook impressive training flights that lasted many hours.

Number 37 Squadron became the next unit to experience the Shackleton and take on maritime reconnaissance work.

Coastal Command had the task of air/sea rescue work from unfriendly waters as well as searching the seas for shipwreck survivors. Unlike its predecessor in oceanic flying, the Sunderland, the Shackleton had no ability to land on water, perhaps in enemy-controlled areas, pick up people and return to the safety of the air. To remedy this drawback, a new airborne lifeboat was in the works, made, fittingly enough, by Saunders-Roe, the firm to which A V Roe had gone in 1928.

The result of their activity was on display at the 1953 Farnborough Air Display. According to one observer, the bright yellow lifeboat 'snuggled up to the weapons bay of the Shackleton . . . introduced a salty new note.'

Flight had previewed the design in February:

> . . . is designed to fit under the bomb bay of the Avro Shackleton. It is 30 ft long and has accommodation for 10 people, for whom there is a 14-day supply of food and a fishing kit.
>
> The engine is specially designed for starting in any weather, and enough fuel is carried for a range of 1,250 miles. In addition sails are provided for use in case of engine failure. To assist navigation, radio and radar aids are installed and the whole boat is designed and fitted out in such a manner that ditched crews would be dependent to only a small degree on the air/sea rescue organisation and could fend for themselves, heading for friendly territory or busy shipping lanes. A small automatic radar homing beacon can be switched on to signal the lifeboat's position to searching aircraft.

Any of the magazine's readers who thought that the lifeboat was too large and superfluous to be useful would possibly have been reassured by the remaining paragraphs. They continued in an optimistic vein:

> Fitting the boat to a Shackleton takes only thirty minutes, and the Dunlopillo gunwale fits snugly to the fuselage. The boat is intended to be dropped from 700 feet, a deploying parachute opening the four main 42 feet canopies. As the main parachutes open, carbon-dioxide bottles automatically inflate the self-righting chambers at both ends of the boat.
>
> As soon as the lifeboat is afloat, immersion switches release the parachutes, which blow away; they also release a drogue, which prevents the craft from drifting. At the same time rocket flares are fired outwards, carrying floating lines on both sides of the boat for the ditched aircrew . . . up.

The lifeboat is boarded by small doors in the side, which open from the outside; the deck is flat and self-draining, and the hull is divided into watertight compartments.

Once on board, the crew can find protective suits, inflatable cushions, sleeping bags, and first-aid kit. Awnings and a screen are provided as a protection against sun and spray.

Made of aluminium, and clearly an inspired design, only about fifty lifeboats came from the manufacturer. In practical terms, the expensive Saunders-Roe item offered little major advantage over the existing Lindholme Gear.

Observers at St Mawgan blinked twice on 10 September 1953 when Shackleton MR2 WL789 arrived with a strange new feature. A boom jutted out from the rear into the airspace. This was, everyone learned, a MAD installation which some thought an appropriate name although it was simply the abbreviation used for Magnetic Anomaly Detection. This smart item could apparently distinguish minute variations in the Earth's magnetic field. A submarine, made largely of metal, disturbs the magnetic field around it. An appropriate aircraft, aligned with the Earth's magnetic field, would create a constant, even tone, heard on the appropriate instruments. An anomaly would immediately be recorded.

Archie Lumsden, an air wireless fitter at St Mawgan's Air Sea Warfare Development Unit, came across the beast some time later. The boom, he noted, increased the landing speed by a significant amount. The technology came from the Second World War when both the US and Japanese Navies towed MAD devices behind ships. Its use was more complicated with airborne searchers. The aircraft needed to be very close indeed to the submarine to detect any irregularity in the tone. Detection range was limited by the distance between the sensor and the target as well as the size of the quarry. Although MAD would one day reach service with the military, it was not to be with the Shackleton. After more than fifty months of extensive trials by the ASWDU, which involved several modifications, the project was abandoned.

On 16 September, Exercise Mariner began. It was the largest NATO air-sea exercise of the year. All in all, some one thousand aircraft and three hundred ships from nine of the fourteen Treaty members became players. In general terms, the exercise recreated a struggle for control of the Atlantic Ocean. This involved protection against surface, underwater and air attacks on convoys and fleets in the Atlantic, the North Sea and the Channel.

Mariner was deliberately planned to be the largest and most important air-sea exercise since the founding of the Alliance in 1949. It gave notice to any potential enemy that NATO had come of age and would fight hard to preserve its freedom. It was described as Castanets and Mainbrace rolled into one.

Shackleton squadrons were dispersed across the whole of the exercise area where they met and flew alongside various NATO equivalents. Number 220 Squadron went to Quonset Point in Rhode Island and Lisbon once again welcomed passing Shackletons. Kinloss became the home of a squadron of Neptunes from the US Navy.

Helicopters appeared to defend the Clyde Estuary, an event which did not pass without comment for Mariner made wide use of smoke and flares to simulate torpedoes, bombs and mines. The 'battle' raged to the pleasure and dismay of the local residents.

Hansard for 28 October 1953 recorded that Emrys Hughes who, despite his name, represented South Ayrshire, asked the First Lord of the Admiralty 'to state the purpose of recent naval exercises in the Clyde; and what was the cost.'

The Right Honourable James Thomas, the member for Ross-on-Wye and First Lord, replied with a touch of disdain appropriate to a Cabinet Minister:

> I assume that the Honourable Member is referring to the exercises in the Clyde which were a phase of the North Atlantic Treaty Organisation's exercise 'Mariner' to test the defences of a large port. Each nation participating bore the direct costs of its own forces, and certain common costs will be shared internationally. The cost of the Royal Navy's participation is accepted as a normal training liability of the Fleet. It is not customary to cost individual exercises.

Emrys Hughes, well-versed in procedure, then delivered what he hoped was a crushing question:

Is the Minister aware of an article written by Mr Chester Wilmot which appeared in last Sunday's *Observer*, in which he said we were spending far too much money on the Royal Navy and that the real danger was rockets? Can the Right Honourable Gentleman say how the Royal Navy in the Clyde can defend us against rockets?

The First Lord replied briefly:

I am prepared to argue that with the Honourable Gentleman another time. I cannot possibly accept the view expressed by Mr Chester Wilmot in last Sunday's *Observer*.

He left unsaid the obvious point that spending on defence matters might be an extravagance but it provided employment throughout the country. As usual in the House of Commons, a member of his own party put in a final comment. Thomas Moore who represented Ayr and would shortly become a baronet, observed:

Will my Right Honourable Friend bear in mind that we are always glad and proud to welcome the Royal Navy to the west coast of Scotland for any purpose?

With the Mk2 Shackleton becoming available, Number 38 Squadron in Malta collected their first aeroplane to start conversion from Lancasters on 18 September 1953. They were the resident maritime reconnaissance squadron in Malta.

The morning papers on 12 December carried short but sombre news items:

It was stated last night that a Shackleton of Coastal Command, from Ballykelly, with nine men on board, was overdue. Other Shackleton aircraft from Aldergrove joined in the search.

A MR2 Shackleton, its identity WL746, with a crew of ten had crashed in the Sound of Mull while on exercise on Friday 11 December 1953. The aeroplane belonged to 269 Squadron but was on loan to 240 Squadron. Its first job had been to conduct radar homings on a submarine followed by a navigation exercise. A radio message was received at 1715 hours to confirm that the submarine phase had finished. Fifteen minutes later, civilians on the Isle of Mull heard an aircraft at low level. The engine noise faded, followed by a loud explosion. The aircraft crashed in a bay near the south end of the Sound of Mull in a rainstorm, shortly after flying over Oban. Searches revealed some wreckage on the Isle of Mull and the adjacent mainland. Expert examination of the remains suggested that the Shackleton suffered an extremely violent impact.

On the Saturday following the accident, the Mountain Rescue team from Pitreavie found two bodies. One was that of the captain, Flight Lieutenant Fielding Chevallier. Atrocious weather then intervened as the rescue team renewed the search. At sea, HMS *Volage*, an anti-submarine frigate, found wreckage that belonged to the aircraft. In January two more bodies were found at Craignure, close to Mull's easternmost point.

Three months later, more wreckage was retrieved in the Sound of Mull. No signs of an impact had been found on the Isle of Mull. This lack of evidence of a ground strike led to the conclusion that the Shackleton had hit the water whilst turning to starboard in a nose down attitude.

Cheering news reached Avro cars in January 1954. The South African Government announced that it wanted to buy eight Shackletons for its air force. They would replace the weary Sunderlands that were the country's arm against hostile submarines. The news did not go down well in a few quarters. Apartheid was a central plank of Pretoria's policy. Some believed that the Shackleton, equipped with an enormous bomb bay, might be used in some unspecified action against the government's political opponents.

The proposed contract had been much aided by four MR2 Shackletons from 42 Squadron which flew to the Union in April 1952 from Ceylon as part of a 17,000 mile round trip from their base at St Eval. South African officials took the opportunity to fully evaluate the aeroplane. Their requirements led to the eventual appearance of the Mk3. Amongst other detail, this incorporated a nosewheel undercarriage to replace the tailwheel of the earlier versions. The South African contract proved to be the sole export order for the aeroplane.

More aeroplanes. Another squadron. To herald the new year of 1954, 204 Squadron came back to life. They returned to maritime reconnaissance duties at Ballykelly with the Shackleton.

Doubters who thought that low-flying attacks on submarines were a dangerous way to make a living justified their fears on 12 February 1954 when news came through of a Shackleton accident in the Mediterranean. Newspaper accounts briefly reported that aircraft of British and United States Air Forces aided by the Royal Navy destroyers, HMS *Chequers* and HMS *Chevron*, searching for an overdue Shackleton had sighted debris in the sea some twenty-six miles north of the island of Gozo.

The Shackleton was an MR2, WL794, from 38 Squadron based at Luqa. It had been with the squadron a mere six weeks. The aeroplane went out on a night-time air-sea warfare exercise in association with the submarine HMS *Tudor*. Unsurprisingly, underwater witnesses at about midnight and some distance from land saw very little. Once again, the consensus from the experts was that the Shackleton had possibly stalled during a steep turn at low level during a practice attack. All ten men on board the Shackleton gave up their lives.

Throughout its years in service, the Shackleton received and incorporated modifications designed to improve its efficiency as a maritime hunter. These ranged from a gadget named Autolycus whose intended purpose was to pick up traces of ionised gases emitted by a submarine's diesel engine to Orange Harvest, a warning receiver able to give the bearing of any radar which picked up the Shackleton. These devices greatly increased the responsibilities of the signallers. In later years, an advanced course turned them into Signallers 'A' with an increase in their pay. Eventually, with the arrival of the three V-force jet bombers, their category tipped over into that of air electronics with an AEOp or AE brevet according to rank.

Shackletons missed out on the 1954 Royal Birthday Fly-past. As a special mark of honour, jet aircraft of the Royal Auxiliary Air Force took part. The Shackleton squadrons took on, perhaps as compensation, an interesting mixture of jobs related to the Royal Family. As they had long endurance and were equipped for rescue roles, it became customary for them to accompany the civil aeroplanes that carried royalty on long flights. Two Shackletons escorted the Queen's aircraft from Aden to Entebbe on the Royal Commonwealth tour. Other jobs included keeping station on Princess Margaret's journeys. 228 Squadron joined the roster on 1 July 1954.

On 26 July 1954, Britain and Egypt agreed that British troops would leave the Canal Zone during the next two years. It was a small step by Whitehall in the slow divestment of imperial grandeur.

Although some felt the shiny gloss had worn from the Shackleton with its origins stretching back nearly a decade, *Flight's* rival, the *Aeroplane* was happy enough to carry the story that pilot training in the Royal Air Force was about to take a gigantic step forward. Its edition of 10 September 1954 enthused about the definite arrival of all jet flying for students. It was not until the end of the piece that any mention appeared of those who would end up flying the heavy piston-engined aircraft that made up a reasonable amount of the Royal Air Force. After describing the flying training course in detail with much geographical reference, the magazine commented:

The courses at Oakington will go, after qualification, to the OCUs at Chivenor and Pernbray, to convert to the Sabre and Venom, and eventually, to the Hunter. For those pilots who, after graduation, opt to go to other Commands, such as Coastal or Transport, their OCU course follows a period at an AFS where they convert to multi-engined piston aircraft.

And the multi-engined piston aircraft would be around for a good while to come.

Ballykelly was now home to three Shackleton squadrons as Jim Hughes, then an engine fitter, recalls:

My first contact with the Shackleton was when I was stationed at RAF Ballykelly, which was to receive the aircraft in the early fifties. I did an engine course at Rolls-Royce Derby Works but with typical RAF planning I was then posted to RAF Mauripur, a staging post in Pakistan, for the next two years. I seem to remember a Shackleton squadron passed through Mauripur on detachment during that time but I never actually worked on them until I returned to Ballykelly in 1954. At that time – 1954, Ballykelly was home to 240, 204 and 269 Squadrons. I ended up with the Aircraft Servicing Unit for the next five years.

Ballykelly had been an important base during the war but even with refurbishment a lot of the buildings were very run-down. Because of its wingspan, the Shackleton could not be moved instantly into the hangars. Tramlines were thus laid on the hangar floor to accommodate special trolleys. The aircraft was then physically manoeuvred by the ground crew until the main wheels of the undercarriage were centred on the trol-leys. Not too difficult – unless there was more than one Chief giving orders. The wartime hangars, incidentally, were hardly waterproof and certainly not windproof although I don't recall any doors blowing off while I was there.

Shackleton squadrons did not take long to learn that, as the air-craft was capacious and had the endurance essential for long flights over the oceans, they were tasked to carry out assignments which, if not vital to the safety of the realm, were guaranteed to bring a little light into the lives of isolated service personnel before the heady days of mobile telephones, e-mail, television and computer provided communication. They soon found themselves employed on ferrying Christmas mail to ships at sea – including Royal Navy submarines that had often acted as the enemy during exercises.

On Tuesday 11 January 1955, 42 Squadron at St Eval sent off Shackleton WG531 to patrol south-south-west of Ireland in the general direction of Fastnet. The aeroplane with nine men on board lifted off a few minutes late at 1041 hours. A second 42 Squadron aircraft, WL743, was scheduled to leave the ground thirty minutes later to patrol the same general area. This also had a nine-man crew and managed to leave a few minutes earlier than planned. In some circles, this would have been an embar-rassment but the navigators soon sorted out the situation to restore the planned thirty-minute gap. Certainly by 2000 hours, when both radioed their standard hourly report, they were eighty-five miles apart.

Nearly one hour later, at 2055 hours, Pilot Officer Len Wood, the captain of the second Shackleton radioed before his hourly report was due to ask for the barometric pressure in the search area. After that call, nothing was heard from him again. Neither was there any contact from Flying Officer George Board, in charge of WG531. It was not a matter of over-riding concern because most people knew that radio communications at the normal operating height were often less than perfect.

Nothing came in during the next sixty minutes. At 2200 hours, neither aircraft reported. The duty Search and Rescue aircraft was promptly brought to immediate readiness and its reserve put on stand-by status. Another Shackleton that had gone out before the two silent aircraft was ordered to return to the area and try to get a message to them. Its signallers tried hard with voice and Morse code. Nothing came back. In the blackness of a dark winter night, in less than perfect weather, nobody saw anything.

At 0129, the SAR aircraft took off. The RAF Rescue Coordination Centre at Mount Batten, Plymouth assumed control of the mission. It seemed unlikely, even to the most dubious, that both aircraft could have been struck down by a mysterious fault. Both had four working engines. Both had trained crews. It was unbelievable that some natural happening or dire structural failure could strike down the pair within minutes so swiftly that neither could raise the alarm.

At dawn, investigation moved into higher gear. Eight Shackletons went out along with a Sunderland from Pembroke Dock. A steamer from the Shaw, Savill and Albion Line, the 8000 ton *Bardic*, reported that she had seen the two aircraft at roughly 2100 hours flying apparently normally some thirty miles south-west of Fastnet.

Hopes were high. Some fishing vessels described seeing flares out at sea between 0330 and 0545 that very morning. The weather was good in the search area, allowing fifteen miles visibility although the cloud base was down to two thousand feet. The Royal Fleet Auxiliary *Wave Duke*, already in the area, entered the hunt while the Royal Navy frigate *Launceston Castle* hurried out of Portsmouth to add its crew to the inquiring eyes. The Eire corvette *Macha* also joined in.

All lifeboats in the area were alerted and other aircraft, including Lancasters from St Mawgan, were added to the exploring team. One of these reported sundry lights and an unidentified object in the water. A Shackleton and the *Launceston Castle* failed to confirm the sighting. By evening, the search area was some 7,000 square miles. Nothing had been found. Confidence of a successful outcome withered.

Murky weather the following day inhibited proceedings. Hopes died. A few sightings of floating items failed to give any positive information. As the conditions worsened, officialdom finally called off the quest. It was formally abandoned on 14 January. The reported lights were finally ascribed to flares fired by searching aircraft.

With no information to work from, the official enquiry failed to reach a reliable conclusion. No blame could be allocated although the Board did consider that a collision between the two Shackletons was 'the least improbable' cause. It seems unlikely that neither crew, nor the navigators in particular, were unaware of the lurking danger of collision.

Eleven years later, in July 1966, a trawler dragged up the starboard outer engine of WL743. The fishing vessel was working between the Bull and Skelligs lighthouses which were some seventy to one hundred miles north of the searched position. Whether the ocean would move a Griffon that far is presumption not evidence.

No bodies were found. Another eighteen men had died.

Shackleton flying had its bad times as well as the good.

CHAPTER FIVE

Fatal accidents, even when two aircraft simply vanish, cannot interfere with the functioning of the Royal Air Force. The loss of the Shackletons was a heartache but work continued. It had to. Apart from exercises, either domestic or international, obligations demanded responses. In the previous year alone, Shackletons were called out on ninety-four rescue sorties. They sought drifting dinghies, broken down fishing boats, missing swimmers or any others in danger from the sea. On top of all that were the detachments, often connected with exercises, but always active in 'showing the flag'.

Appalling weather gave the marooned inhabitants of Braemore in Caithness a wretched beginning to their year. Snow cut off access and, inevitably, supplies of food and fuel. After four days, Avro's submarine killer took on the role of a saviour. A Shackleton dropped provisions and necessaries to the forlorn community.

The condition of the Royal Air Force gave concern to some. Apart from the Shackleton and the Canberra jet bomber, few new types had reached the service for many months. The worse reality was that the air arm was almost totally reliant on conscripts for its ground trades. Transport Command was dangerously small and had no long-range aircraft. Britain had no capability to ferry troops to any trouble spot on the globe nor enjoyed the luxury of having aircraft that were also suitable for airborne operations. It was a blessing that the Shackleton could be used to carry some thirty troops over long distances. It would not be too long before Roy Chadwick's design displayed that particular virtue.

For many people, military or otherwise, the big news of 1955 was the retirement of Winston Churchill as Prime Minister at the age of eighty. As Head of the British Government for nearly the whole of the Second World War, he held a special place in public affection. He remained a Conservative Member of Parliament but his position was filled by his widely-agreed successor, Anthony Eden. He quickly called an October election although few knew of his wretchedly ill health.

Churchill's departure rather overshadowed the foreign news of troubles in Cyprus. On 1 April 1955 sixteen bombs exploded in four towns in Cyprus. EOKA – which was quicker to say than Ethniki Organosis Kyprion Agoniston – claimed the credit. The Greek Cypriot organisation wanted both self-determination for Cyprus and union, or *enosis*, with Greece. This later aim was anathema to the Turkish minority on the island, while the British garrison served, in London's eyes at least, as a substantial deterrent to Soviet expansion in the region.

With the British planned withdrawal from Egypt as well as actual evacuation of the garrison in Iraq, both part of an ongoing attempt to stop the spread of Communist influence, Cyprus was the clear choice to become the headquarters for a strategic reserve in the region. Britain, along with Pakistan and Iran, had joined the Baghdad Pact in February, originally an agreement between Iraq and Turkey.

Cypriot requests were met with refusal. EOKA joined Kenya's Mau Mau and other freedom fighters in British territories as no more than an irritation to the politicians in Westminster. Although in nearly all of the territories the local population showed a disturbing degree of support for independence, Britain's colonial administrators firmly retained a touching belief that native inhabitants swiftly succumbed to shows of force. Should terrorists desire British rule to end, the arrival of troops with guns and aircraft with bombs would persuade them otherwise. Britain had the will and the means to impose its own solution.

Coastal Command slogged on, training crews for its maritime

operations as well as carrying out all the other tasks dropped on it by Whitehall. The School of Maritime Reconnaissance at St Mawgan and 236 OCU at Kinloss remained as busy as they had ever been. Douglas Wilson describes his signals training:

I entered training at Swanton Morley, near Dereham, in Norfolk in 1952. National Servicemen had been trained at Halfpenny Green prior to this time but, as National Service was coming to an end, both courses were amalgamated at Swanton Morley. No1 Air Signaller's School (1ASS) trained Signallers for Transport, Bomber & Coastal Command replacements, although, at this stage, most people went to Coastal Command which was building up the Shackleton fleet. The main area for training was learning Morse, as all long range communications were in Morse. This was a long and boring process involving receiving and sending in Morse code to a minimum standard of 18 wpm. And took up most of the year's course. Radio Equipment (Marconi T1154/R1155), Radio Procedures, Electronic and Radar theory, Airmanship, Rescue and Survival and General Service Training occupied most of the Ground School time.

The potential aircrew signallers at least had the pleasure of not spending every hour of each day's training in a stuffy classroom. Bitter experience had taught the service that every crew member had to be able to function whilst in the air, irrespective of the comfort of the ride provided. It was not a short training course either:

Swanton Morley was a grass airfield and the flying phase was in Avro Anson and Percival Proctor & Prentice aircraft. The Anson was the flying classroom where an Air Screen monitored the student who sent position reports and received broadcasts and weather reports flying along the designated training route. The Prentice was used for solo flights as a Radio Operator. The whole course lasted approximately a year and at the end of the course the student was awarded his coveted Signallers brevet and his Sergeant's stripes. The only really noteworthy event during my time at Swanton was being sent on Flood Relief duties along the Norfolk coast after the floods of 1953 and getting half a day off for the Coronation – after a parade in the morning.

The next step in the process was Gunnery School at RAF Leconfield, near Beverley, in Yorkshire. This was a three-month course flying on Lincoln aircraft to learn the basics of aerial gunnery, firing Browning 0.303 and 0.5 machine guns. At the end of the course you received a Gunner's Brevet. Air Gunners were being phased out at this time and the few that did remain on flying remustered to Air Signaller. Gunnery on the Shackleton Hispano Suiza 20 mm cannon was done by qualified Air Signallers.

After months of training, Douglas Wilson was posted yet again but this time it was to learn all about the actual task he would do in the RAF:

The next phase in training was attending the School of Maritime Reconnaissance (MRS) at RAF St Mawgan. This was a four-month course, flying on Lancasters, to learn the basics of Sonics, Anti-Surface Vessel Radar (ASV13), Ship Recognition, Maritime procedures, photography and all the subjects peculiar to flying in the maritime environment. Then at last, after some eighteen months training – the Shackleton. A three-month course at the Maritime Operational Training Unit at RAF Kinloss. This was really about forming up into a crew and familiarising yourself with the Shackleton and its Cold War role. The part was Anti-Submarine Warfare, Anti-Surface Vessel Warfare, Reconnaissance, Search and Rescue, with a secondary role of Trooping and any other odd-ball task that came your way.

The equipment was for the main part obsolescent, Radio – T1154/R1155, Radar – ASV13 (later ASV21), Mk1C Sonics. The Radio Operator usually flew in the Radio station for the whole sortie, the Radar Operator did a nominal forty-five-minute stint, the sonics was manned as required. In between times the signals team, headed by the lead signaller, manned the beam look-out stations, cooked in the galley, took photographs, dropped smoke floats, loaded flares and were general dogsbodies.

Potential Coastal Command signallers had been in training for almost two years before they were ready for active employment. Douglas Wilson was one:

> My first Squadron was 220 Squadron at RAF St Eval, Newquay, Cornwall, flying Mk1 Shackletons. Duties on the Squadron were much as we had been trained for – anti-submarine training with submarines from our own fleet, taking part in NATO & Naval Exercises. We occasionally operated against Soviet submarines, Soviet warships or Soviet fleet auxiliaries that entered the Southern Maritime region defined as the Western Atlantic, Channel and Southern North Sea areas from 35N to 52,30N and jutting out to 25W.
>
> The bulk of the time was spent in training – long boring hours. Radar homings on the radar buoys, Radar homing and bombing runs on a skid towed by a launch from the Marine Craft Unit, Stage II Sonics training, practise creeping-line-ahead navigation for Search & Rescue training, long-range navigation exercises to Jan Mayen Island, fire drills, engine failure drills and long periods of circuit bashing for pilot training.
>
> The galley was generally run by the 'siggies'. At one stage we had tinned meals probably left over from the war and uniquely horrible. The most favoured meal was 'honkers stew' – this consisted of all the various tins supplied by the catering section shoved into a large pot and stewed up on the galley. Just what you needed on a bumpy trip when your guts already felt queasy! This was generally the main meal with bacon and egg or doorstop sandwiches plus plenty of tea in between times.
>
> It was said that you could always tell a 'siggie'. He had long arms and rounded shoulders from carrying the Crew Box, the flying rations, the KL7 cipher machine, the codes and ciphers to go with it and his own crew bag.

An Air Ministry statement to the newspapers returned the Shackleton to more public notice:

> On the Sovereign's official birthday, June 9th, it is customary for a ceremonial fly-past to be staged by one of the operational

commands of the Royal Air Force. This year the honour falls on Coastal Command who last performed the duty in 1952.

Eighteen Shackletons will accordingly fly over Buckingham Palace at 1 pm while Her Majesty takes the salute from the balcony. Three aircraft will be provided by each of six squadrons . . .

Of the six, 120 Squadron, was based at Aldergrove. Numbers 240 and 269 were stationed at Ballykelly whilst the final three, 226, 206 and 220, all came from St Eval. The official proclamation explained that the aircraft would fly in two close arcs of nine aircraft. There would be a half minute interval between the two groups although both would fly over the Palace at one thousand feet.

Shackletons were kept in the public eye with appearances at suitable events. The Golden Jubilee Flying Display of the Royal Aircraft Establishment was one that proudly boasted of appearances by the advanced submarine hunter.

On 2 September 1955 the prototype Shackleton MR3 numbered WR970 made its initial flight. Three days later it appeared at Farnborough for the 1955 SBAC Display. *Flight* magazine of September 16th 1955 commented:

The big grey Shackleton 3 is much heavier than its predecessors. The elimination of the dorsal turret and increased power from the Griffons have led to a notable increase in speed which was demonstrated to the full during the show. Noise level is much reduced. Tab-assisted ailerons, in four sections on each wing, have improved lateral control. The aircraft flew past each day with three airscrews feathered.

Immediately the show finished, the Mk3 returned to Woodford for manufacturer's handling trials which lasted for nine months. AAEE would not see the aeroplane until September 1956.

In January 1956, the Shackleton was called into service as a troop transport. On 12 January, the aircraft flew 1,200 men and personal gear to Cyprus. These were mostly paratroopers. Contrary to some wild speculation, they did not jump out at height when the aircraft reached its destination. Each flight was airborne for a total of fourteen hours with a break at Luqa to change aircrew. It took some flying to move all the soldiers. The flight crews were reduced to the two pilots, one navigator, one signaller along with the indispensable flight engineer.

RAF North Front in Gibraltar received some fresh ground crew that same January. Amongst them was Trevor Dobson who cheerfully anticipated his first journey out of Britain. He duly collected a mound of tropical khaki kit and endured an array of vaccinations. Trevor recalls:

> One cold winter's morning a group of servicemen boarded an Eagle Airways aircraft bound for Gibraltar, one thousand miles away. Once we were airborne the pilot informed us that Gibraltar airfield was fog bound and that we would be landing at Biarritz, a French town close to the border with Spain. General Franco was in power in Spain at the time and British flights were not allowed to overfly Spanish territory. Stopping over in France just added to the excitement. After spending the night in a hotel we were again on our way to the Rock.
>
> The runway in Gibraltar starts and ends in water with Algeciras Bay at one end and the Mediterranean at the other. It has been known for aircraft to overshoot the runway and end up in the sea! Another unusual feature was that the main road from La Linea, the Spanish border town, to Gibraltar goes across the centre of the runway which meant it had to be closed for all take offs and landings.

Trevor, like most junior tradesmen, had no firm idea of what his job would be at the new station. Sometimes it proved to be a humdinger; on other occasions, it was less than inspiring:

> My first job was to service bomb carriers in the maintenance hangar. This is not what I wanted to do for two years so I put out feelers for a transfer to 224 Squadron who flew MR2 Shackleton aircraft in anti-submarine and rescue roles. Thankfully a transfer was arranged about one month after my arrival. At last I was back working on aircraft albeit a lot different from Canberras.
>
> By this time the amalgamation of 'bombs' and 'guns' had

taken place. We were expected to service 20mm Hispano guns without any tuition but all armourers soon picked up the information from those who had received the training. Around ten aircraft made up the Squadron with them being in constant use both day and night, with up to twelve-hour training sorties over the Atlantic. Ground crews had to be available to work shifts to suit the flying hours. Some long hours could be spent just waiting for the Shackletons to return and be serviced ready for the next exercise.

To overcome this long wait, we used to pass the time in the armoury playing cribbage. For safety reasons it was situated away from the main service buildings, right next to the border post which it backed on to.

Once the aircraft had arrived, there was no time to finish a hand of cards. Timing was all:

On landing, the aircraft had to be refuelled and rearmed. Any faults, however large or small, had to be fixed so it was all go when we were working.

Luckily, the armament caused little trouble apart from the guns occasionally jamming. These were reloaded with belts of 20 mm ammunition. At the same time the bomb bay was loaded with a variety of supplies such as five-feet long sonobuoys which floated in the sea after being dropped in a pattern to detect submarines. These were used extensively together with practice bombs which gave off smoke. Flares were inside the aircraft in a rack near the door and were despatched manually down a flare chute. Now and again real 500 lb depth charges were used.

One day while one was being manually winched into the bomb bay it dropped to the ground. Fortunately nobody was underneath it!

The bomb aimer's position in the nose contained banks of switches to allow selection of the correct armament to be released. If these went wrong it created a headache for the armourer as it was his job to sort it out, not the electrician's. Also carried in the bomb bay were tarpaulin panniers used for carrying spares when the aircraft was on detachment. Very pistols had to be checked but were not used much as they were for emergency use.

Four aircraft went out to Australia to begin daily weather-spotting patrols before the projected British atomic tests in the Monte Bello Islands in April. The aircraft had meteorological instruments fitted on a special panel in the nose. The psychrometer, often called a wet and dry bulb thermometer, designed to measure humidity, was not accessible from inside the aircraft. The meteorological observer attached to each aircraft became wearily accustomed to the regular Shackleton crew gathering to watch as he climbed a ladder before each flight to change the wick on the wet bulb thermometer.

On 23 February, the estimates for RAF expenditure by the Government appeared. Of the £479,500,000 allocated, the money for new airframes and engines fell from 160 million pounds in the previous year to 140 million. As an accompanying memorandum explained, there had been 'serious underspending' the previous year because of cancellation and readjustment of orders. Fuel provision also fell by some twelve million pounds from sixty-three million to fifty-one million. The demand for armaments, ammunition and explosive fell from thirty-seven million pounds to a fraction above thirty million. Belts would have to be tightened by more than a single notch or so.

Despite many other tasks, eighteen Shackletons flew in formation over Buckingham Palace on 31 May 1956 to mark the Official Birthday. Douglas Wilson, having finished his training, was now a signaller with 220 Squadron. As he recalled, 'flying in the middle of a nine-man box of Shackletons lumbering and groaning, trying to keep close station in a fly-past – very scary.' He held the view that 'despite what you may have heard, the Shack was a dirty, noisy, smelly beast at the best of times.'

The Secretary of State for Air, Nigel Birch, soon received the customary Royal message of thanks:

Please convey to all ranks of Coastal Command who took part my warm congratulations on the exact manner in which they carried out their fly-past today. I greatly value this salute from the Royal Air Force in celebration of my birthday.

In Egypt, Colonel Nasser sought financial aid to build the proposed Aswan High Dam. An original offer of fifty-six million dollars from the United States fell by the wayside when Egypt continued to cosy up to the Communist authorities in Russia and China. Nasser was not pleased by this prevarication. On 26 July 1956, in a near three-hour speech in Alexandria, Nasser announced the nationalisation of the Suez Canal in order to raise funds for the dam's construction. All company assets, he said, had been frozen but holders of shares would receive their value according to the closing price on the Paris Stock Exchange.

Both France and Britain relied on the Canal for moving their oil supplies. They considered Nasser to be a menace to their remaining Middle East interests. Anthony Eden wanted to attack Egypt without delay but he soon learned that this was not a viable proposition. Nonetheless, he firmly believed that Nasser had to be brought down. London began secret talks with Paris and Tel Aviv. Agreement soon arrived. The three countries would make a joint attack on Egypt.

As so many non-expert observers considered the Shackleton to really be the Lancaster from the Second World War, it came as no surprise when they featured in a film. Trevor Dobson, with 224 Squadron in Gibraltar, recalls:

> During 1956 a film crew arrived to make part of the film *The Silent Enemy*, a story about Buster Crabbe the wartime frogman and his exploits. This was being produced by Herbert Wilcox and his wife, Anna Neagle. Laurence Harvey and Dawn Addams were the stars. Part of the shoot was to involve the Shackletons which were substituted for wartime aircraft so some extras were required from the ground crew. My claim to fame ended up with me walking away from the camera and disappearing into the distance! The actors were most co-operative where photographs were concerned and were very approachable. It was great fun and a new experience.

The MRS at St Mawgan and 236 OCU at Kinloss, impelled by a desire to save money, amalgamated into one single training school on 1 October 1956, the Maritime Operations Training Unit, immediately abbreviated to MOTU. The course became a five-month slog that required twenty Shackleton aircraft although the initial holding was sixteen. It became clear that the whole course would be easier for instructors and students if a specific training aircraft filled the vacancies. Plans were made, letters were written. The first Shackleton T4, simply a modified Mark One numbered VP258, eventually appeared at MOTU. The major change to the naked eye was the removal of the mid-upper turret, which gave room for additional radar- and radio-operator training positions.

Ted Gregory, considering the new MOTU, confirmed Douglas Wilson's earlier impressions of the Kinloss OCU. Some things change only slowly:

> For many Air Signallers straight out of training school in the 1950s, the MOTU at RAF Kinloss was the first taste of the real air force. Many of the training staff together with the pilots, navigators and engineers on the conversion courses had seen war service; they were converting to the Shackleton from other operational aircraft types such as Sunderlands, Neptunes and Lincolns. As a result there was still a strong, carefree, wartime spirit when it came to the social side of life. Add to the mix the presence of South African Air Force crews converting to the Shackletons purchased by their government, and it produced a halcyon time of party, party, party. We could all afford it; we were on full aircrew pay for the first time, and life was a great adventure.

Disillusionment, if that is the appropriate word, for a return to realistic assessment of what the Royal Air Force demanded in return for status, soon arrived:

> I soon realised that the air signallers on the crew were the general dogsbodies. We did everything other than navigate and fly the plane; we were radio operator, radar operator, sonics operator, Autolycus (sniffer) operator, nose gunner, flare dispatcher, visual look-out and galley cook. The team of five took turns at all these duties, and not until the early 1960s did the duties become specialised into 'wet' and 'dry' operators. The expertise and professionalism of the signals team on

any crew determined whether or not that crew was a successful one, for it was the team that performed the most important submarine-hunting duties.

The interior of the Shackleton had a unique smell. It was an amalgam of leather, oil and fried food. The fried food smell came from the galley, which consisted of an electric oven, hotplate and urn alongside a sink with draining board. For many crews this was the most important piece of equipment on board. Dedicated cooks (always an air signaller) could produce three-course meals for a crew of eleven. After such a feat, in the usual turbulence at low level, the duty cook was physically shattered. Each crew had their own lockable galley box that contained their crockery and cutlery together with unused 'goodies' left over from each sortie, and it was the air signaller team's job to lug this great box to and from the aircraft, together with all the food. There were two favourite delicacies that were sometimes issued in the rations; these were tinned ham and tinned whole chicken. One crew I was on had a rota where we took it in turns to take such tins home unless, by majority vote, it was agreed to use them in a meal.

Geordie Marsden, veteran of two tours on the Shackleton, discovered he was the ideal candidate to be an instructor, first at 236 OCU and then MOTU. Moving to Kinloss from the green fields of Ireland could have been a cheerless chore but luck, as usual, seemed to find its way to him. He was offered a lift on a Shackleton that was going to Kinloss. All he had to do was to put himself and his kit on board. The problem was he had a motor-bike, a difficulty he pointed out. The flight engineer gazed at him thoughtfully, mentioned that all that was necessary was to wheel it on at the back and the job was done. It was rather simpler than going by train and ferry boat.

Geordie arrived at his new unit complete with gear and a motor-bike. He recalled a particular hazard during training at the OCU:

This happened at least twice during 236 OCU times. The Shackleton had a special clock mechanism in the bombing

79

set-up which enabled a series of bombs to be dropped in order, as if they were depth charges, on a submarine.

The apparatus had to be ground tested before any bombing practice but without the master switch ON. No matter how many times this was pressed home, there was always one who had his own way of doing things.

Result? A great cloud of smoke underneath the bomb bay when twenty-five practice smoke bombs fell flat on to the tarmac. A whole bunch of fresh bombs had to be loaded up again.

No doubt somebody was put on a charge but fortunately did not have to pay for the bombs. So they said.

The Shackleton became operationally active as a long range troop transport. Cyprus was chosen as the assembly area for Operation Musketeer, the planned assault on Egypt which officially began on 31 October 1956. The Shackletons had started their life as troop transports for the action rather earlier than that.

Soldiers flew from Blackbushe to Nicosia. The Shackleton gained the reputation amongst soldiers, both fighting and support troops, of being a flying sardine can. For the crews, reduced to the essential minimum of two pilots, one engineer, one navigator and a signaller, the passengers varied wildly in their ways. The paratroopers, in general opinion, proved perfect travellers, well behaved and properly disciplined. Soldiers from less meticulous regiments made the aircraft look untidy even on the ground.

Squadron ground crew for the bombing squadrons also flew out in Shackletons. They often enjoyed a less exhausting route and they did not always go to Cyprus as Jim Watts remembers:

I served with 207 Bomber Squadron during the Suez Crisis. In October 1956 my squadron, along with other Valiant squadrons from RAF Marham in Norfolk, was posted to RAF Luqa on Malta. We, the ground crews, went in Shackleton aircraft. We were issued with dog tags, ear defenders and sick bags. There were no seats, just single bed mattresses placed on the floor with an Elsan chemical toilet standing in the middle. I do not remember anyone using it.

The flight to Malta took nine hours. We flew south from

Marham and then flew over the south of France and the Mediterranean. This was to confuse anyone of our destination. A member of the aircrew informed us that we were flying over Bordeaux. He said that we could take a look, but not all at the same time.

After the hostilities were over we also flew home in the Shackleton, the return journey taking seven hours and thirty minutes. Again we had the bed mattresses and the primitive toilet.

For a reason that no doubt seemed excellent at the time, some Musketeer Shackletons and other aircraft received three painted yellow stripes around the rear fuselage, reminiscent of the black and white stripes used for immediate recognition during the 1944 Normandy invasion.

British and French forces swiftly gained control of the principal facilities of the Suez Canal but the Egyptians made that meaningless by simply sinking ships and other obstacles in the Canal. The attack took place in co-ordination with an Israeli armoured assault into the Sinai.

Reaction from the rest of the world was savage. The Soviet Union promptly made military threats against Britain and France while an oil embargo began in the Middle East. The United States, despite Eden's fervent hope that they would loathe Nasser's Communist links, believed the right of self-determination for small nations was paramount. Their financial and diplomatic pressure forced Britain to unilaterally declare a ceasefire at midnight on 6 November 1956, an action they took without warning their Israeli or French allies. Eden and the country were humiliated. Before the year was out, a United Nations Force replaced the occupying troops.

Once again the Shackletons served as troop transports and brought back the returning soldiers. Its initial foray into active operations would not be its last.

The USA also suggested, giving little room for manoeuvre, that the aircraft supplied on friendly terms to help Britain's NATO commitments, would be better employed by their country of origin. This impinged on Coastal Command for the Neptunes had to leave the RAF.

The Mk3 Shackleton prototype, WR970, crashed on 7 December 1956 when under the control of an Avro works crew. The aeroplane had spent twelve months with the manufacturers after its Farnborough appearance followed by a mere two months with AAEE and the Ministry of Supply. *The Times* reported the affair briefly in a short news item:

> The four occupants were killed when a Shackleton aircraft crashed outside the village of Foolow, Derbyshire, today. Villagers saw the aircraft skim over rooftops and crash into a field about 100 yards from the main street. There was an explosion and the aircraft was enveloped in flames. Firemen from four towns were called.
>
> Mr Bernard Pursglove, licensee of the Bull's Head at Foolow, said tonight: 'People who saw the aircraft are sure that the pilot was trying to avoid the village.'
>
> The Shackleton was flying from the Avro Aircraft works at Woodford, Cheshire. An official of the Hawker Siddeley Group said that four bodies had been recovered, including that of the pilot. He was Mr Jack B. Wales, a test pilot for Avro, who took part in the tests of the Avro 707 delta-wing aircraft and of the Vulcan bomber.

Peter Bardon who ended his RAF service as Chief Test Flying Instructor at the Empire Test Pilots School with wing commander's rank allied with a Distinguished Flying Cross and an Air Force Cross adds substantially more particulars:

> In 1956, after completing the Empire Test Pilots School course at Farnborough the previous year, I was posted to B (Heavy Aircraft) Test Squadron at the Aeroplane and Armament Experimental Establishment at Boscombe Down in Wiltshire.
>
> My first job on arriving at the squadron was to participate on the handling trials of the prototype Shackleton Mk3 WR970 prior to its introduction into service. My particular task was to test the aircraft's stalling characteristics.
>
> During the test programme I found that with the bomb doors open and the radome extended in turning flight, there was a continuous mild buffet when the speed was reduced by

pulling back on the control column with the engines at high power. This buffet masked the onset of the stall which, when it occurred, was marked by a violent snatch on the ailerons which could not be held on the control wheel and the aircraft rolled on to its back.

This behaviour was both frightening and dangerous, particularly as it took some while to bring the aircraft back under full control:

Before level flight could be restored some 2,000 feet of altitude was lost. This was clearly quite unacceptable for an aircraft that would be operating in this configuration close to the sea during anti-submarine attacks. It was decided there and then that the aircraft was unsafe for service use and the aircraft was returned to Woodford for them to sort out the problem.

Avro's test team regrettably picked a day when the weather was particularly bad. They took the aeroplane up above the clouds to try out the turning stalls.

The aircraft was observed by a passing BEA Trident to be carrying out a steep turn close to the cloud tops, when it suddenly rolled over on to its back and disappeared into the cloud inverted. The wreckage of the aircraft was later found on high ground near Woodford. The investigators determined that on impact the aircraft was the right way up when it hit the ground but all four engines had stopped because of fouling of the plugs by oil when it had been inverted. All on board were killed.

One could only be sickened, as we all were at Boscombe, by this loss of life. The problem was eventually sorted out but I need much more space to detail how it was done!

During the next four years I did a fair amount of test flying on all marks of Shackleton, mostly equipment trials. Of the seventy or so types of aircraft I flew during this period the Shack (whatever the mark) was always a pleasure to fly, though it was a tad noisy.

A flight engineer of a Lincoln bomber also saw the start of the Shackleton crash. His aeroplane was at 8,000 feet. He saw the

Shackleton about 1,500 feet below his own aircraft enter a climbing turn. This became a spin and WR970 went through two revolutions before it vanished into cloud at about 5,500 feet.

The Shackleton came out of the cloud north of Foolow village. Eye witnesses described the aircraft as flying very slowly and sinking quickly in a nose-down attitude. The engines made banging and popping sounds and were running roughly. The Shackleton passed slowly over the village, made a slow turn to port and stalled. The port wing tip hit the ground close to a stone wall. The aircraft cartwheeled, destroying the wall in its path, and burst into flames. As a macabre finish, the rear fuselage pitched into the middle of the field with more fragments ending up at an adjoining wall.

Engine oil had entered the intake manifolds. Forced into the cylinders, it fouled the spark plugs. The cylinders could not, as a result, fire. The only explanation was the simple one that oil had flooded the area around the cam shafts and went into the inlet system as the Griffons had been inverted.

Shackletons continued to bring home soldiers and airmen from Operation Musketeer, the Suez adventure. One of the more wearying journeys was the province of a bunch of mostly conscripted ground staff from various RAF units who were sent to Episkopi base at short notice. Unlike the members of organised groups, they had all flown out to Cyprus in chartered civil aircraft.

Once in Cyprus, they were swamped with work before and during the action. Despite hopes of returning home once their slog was over, inevitably fortified by wild whispers, some doubted they would ever see Britain again. They lived under canvas, which sounds fair enough for Mediterranean living but Cyprus has the ability to be wet and chilly during the winter months. Their tents steadily became colder and wetter. Christmas approached. An optimistic story that they might fly home in time for the holiday was confirmed on 21 December. With no warning, they received the instruction to pack their gear and be ready to leave at the end of thirty minutes.

Although several of the group nursed hangovers, they all managed to make it in time. Three-ton trucks bumped out of Episkopi and took the less than smooth main road to RAF Nicosia. Most of the men lay on their kit bags enduring their severe headaches and idly hoping that EOKA would finish what alcohol had wrought. At Nicosia, they found themselves in wet tents, pitched in the middle of a muddy plain. It was, some thought, eerily reminiscent of the First World War.

They went down to the airfield the next afternoon. Most of them were astounded to see three large four-engine aircraft. As National Servicemen, the majority of whom had not been on flying units in the United Kingdom, the first thought was that the aeroplanes were Lancasters or Lincolns. Eventually, with help from a permanent staff member, they agreed they looked at Coastal Command Shackletons.

The party were marshalled into groups of more than thirty men. Each one received a Mae West to wear there and then. As they also wore greatcoats, the final result was bulky aircraftmen. To add to the excitement, each one received a white cardboard lunch box with sandwiches inside. Nearly all scoffed the food at once for that was the service habit. It was better to eat when the chance arose rather than cling on to sandwiches that could easily go stale.

Each group received a lecture from a crew member. The captain, irrespective of rank, was to be obeyed at all times. Smoking inside the aircraft was forbidden nor should they upset the trim by running up and down the aeroplane.

For one particular bunch, matters did not go well. They endured a wait that ended with a banging sound. One Griffon started. Noise crept into the fuselage. Two more engines added their clamour. The fourth engine resolutely failed to start. After several tries, it still refused to add its noise to that of the other three. Eventually, the flight engineer told the passengers to exit the aeroplane. This was not a welcome order. Rain had arrived. The group stood outside the Shackleton, water beating into their miserable faces.

After a while, an engineer officer arrived on a bicycle. He had the ultimate tool – a hide-faced hammer. A sudden calculated blow on the recalcitrant engine failed to persuade it into action. Ground crew came to fiddle with the Griffon. After some while, which most of the wet and shivering passengers believed had to be several hours, they filed back on board. This time a familiar roar resulted. Everything seemed well.

The Shackleton thundered down the runway and climbed to 8,000 feet to roar and vibrate its way to Malta. The heaters failed. Draughts penetrated the fuselage through any aperture they found. The aeroplane became steadily colder. The returning tradesmen reached Luqa at about 2100 hours in time to step out into the torrential rain that arrived just as they landed.

The weary aircraftmen endured another sleepless night in a leaking marquee. They left the island soon after lunch the next day. The Shackleton, they all believed, was to head for its base at St Mawgan in Cornwall. Night fell. Half dozing, conscripts with watches told their yawning companions that it was now 2100 hours. The date was 23 December so it was clear that nobody would reach home by Christmas Day. Except, some said darkly, for the crew because they would all live near St Mawgan.

The men closest to the front of the aircraft jerked awake at a sudden flurry. The navigator spoke with someone over the intercom before he abruptly pushed his charts to the back of his table. He then sat back with folded arms. The aircraft turned to starboard. The flight engineer demanded that every passenger sit down. When the signaller put his knees against his table and buried his head in his arms, several onlookers thought the aircraft was in trouble. The engineer steadied himself with an outstretched hand. Without warning, the engine sound died away. In the deathly quiet the passengers heard the wind rushing past the fuselage. The pessimists decided the end of their lives had arrived. Most tried to cling to something or someone even if it was only another conscript. Christmas clearly had been cancelled.

The thump sent some hearts sky-high before they realised the aircraft was rolling along a hard surface. The rumbling and bumping stopped. Silence washed through the fuselage. A sharp command. One by one people stood up and filed slowly to the rear exit. From there, across the wet tarmac over which a cold wind blew and cold rain fell, they could see a sign. It said 'RAF Lyneham'. Far more convenient for the conscripts than St Mawgan. They would be home for Christmas after all.

CHAPTER SIX

Despite the December 1956 accident, production of Mk3 Shackletons continued without much apparent impediment. In February 1957, Commandant M. J. Uys, in charge of South Africa's 35 Squadron visited Woodford to formally accept the first of their eight Shackletons although the initial aircraft of the batch did not fly until late March.

The new version of the Shackleton attracted many of its crewmen for it was a more handsome aeroplane than earlier versions. It looked more purposeful, for the improved canopy escaped from the old-fashioned cast of its predecessors. It had a tricycle undercarriage with smaller twin wheels, nosewheel steering, a nose hatch and wingtip fuel tanks. It enjoyed Maxaret brakes and power-assisted controls, features that pleased most of its pilots.

The Maxaret brakes worked through the parking brake, an interesting feature that gave many pilots a moment of panic when they landed with the parking brake in the 'On' position. It allowed the Shackleton to have an amazingly short landing run which had the extra advantage of depositing any loose articles dropped in the fuselage into the bomb-aimer's nose position.

The nosewheel gave a handful of problems. Landings did happen with the nosewheel unlocked. Some instances seem to have been the result of hydraulic failure because of leaks but other factors included a slight airframe distortion in the nose-wheel bay. Once open for retraction the lock sometimes failed when needed to secure the nosewheel in the down position. Other early difficulties included Griffons that faded or failed.

Coastal Command steadily gave back its Neptunes. The crews transferred to Shackletons, a move that kept MOTU at Kinloss extremely busy. Bernie Donders recalls:

I was posted as a pilot to 36 Squadron at Topcliffe in April 1954, being very pleased that I had passed the Neptune OCU course and looking forward to a Coastal Command tour on a very new, shiny and relatively modern aircraft. At the same time I gave thanks that I had not been sent to fly that smelly and very noisy old variation of the Lancaster, namely the Avro Shackleton.

After three years on the Squadron, the Neptunes were returned to the USA.

Most of the Squadron aircrew were posted to Kinloss on what was called a Nep/Shack conversion course. For me this started in April 1957 and also commenced my personal con-version to respect and then develop a fondness for the 'Old Grey Lady'.

My initial impressions were as expected; the Shacks defi-nitely were smelly, noisy and not very comfortable compared to the Neptunes but they were strong and powered by four engines as opposed to two on the Neptune. These were of course those very reliable old Rolls-Royce Griffon Engines. That smell, incidentally, still evokes lots of fond memories whenever ex-Shack aircrew step on board a static display one.

With a good number of flying hours in his logbook, Bernie had few problems with the Shackleton although one feature did cause a little head scratching:

I found the Mk1 Shackleton heavier on the controls and nowhere near as easy to manoeuvre as the Neptune but nev-ertheless it gave a feeling of good old British workmanship and trustworthiness. It was also good that there was proper provision for a flight engineer. The Neptune only carried a flight engineer as a Royal Air Force requirement and no station was provided. In fact the poor guys had to carry their own chairs aboard to place behind and between the two pilots. Who cared about strapping in and safety then?

My biggest problem was converting back to a tail wheel aeroplane which seemed much more difficult to land. After a few weeks and about twenty-five hours' flying I was posted to 120 Squadron, then based at Aldergrove, now the civilian airport Belfast International. The squadron was equipped with Shackleton Mk2 which I found not to be dissimilar to the Mk1 in flying characteristics. It was at this time that I realised just how noisy those Rolls-Royce Griffons were. I lived in Belfast so, after a sortie, I would drive home in my very old Ford Prefect which had 'big end' trouble and seemed to use more oil than petrol. It was also very noisy but after twelve or fourteen hours in a Shack it sounded like a Rolls-Royce – that's the car not the aero engine!

For Bernie, as for every single soul who was involved with Shackletons, there was plenty of work still to come.

Operation Musketeer had done little to enhance Britain's reputation for it was almost universally condemned by other nations. In truth, the country itself and the Government had been divided over the decision to use force.

Anthony Eden addressed a final cabinet meeting on 8 January 1957. His failing health, exacerbated by the pressures of the Suez adventure, simply did not allow him to continue. The Queen accepted his resignation the following day and invited the Chancellor of the Exchequer, Harold Macmillan, to form a new administration.

Nasser immediately became a hero both in Egypt and the whole Arab world. He had faced down the lofty desires of Britain, France and the hated Israel. Many in the Middle East questioned both Britain's policies and her ability to maintain them.

For Coastal Command, matters had inched forward. It was still a life of exercises, of preparation to hunt submarines or to rescue distressed mariners or downed aircrews in the ocean. With the Neptunes rapidly vanishing westward, Britain's own maritime reconnaissance aeroplane had plenty of work to do. Added to which, Shackletons now had trooping responsibilities. Transport Command simply did not have long-range aircraft that could do the job. Nor did they have the 1957 Royal Birthday fly-past to distract them. Bomber Command picked up the job for the first V-bomber, the Vickers Valiant, had finally reached squadron service.

The Middle East was a never-ending collection of trouble spots. Fighting broke out on the border between the Aden Protectorate and the Republic of the Yemen. Communism had permeated the Republic of South Yemen. Warring splinter-groups in Kuwait, Oman and Muscat needed regular policing. Although there were little more than raids, both the Army and the Royal Air Force became involved. 42 Squadron sent four Shackletons to RAF Khormaksar just north of the town of Aden which became an operational home for a variety of aircraft during the next two years. The Shackletons carried out bombing attacks on the troublemakers. Their enormous bomb bay held a large number of 20 lb practice bombs that banged in an intimidating way when they reached the ground. For more formal occasions, the aeroplane could use twenty-five 500 lb or twelve 1,000 lb bombs on enemy fortified positions. One participant was Mike Rogers who did, however, collect an extra occupation that at least suggested the Royal Air Force was not entirely grim even if there were ulterior motives:

In the early part of 1957 I was sitting in the coffee bar of 42 Squadron at St Eval, when somebody wandered in and asked me if I would like to go on a photographic course at the Air Ministry in London. This being winter in Cornwall, I jumped at the chance. After a week wandering around London with a couple of cameras it was off to Aden via St Eval. Out there, apart from normal flying duties, I was taking photos, still and cine, for my lords and masters in Whitehall and sending the unprocessed film back to London.

I never saw the finished product apart from one trip when I, with the authority of Whitehall behind me, commandeered

90

a Pembroke to take me to Dhala, which was about sixty miles north of Aden, to take some cine of skirmishes with rebels who were just across the border in Yemen. My memory of that was trying to concentrate on holding my camera steady and to ignore the ricochet noises coming from the rocks I was trying to hide behind. The Aden Protectorate Levees had arranged a little punch-up with the bad guys across the border without telling them that a devout coward wanted to make them movie stars and would have no objection to them using blanks. On reflection, the thought of firing a rifle with blanks would probably strike them as being stupid and a complete waste of time. When we got the processed film back from London and showed the local militia how brave they looked on film they thought it was wonderful.

As in a lot of cases the rebels eventually won and now Aden is part of the Yemen.

Although the squadrons all had the normal range of duties on their list, they often had to make goodwill visits. These were generally to parts of the world that rarely featured on RAF detachments or postings. Frequently there was a not too subtle Government reason for the journey. One major showcase journey came the way of 224 Squadron in March 1957. Named, not subtly, Southern Cross, 224 Squadron was to range across South America with four aircraft. Another remained behind as back-up if needed. This was a particular prestige project with the Air Officer Commanding RAF Gibraltar and his Senior Air Staff Officer acting as Force Commander and Deputy.

The trip gave all those who went on it scope to hone their craft in unfamiliar surroundings. It also gave expatriates who lived or worked in the area an opportunity to rub shoulders with 'our boys'. To ensure that the planned displays reached the standard the potential audience anticipated, the squadron concentrated on seriously polishing their formation flying.

Each aeroplane had a face-lift to better its appearance. The squadron number appeared on either side of the fuselage together with a number, 1, 2, 3 or 4, on each side of the nose. Number 1 was WL758, WL753 was Number 2, while WL751 and WL752 were 3 and 4 respectively. Each Shackleton on the month's trip would carry its normal crew of nine together with twelve ground crew. The total flying time for the tour was estimated at just ten minutes under 100 flying hours.

Almost every man in the squadron's ground crew hoped to be chosen for the trip. Trevor Dobson was appointed to Number Two as one of the four selected armourers. They would have, amongst other demands, the responsibility of winching panniers and spares out and into the bomb bay on arrival and departure. Trevor recalls:

Apart from the aircraft being spick and span, the ground crew personnel were also very smart, being issued with white overalls. Those below the rank of sergeant were promoted to acting unpaid sergeants for the duration of the tour only. This naturally raised questions from our hosts as to why 'ordinary airmen' were not included.

This was difficult to answer truthfully as we had been told that many of the host countries had very poor billets and food for personnel below the grade of sergeant. Accordingly, it was felt prudent to make that the lowest rank.

Each three-day visit took the same pattern. First full day – service the aircraft. Second day – demonstration flights for the local dignitaries. Third day – free for sightseeing and the like, provided the Shackletons were serviceable. Local money could have been a problem but with true Air Force efficiency, appropriate currency was issued on each inward journey so there was cash for mementoes.

The trip began with a staging flight that left at 0830 from Gibraltar. The destination was Dakar, Senegal. The next morning, the Shackletons had an 0730 departure for the long haul across the Atlantic. They went to Recife in Brazil which acted only as an overnight staging post. The next morning, the four Shackletons flew on to Rio de Janeiro to begin the tour proper. With no posers popping up on the aircraft, the flying display passed off with no trouble. Trevor Dobson remembers:

This consisted of a single aircraft doing a three-engine fly-past, then a two, then a single-engine fly-past which is quite impressive. Afterwards a slow fly-past with bomb doors open and scanner down plus wheels down took place, then a fast low fly-past and to finish a formation of the four Shackletons.

The goodwill visit moved on to Montevideo in Uruguay after which a short flight across the River Plate found the Shackleton teams in Argentina at Buenos Aires. The Shackletons drew large crowds who cheerfully joined long queues to look inside the aircraft.

The next stop was Chile. This involved a journey over the Andes. Chile was much cooler than the earlier destinations so everybody changed en route into standard blue uniforms. After Chile came Peru. The highlight for many was a train trip on a line that ran upwards, ever upwards into the mountains where it reached a height of 11,502 feet above sea level. After Peru came Ecuador. The aircraft staged through Guayaquil. One flew to the capital Quito to test performance at the airfield, one of the highest anywhere at 9,350 feet above the sea:

> Take-off turned out not to be a problem, so as far as memory serves all aircraft departed to Quito. This was very different from other visits. The locals were all Indians with the ladies wearing trilby hats and shawls, carrying their babies on their backs. Quito is on the equator so a visit was arranged to go to the monument bang on the equator. I had a photo taken with one foot in either hemisphere.

To make the Quito visit less demanding, heavy items were left at Guayaquil. The aircraft returned there to pick up full fuel and their normal loads before they set off on the eleven-hour haul to Key West in Florida. One Shackleton developed a fault in an engine starter motor so the spare aircraft flew out from Gibraltar to take part in the final appearance in Bermuda.

On 16 April, 224 Squadron returned to its home base in Gibraltar. Flying first non-stop to the Azores to overnight, the four Shackletons reached their home base on 18 April 1957. The total flying time came out at 99 hours and 40 minutes, a whole ten minutes under the pre-tour estimate.

Duncan Sandys, the Conservative Defence Minister, on

behalf of the Government had introduced a new defence policy in April 1957 which was, in the eyes of many, muddle-headed and wrong. Manned aircraft would slowly disappear as the country would eventually employ missiles to intercept incoming attacks while Britain's own striking force would use nuclear strike rockets. This anticipated the introduction of Bloodhound surface-to-air weapons as a defence and the Thor Ballistic Missile as a deterrent for use by Bomber Command. This new approach forced the cancellation of almost all projects for new front-line military aircraft.

At 1036 hours local time on 15 May 1957, a Vickers Valiant at forty thousand feet dropped a hydrogen bomb. It took nearly a minute to fall to eight thousand feet and detonate. It did not reach the promised yield but Britain had shown the world that it had entered the Age of the Deterrent. The tests at the Monte Bello Islands the previous year were the groundwork. Shackleton WB828 photographed the mid-air blast south-east of Malden Island, an uninhabited atoll 400 miles south of Christmas Island. Their cameras clicked five minutes after the awe-inspiring flash of what was planned to be a one megaton yield but proved to be just half of that. Two further drops also failed to meet designed yields. The last of these took place on 19 June 1957. It was kept within official circles that the weapons had not reached their designed yields. Scientists made new efforts to produce a fearsome bomb for the next tests. Christmas Island and Operation Grapple would now feature on future Shackleton detachments.

Concerns that the flash of the explosion could damage eyesight led to a temporary addition to the Shackleton's equipment. The cockpit windows were covered with silver-painted canvas. It worked but the cockpit duly suffered. Silver flakes fell everywhere after the bang.

Both pilots on the expedition became recognised later for their varied Shackleton exploits. Docree Foster who served for thirty-three years was the first to make a Shackleton flight of more than twenty-four hours. He exceeded the target by twenty-one minutes although his co-pilot Bill Houldsworth later capped it in March 1963 with a time of twenty-four hours and thirty-six minutes in a Mk3.

On 16 July 1957, the Sultan of Oman requested British help

to deal with dissident tribesmen under the provisions of a treaty with Britain signed six years earlier. His army, numbering 620 men, was unable to fight a bitter campaign against rebels. The Sultanate believed in oppressive rule. His regime was undemocratic and wildly unpopular. Despotism does have drawbacks.

After the catastrophe of Suez, Russia and most Arab states viewed Britain with hostile scrutiny. Despite the unpopularity of the Sultan, Britain risked potential political danger and responded positively. The Masirah RAF base between Muscat and Salalah was one factor that swayed Whitehall. More important was the fervent hope that the Omani ruling clique would further British commercial interests, particularly where they involved oil. In any event, to refuse the request called into question the whole British presence in the region from Aden to the Persian Gulf. Britain's positive response demanded a change in the Sultan's attitude. Approval of his request came, given on condition that the Omani leader changed the worst aspects of his government and agreed to more British presence in his country. A company of Trucial Oman Scouts appeared and were rapidly joined by three companies of Cameronians and a troop of Hussars.

More immediate was air attack. Shackletons from Khormaksar bombed the Jebel Akhdar plateau with 1,000 pounders. This had little effect for the crews diligently followed their orders to bomb only caves and the water system and to leave the villages alone. That date gardens, the crop of which provided income for many rural inhabitants, also suffered gave much pleasure to the Sultan.

Crowds gathered at RAF Gibraltar, home of 224 Squadron, on 14 September for the annual Battle of Britain display. A wide-ranging collection of aircraft, both British and foreign, were on parade either in the flying display or as ground exhibits. The 224 Squadron Shackleton WL792 took off for the completion of the show. To close its own competent display, the aeroplane prepared for the regular finale of a fly-past. The Shackleton pointed its nose at the runway. The grumble of four Griffons reverberated off the immense 1,300-foot-high limestone Rock that gave Gibraltar its most recognised feature. One propeller ceased to revolve as did its neighbour. The undercarriage stayed up as the straining aircraft reached the runway and touched down. A slithering, screeching grinding of metal hit every ear as the aircraft slid on its belly along the tarmac surface.

One squadron pilot, Tom Holland, gave an insider's view:

We did have one accident due to contra-rotating propellers and that was on the starboard wing – the critical starboard wing. One of the engines had an overspeeding propeller. Unfortunately, the co-pilot put out his hand and pressed the button to stop it at the same time as the captain put his hand out. The captain hit the right button, the second pilot hit the wrong button and both engines on the starboard side stopped.

The two hydraulic pumps are one on each engine on the starboard side so they got a total loss of hydraulics. They were about a mile from the runway, coming in on a Battle of Britain Open Day low-level demonstration of a fly-past, full flap. They had got the flaps down and there they were with only two engines. All you can do with only two engines, really, is just land straight ahead and that is what the captain did. He landed straight ahead. He'd managed to control the aircraft sufficiently well to – bear in mind they couldn't put down the undercarriage, couldn't do anything – stay on the runway. The tail wheels broke off and my wife tells a very interesting tale of what it was like, in the Officers' Box on the edge of the runway, watching the display when a tail wheel came bowling towards them at high speed. Frankly, they all stood up and they gasped. It could be heard practically from end to end of the runway. But, fortunately for them, it fell over. It didn't go into the crowd.

By October 1957, British and local troops in Oman had recaptured the main centres of population. Talib, the leader of the rebels, and about fifty of his followers then went into the Jebel Ahkdar mountains. They quickly gained the support of many hill tribesmen. A prolonged and bitter struggle loomed.

On 8 November 1957, a final test at Christmas Island vindicated the scientists. A bomb that burst in the air produced a 320 kiloton blast. This was sufficient to persuade the Government to go ahead. 1958 would be a busy year. Throughout the whole testing sequence, Shackletons had kept constant patrols around the island.

These were both to dissuade any inquisitive seafarers and take weather readings, for the age of the satellite was still in the future.

Appointed Shackleton outfits were warned of the forthcoming detachment. This meant a good deal of work for the chosen squadrons. Chadwick's team had never designed the Shackleton as a cargo hauler. Ground crews perfected a range of devices to fit in the huge amounts of stores and kit that had to be taken out to the Pacific for the tests. Normal servicing also had to be either advanced or delayed so that transit periods did not affect it.

Shackleton crews frequently built friendly working relations with people they never met. In patrols over the Atlantic, the aircraft repeatedly spoke with ocean weather stations. These were generally converted corvettes which gave periodic weather reports to the British Isles and Europe. A more important job as far as aircrew were concerned was their ability to provide direction finding and lay flare paths as well as do a 'talk-down' in an emergency. Every type of Coastal Command aircraft exercised with them on many occasions. Shackletons would try simulated ditching to make sure the ship's Ground Controlled Approach operators stayed competent at talking down aircraft. Additionally, search and rescue aircraft habitually practised their role, often enough with their favourite weather ship.

This all came to a head in December each year when the Shackletons delivered letters and parcels. They regularly took post to ships at sea but Christmas was always special. The ocean weather ships anticipated the arrival of their post bags and sat in the water with every deck light switched on to outline the vessel. After a mutual exchange of greetings, the delivery aircraft made a dummy run. The captain would ask for the mail containers to be dropped off his port or starboard bow and the aircrew would usually see a ship's boat standing by.

As the Shackleton lined up, the captain would bring the aircraft down to 100 feet and reduce speed to less than 120 knots, giving the despatcher a steady commentary – 'Coming up in 30 seconds . . . 20 seconds . . . 10 seconds . . . ' A final 'NOW' was the executive command for the mail containers, usually part of the Lindholme survival and rescue gear – to tumble out of the bomb bay. A flame float would go with them to give the boat's crew a good sight of their prize.

Tom Holland, with 224 Squadron in Gibraltar, collected a number of trips which broke up the consistent round of training operations in which Shackletons and submarines had a jolly time:

Occasionally we got what you could almost call 'funnies'. In 1957 there was a tremendous plague of mosquitoes in Gib. It was thought that there was a possibility these could be malarial so we picked up five thousand mosquito nets in the UK. I flew them back to Gib – five thousand nets for the whole of the garrison, their families and so on – but there was no malaria!

One other load came along at Christmas. It was decided that the garrison should have Brussels sprouts, fresh Brussels sprouts, with their Christmas dinner, so I went off to the UK to pick them up.

There were five tons of them! We had pallets which could be put in the bomb bay in place of the warload. Essentially they were great frames with nets and supports and you could load goods on to them, your own personal kit, anything. If you were going away on a detachment, you could load up your spare parts, all that sort of thing.

The sprouts came from a cool place so that they stayed as fresh as when they were picked. We were flying south, out of England into sunshine. By the time we got to Gibraltar it was quite warm. When we opened the bomb bay to offload the sprouts – I have never seen an aeroplane vacated quite so quickly! Being the pilot and furthest from the door I was last out but the stench from five tons of rotting sprouts has to be smelled to be believed. It was hideous! Sad to say, the garrison didn't get its fresh Brussels sprouts for Christmas dinner!

Swanton Morley's role as the training school for signallers finished at the end of 1957. The school had been renamed as the Air Electronics School on 1 April 1957. It catered for officers who did not mix with the remnants of NCOs still taking the signals course. At the end of the year, the whole operation closed and the training moved to RAF Hullavington.

The new year of 1958 was just ten days old when MOTU at RAF Kinloss suffered casualties. A Shackleton training aircraft with the serial number VP259 crashed while practising night-time approaches. The weather was not good. Scotland in January often suffered with ice and snow but the Royal Air Force knew pretty well all that anybody needed when it came to flying in such conditions.

The Shackleton T4 flew into eight hundred feet of ground at Monaughty Forest near Alves which is between Forres and Elgin. The aircraft was on roller landing practice of night circuits. Although no cause was declared, the general suspicion was that low cloud played an important role in the accident. Perhaps astonishingly, the aircraft did not break up when it hit. Four of the crew escaped from the burning fuselage. One of them was Sergeant L. G. Birnie, who preferred his second name 'George' to his first, more pedestrian, 'Len'. He realised that the flight engineer was trapped under a blazing engine. His citation tells the story:

On the night of 10 January 1958, Sergeant Birnie was detailed to fly as a member of the crew of a Shackleton aircraft on a night-training exercise. The aircraft returned from this exercise at about 11 pm, when bad weather conditions led to its crashing into the top of a thickly wooded hill, where it burst into flames. Two members of the crew of nine were killed and others were injured. At the time of the crash Sergeant Birnie was occupying his routine position and looking forward, he saw that the whole of the front of the aircraft was a sheet of flame. He went aft and with three others, escaped through a hole in the fuselage. He then realised that two members of the crew were not accounted for and at once went back to the wreckage to look for them. He eventually found one of them lying severely injured and burned on the mainplane between Nos 3 and 4 engines. Both of these engines and the mainplane were on fire and the risk of fuel tank explosion pressed closely. Completely disregarding his own safety, Sergeant Birnie secured the injured man and dragged him through a tangle of broken trees and wreckage clear of the flames. Soon after this the petrol tanks exploded. There is no doubt that Sergeant Birnie's gallant action, which critically endangered his own life, saved the life of his comrade.

Sergeant Birnie received the George Medal for his gallantry.

The Shackleton's size could give even its devoted ground crews unusual problems. As Stuart Law, an engine fitter at Luqa in Malta, recalls:

Straddling each side of the peritrack on our side of the airfield were numerous spectacle-shaped dispersals or pans. We could leave the aircraft to rest here after a flight, service them or prepare them for some visiting VIP to look at.

Dug in one of these pans was a hole about six feet square and eight feet deep. This was deep enough to allow the ASV extendable radar to be dropped delicately down for the tradesmen to inspect. The three positions of 'Search 1', 'Search 2', and 'Attack', extended about six feet or so beneath the belly of the aircraft.

The hole was normally covered with railway sleepers to stop the various bodies working on or around the aircraft from falling in it and to allow us to drag the aircraft into position over it. Sometimes, sometimes, when uncovered a misalignment would occur.

As most people know, if something can go amiss, it usually does. Holes in the ground present a hideous trap for the unwary:

Back in those fascinating days of National Service, there were a great number of willing conscripts who were not blessed with a terrific amount of brains. One of them, generally known as Jacko, became my 'assistant'. He had an amazing talent for doing it wrong, losing it, or dropping it. No matter where you had been, or what you had got, his was bigger, better, newer or older and he had been there before you and stayed longer.

When working on a Shackleton under sunny Maltese skies, it did tend to get rather hot. The normal procedure was to open everything from doors to windows and escape hatches to allow a little bit of air to circulate. When the cry of 'NAAFI!' went up, various trades appeared at all of these openings which allowed them to take the quickest way down. From the escape hatch over the wing, you slid down and dropped over the trailing edge. This normally left you in a standing position, poised like a greyhound in the starting blocks and hopefully heading in the direction of the NAAFI wagon.

On this occasion, I was underneath an engine and taking out the oil sump filter. When the cry and general exit happened, I was one of the first in the queue. Once we were all sat on the ground, drinking our tea and eating a cheese wad – that was all you could get – I asked where my mate Jacko was. Nobody had any idea but as he was required in the flight office we did a search. We eventually discovered him piled in a crumpled heap at the bottom of the radar hole. My man had done as expected. On hearing the cry, he dived out of the escape hatch on to the wing and slid down on his backside. The flap was lowered so he didn't have to drop the last few feet. Sadly, the aircraft was not quite correctly positioned. With the covers off the hole, bingo! Down he went, knocking himself out when he landed.

For a few brief seconds we considered putting the covers back over but finally decided to drag him out. Following a short spell in the sickbay, he returned to us. As the hole was undamaged, no action was taken against him.

This was not his only adventure. A further incident might have resulted in far worse consequences:

The Griffons were large and impressive with a very distinct sound that eventually deafened you. They also enjoyed very high compression. If you felt adventurous, another interesting way to get down from the top of an engine was to walk out to the props, step on the rear one and very gingerly walk outwards until your weight overcame the compression. At this point you started to go down. The front prop came up to meet you. This was extremely useful as it was something you could hang on to. Eventually, all things being equal, you could either leap off with all the grace of a pregnant gazelle or just drop.

There were obviously a couple of points to remember before trying this. It was not recommended if the magnetos

101

were switched on. Trying it then could elevate you to new heights unless the fuselage was in the way or you were pointing downwards. Both of these did tend to bring you to a very sudden stop. Another time to avoid it was if the plugs were out. You did not try it either if the cowlings were up which was usually the case during a normal service.

One day, my amazing Jacko was on top of the wing, either sunbathing or sniffing the avgas, when along came the Naafi wagon as per normal. Up went the cry. Bodies appeared at every exit. And our hero rushed along the top of Number Two engine. To give him his due, the covers were down. He grabbed the rear prop and headed outwards. And you will have already guessed that the plugs were out.

As he went rapidly downwards, he did manage a grab at the front prop blade as it sped past in the opposite direction. He missed. His feet arrived on the ground. He must have realised that a rear blade was heading towards him for he threw himself flat on the tarmac beneath the free spinning prop. The rest of the ground crew, it is fair to say, were now in a state of hysterical laughter.

Jacko, realising both that he was unhurt and centre stage, sat up. That's when the front blade finally got him.

When he came out of the sickbay this time, he was a whole lot quieter.

The first two aircraft for the Christmas Island tests left Britain in February 1958. They would have a busy time as would other Shackletons who were there to witness the birth of Britain's nuclear deterrent.

Jim Hughes, now a crew chief with 240 Squadron, gives some background and recounts an associated adventure:

I was involved in this operation, though as crew chief on the reserve aircraft, I did not expect to travel out until the end of the affair. The aircraft travelled from Ballykelly in pairs with the first leaving in February. They made it as far as Travis airfield near San Francisco when one aircraft developed serious engine trouble. A spare engine had to be sent out immediately on my reserve aircraft. At that time Shackletons could carry a spare engine but it meant fitting special bomb doors with a slot for the engine to poke through. Of course all this happened at a weekend. Only a very motley crew of tradesmen could be found to do the job while myself and my crew prepared to leave.

Arriving at the aircraft in the early hours of Sunday morning, we found to our horror that the bomb doors had been fitted back to front. Everything was delayed twenty-four hours while a new crew of tradesmen fitted the bomb doors again – hopefully the correct way this time. We eventually set off on Monday morning with a very overladen aircraft. As well as the normal aircrew we carried four spare aircrew, eight ground crew plus another four ground crew for changing the engine.

Obviously there were not enough seats for everyone but some bright spark had organised a huge roll of carpet underlay to ease our bones while lying on the metal floor. As well as the engine, the bomb bay contained panniers of aircraft spares and personal kit. The engine change team brought a huge coffin-like box containing a propeller change kit. This had to be placed in the middle of the fuselage, adding to the already dangerous main spar when clambering up and down the aircraft.

At that time, Shackletons travelling to America went via Canada in the summer and the Caribbean in the winter. The first stop was Lajes in the Azores but by the time we reached the Bay of Biscay it was obvious we could never make it against the February gale. We diverted to St Mawgan where we stayed the night and set off again the next day, finally landing at Lajes and into the welcoming arms of the Portuguese Air Force.

The Shackleton still faced a long journey across the grey Atlantic:

Another night of waiting until it was decided to face the long haul across the Atlantic to Bermuda. This involved thirteen hours of gazing at a wintry Atlantic and cooking up various meals in the galley. Shack crews, both air and ground, usually had at least one budding cook who liked nothing better than trying to produce gourmet meals from the motley collection of flying rations on board. We got a bit worried when one of the pilots came back and asked us to dump some of the many tins we had on board. If we were having trouble through excess weight we thought the engine in the bomb bay should go before our grub.

It took thirteen hours and twenty minutes before the Shackleton's wheels kissed the runway at Bermuda. The extra delay was down to a US Navy blimp which had to be collapsed because of gales before it could be tethered. After a rest period, the Shackleton and its collection of crew and passengers set off once again. This time they aimed for Charleston in South Carolina:

This huge base was used for some routine servicing but when we set off after a couple of days we had a complete engine failure. Our trip to Texas was cancelled and we had to land at Barksdale in Louisiana. A quick check soon revealed that an engine change was necessary – lo and behold, we had a spare in the bomb bay. The base personnel could not have been more helpful despite being rather bemused by this relic of the piston age parked among their latest jets. We did a smooth engine change, carried out a quick air test and we were away to California. The fact that we carried a duff engine to Travis Field did not worry the stranded crew too much. Obviously the Californian sun and local atmosphere was more enjoyable than Christmas Island.

We gladly got rid of our spare, now duff, engine and changing crew – especially the prop change kit. We now faced another thirteen-hour trip to Honolulu with only a brief stay there until Christmas Island.

The stranded Shackleton in California eventually received a working engine delivered by courtesy of a Transport Command Hastings. More troubles nipped at the Shackleton and Operation Grapple was nearly finished before it finally reached Christmas Island.

Over the next month the squadron came out two by two until we had nine aircraft, all very busy patrolling the Pacific.

By the end of April the Island was packed with RAF, Army and Royal Navy and we had settled down to the rather odd routine.

Christmas Island had the usual tropic climate sun and rain. We did shift work made strange by the authority's idea of putting an extra hour on the local time. As we were near the Date Line we heard the English football results on Saturday morning.

The tented accommodation was rather primitive and dangerous when the electrics fused and set the tent on fire. There was not much spare time but we managed to swim inside the reef – the sharks watched from outside. The local wild life was mainly land crabs, which were constantly crunched under our truck wheels. We had a very good mail service to and from the UK. A lot of guys sent home decorated coconuts, the equivalent, I suppose, of present day e-mails.

As Sunderlands vanished from active service, Coastal Command needed new squadrons, a situation exacerbated by the forced withdrawal of the Neptune. The only contender for maritime reconnaissance was the Shackleton. Number 205 Squadron, based at Changi in Malaya, became the next squadron to receive the Avro Growler, the first arriving in May 1958.

Things were not going too well with the British military. Restrictions on Defence spending grew apace. Cold War requirements were not always imperatives as the three services had started to learn.

CHAPTER SEVEN

Problems arose once more in the Middle East in the summer of 1958. This time, the Lebanon took all the attention. Inspired by the creation of the United Arab Republic, the union of Egypt and Syria, Lebanese Druze and Muslim activists demanded that their country join the new grouping. Their revolt took on a tasteless religious aspect that pitted Muslim against Christian.

Lebanon appealed to the major Western nations for help. Britain decided to send troops to Cyprus. Once again the Shackleton put on its troop transport coat, heaving aloft thirty-three soldiers with their kit from Abingdon. As usual, Malta became a staging post on the passage. The lack of suitable long-range aircraft for Transport Command use was painfully evident.

Colin Whiting, an armourer mechanic, was already serving at Nicosia. He remembers:

I was based in Cyprus from March 1958 during the very unfortunate EOKA terrorist campaign. A Shackleton detachment from 38 Squadron, based at Luqa, was used on anti-smuggling patrols. They were to try and stop arms, ammunition and explosives being imported/landed illicitly around the island. Somehow arms, ammo and explosives were landed, in spite of the air and sea patrols.

The Shacks would fly round the Island and then along the

southern coast of Turkey before returning to Nicosia. They would fly only at night, which involved calling by radio all ships for their identity. Flares would be dropped if needed. The patrols lasted about four hours.

RAF personnel were encouraged to fly on these operations to act as observers, which I did once with some others. Oh dear, the noise and vibration was uncomfortable but when we returned to Nicosia, it took four tries to land. Three attempts appeared to be 'circuits and bumps' or maybe the crew were just having a bit of fun!

Danger did not necessarily always lurk in areas where Shackletons and crew went on active service. As in the War, sensible commanders kept their valuable assets some distance from danger when they were at rest. Not that it was necessarily an easy existence as Mike Rogers explains:

In 1958 back in the Gulf area, a lot of Shack crews found themselves in Masirah preparing to drop some bombs on a different bunch of rebels from the ones operating in the Aden area. (There was a rumour that it was something to do with the probability of oil in the area but I cannot believe that.)

One of the problems with Masirah was the lack of refuelling facilities, which was solved by arranging for a freighter to bring the fuel to Masirah in forty-gallon drums. Unfortunately the freighter could not get close enough to the old wooden pier on the beach to unload them so dhows were hired to bring them to the shore. To get them out of the dhows and on to the old wooden pier, a block and tackle was used, moving two at a time. They had to be hoisted up to the height at which I was taking the photograph, then swung on to the pier. This was very slow.

Somebody had a bright idea. Oil floats on water so a logical answer was to put the oil drums in the water and use the dhows as sheepdogs to drive them on to the beach. This worked fine until the wind shifted. Some got away, drifting off into the Persian Gulf.

Despite their ongoing role as troop carriers, Shackleton crews also had to stay on normal duties. Maritime patrols, reconnaissance, search and rescue and, as always, exercises kept everyone ready for action should the Cold War ever decide to warm up. On top of all that was the hardly negligible matter of upgrading skills as new equipment arrived. Bernie Donders found himself moving from tailwheel to nosewheel:

> In August 1958 two crews from the Squadron, mine included, were sent to St Mawgan for conversion to the Mk3 Shackleton. Well what luxury; it was much quieter, with sound proofing, a steerable nosewheel, lighter flying controls and generally much more comfortable to fly. I found that the Mk3 was certainly easier to land than the previous versions. I particularly remember one occasion when the crew were called out for SAR duties the only aircraft available was a Mk2. This flight was my first in the Mark for about two months. On return to base and at the pinnacle of the 'landing bounce' my navigator, Jimmy Horne, asked if we should file another flight plan!

Like all Kipper Fleet members, Bernie Donders and his crew needed to be highly proficient when it came to search and rescue. Guiding lifeboats to the aid of vessels in distress needed skill and patience:

> Search and Rescue was, of course, one of our most rewarding duties. Unfortunately, it often called for flights in the worst weather conditions and the most unsociable hours, with mostly nothing to show for our efforts. Although the total number of incidents was probably large, as individual crews we seemed to do little. One crew was always on immediate call and slept in the Squadron HQ, with a fully prepared Shackleton standing by.
>
> On 4 October 1958 my crew were called to rendezvous with a Sabena, Belgian Airlines, DC7C aircraft, which had engine trouble whilst crossing the North Atlantic. The weather was not very good when we took off from Aldergrove but we broke out into absolutely clear skies over the ocean. Eventually, we were able to communicate with the Sabena captain on VHF radio and get a good idea of his position and

track. Remember that this was long before accurate navigation aids like Inertial Navigation and GPS. We were using things like LORAN and Astro. My Nav at the time, Jimmy Horne, said, 'turn right now, fly XXX degrees and if we are very lucky you might see something'. Well I did turn right and as I rolled out I saw a little speck in the distance which turned out to be the aforesaid DC7C. We soon tucked in alongside. Although he was struggling on partial power we had trouble keeping up! We did manage it with the use of a lot more power and then, would you believe it, our H/F or long-range radio failed. So there we were, using a lot of petrol to keep our station with the distressed aircraft and that crew was passing our position reports for us. I recall that we were wondering exactly which of us was in trouble! All ended well though, the DC7C landed at Shannon in the Irish Republic and we went home to Aldergrove.

More active service awaited many in the military. The Government, no matter how much some resented its policies, could always rely on its armed forces. Irrespective of private beliefs, they forswear public political allegiances. British service-men nonetheless also appreciated that politicians had to make choices. As far as Oman and the Middle East went, service personnel generally understood that the resident populace wanted to remove British influence in the area. Apart from any other consideration, it was a matter of who controlled the emerging oil supplies. In the era of the Cold War, Britain additionally found it essential to supervise the adjacent seaways. It can be argued that the modern pro-Western states in the region result from political decisions by Whitehall.

Four Shackletons of 228 Squadron left St Eval on 3 September 1958 for the long haul to Aden. After some ten hours in the air, they stopped overnight at El Adem, the RAF's main base in Libya. The next morning, WR959, WR969, WR957 and WR961 went on to Khormaksar. Over the next few days, with the aid of 37 Squadron's hard-working ground crew, the four aircraft received some minor but important modifications. Fully prepared, they took off for Sharjah which took another six hours' flying time. The Sultan of Oman still needed help.

The rebels who had vanished up into the Jebal Akhdar were stronger and more active. Shackletons had bombed the area unceasingly for more than a year but the rebellion carried on with little apparent hindrance. The Shackletons were impressive enough as bombers although they proved to be less than militarily effective. Sharjah, their temporary base, was little better than a slum. At best, it was cramped but just bearable. Venoms of Number 8 Squadron, normally based at Khormaksar, also flew out of Sharjah. They worked in conjunction with the Shackletons, attacking rebel positions with rockets before the big aircraft dropped their 1,000lb bombs.

The first operation by 228 Squadron happened on 13 September and it effectively proved a template for those that followed. The aircraft took off in the coolest part of the day, just before dawn. This helped the crews and the Griffons both. Each aircraft carried six 1,000 lb bombs although this later became twelve. They had an outward journey of some 200 miles to reach the target area. The bomb load was heavy enough to keep the Shackleton labouring for some thirty minutes to reach six to eight thousand feet. When the aircraft reached the target, smoke was dropped to calculate wind speed and direction. One of the essential modifications carried out in Aden had been the swapping of the low-level depth-charge-sighting device for a medium-level bomb-sight which needed wind direction and strength to be effective.

On the second pass, the aircraft dropped its bombs. The whole unhurried performance was, most crews considered, enough to ensure that any self-respecting terrorist, or indeed civilian, would have taken to a local mountainous cave when they heard the first growl of the Griffons.

Ted Gregory flew with 228 Squadron on these raids. As the winter and rainy season approached at the end of October, the Shackletons exchanged the shanties at Sharjah for the even less desirable hovels at Masirah. He recalls:

RAF Masirah was a small staging and communications post with a permanent staff of about thirty personnel. It was not really equipped to take a whole squadron of Shackletons but we fitted in wherever we could, mostly in tents. In addition,

110

a detachment of Aden Levies were there to guard us. The quiet backwater became a hive of activity.

The two main tasks for the squadron were desert reconnaissance and tactical bombing. The reconnaissance was carried out at low level, flying into the Rubh al Khali desert to the west of the mountains searching for rebel camel trains or lorry convoys moving eastwards from Saudi Arabia or the Yemen. We were not allowed to attack them but would alert the Trucial Oman Scouts by radio so that their patrols could intercept and determine whether the convoy was friend or foe.

One of the problems in dealing with the insurgency was the difficulty in deciding who supported the Sultan and who was a rebel. As Ted explains, this did call for the occasional change in tactics:

An unusual reconnaissance task was the requirement to fly over a nominated village or desert fort and determine whether the flag being flown was that of the sultan or the rebels. If the rebel flag was flown, again, we were not allowed to attack in order to prevent injury to the innocent population but we were allowed to 'fly our flag'. This meant roaring in at full engine chat, bomb doors open and nose guns swivelling, just over tree-top height. The nose guns were twin 50 mm Aden cannon intended for strafing surfaced enemy submarines. We never did fire them in the Oman because of the high risk of ricochet off the rocks, then flying into your own shells. Not that the rebels were aware of this restriction.

Tactical bombing targets were mostly on the tops and upper valleys of the Jebel Akhdar. The Shackleton could carry twelve 1,000 lb bombs in a bay designed to take depth charges, torpedoes and sonobuoys. Each bomb had to free-fall 6,000 feet to arm. Sometimes the target itself was 6,000 feet high so we flew at an altitude of 12,000 feet over these targets. Flying rations were provided for sorties expected to be airborne over a mealtime. Unfortunately, flying rations always seemed to be the same – cream crackers, tinned pineapple and orange juice.

As the Sultan's opponents maintained their happy hold on the Jebel Akdhar, the military decided to impose firmer measures. The Special Air Service turned up. They flew in from Malaya in a Hastings transport aircraft, promptly transferring to a waiting Beverley that took them to an airstrip closer to the rebels.

They became mildly contemptuous of the rebels who shouted down to them from their defence positions, 'Come up, Johnny, and fight.' In December they did, with a night attack which killed some twelve rebels. Despite this setback, the opposition was wily, strong and stubbornly determined. The SAS had no casualties yet had to eventually call off their only partially successful foray.

The 228 Squadron Shackletons continued to make pinpoint raids in support of the SAS when they could but they were withdrawn with little warning in the middle of December. They arrived back at St Eval on 20 December 1958. A single Shackleton, WL800, from 37 Squadron continued a forlorn air campaign with daily bombing attacks on rebel positions. The crew of this aeroplane possibly invented the ruse of flying at night to drop their bombs on camp-fires that had no business being in such a place. The terrorists soon associated the growling engines with the arrival of damaging explosions. They countered by vanishing into nearby caves. This let the Shackleton squander flying time and expensive bombs, wasting effort and money. Some genius, unknown to history, discovered that a pint bottle of lager, especially Carlsberg, with its crown cork in place, dropped from one thousand feet, sounded exactly like a falling 1,000 pounder. When the lager failed to produce havoc, the terrorists cheerfully returned in ideal time to be greeted by real bombs from above. This helpful technique found its way to Middle Eastern trouble spots whenever Shackletons needed to go into action.

Number 201 Squadron reformed at St Mawgan on 1 October 1958 by the simple process of renumbering 220 Squadron to the familiar Two-Oh-One. This procedure of shifting a distinctive identity, possibly specifically designed to confuse ancient female historians, was not confined to Coastal Command. The practice, occasionally frustrating, does nonetheless retain hallowed titles.

Shackletons went to Christmas Island in the second half of

the year for the final H-bomb tests of Operation Grapple. The aircraft from 269 Squadron spent their time on low-level sea searches to ensure complete clearance of the area. John Perigo remembers:

On 2 September 1958 I was a sergeant signaller aboard WB835 out of Christmas Island as part of Operation Grapple, the UK's nuclear bomb test programme. Our task was to carry a cameraman from the Atomic Warfare Research Establishment to film the detonation, scheduled for dawn, and later to take radiation samples from the area of Ground Zero.

Approaching detonation time we were positioned fifty miles from Ground Zero with the camera set up in the port beam window. The crew were all heads down, eyes covered as protection from the flash as I counted down the radio signal to detonation over the intercom. After a further ten seconds for safety we were allowed to look out.

A huge cloud rose into the clear blue sky and towered far, far above us. I turned to the navigator now looking over my shoulder and said, 'We are supposed to be fifty miles from that!' He replied in a very low flat voice, 'We are!' Such was the impact of those weapons.

Three weeks later, 23 September, was my birthday and the last of the four bomb test series. Many people have fireworks for their birthday but I got a nuclear bomb for mine.

Number 203 Squadron became the next to fly Shackletons. Its Neptunes vanished from charge on 1 September 1956. Coastal Command's renumbering system came into action again when the squadron reformed and 240 Squadron blossomed into 203 at Ballykelly on 1 November 1958. It received its first Shackleton later that month and was immediately known as Two-Oh-Three Squadron by everyone there.

They were joined on Ballykelly's Order of Battle by 210 Squadron which, in accordance with local usage, became Two-Oh-Ten. This was another renumbering for it had previously been Number 269 Squadron.

Archie Lumsden had moved on from the Air Sea Warfare Development Unit at St Mawgan to Singapore in January 1958.

He was part of 205 Squadron which was about to convert from Sunderlands to Shackletons. A delay in aircraft arrival meant 205 went without Shackletons for a few months. He makes the following observations:

In May 1958 I flew with a small party to Ceylon to meet the first aircraft staging in from Aden. This was VP254. This was the first production MR1 which first flew on 28 March 1950. It had been retained by the manufacturers for various trial installations and had been in storage at Aldergrove from January 1958 until May.

On 19 May we all flew back to Changi with the aircraft with a flight over the whole of Singapore accompanied by two Sunderlands. VP254, coded B, was the first to undergo a major servicing at Changi and emerged from this just prior to the flight to RAF Labuan, Borneo, 8 December 1958, to take part in a demonstration of anti-piracy patrols with a representative of the North Borneo Police. There had been problems during the servicing and the aircraft was delivered back to the Squadron without a compass swing being carried out.

Labuan is the largest in a group of islands some five miles off the coast of Borneo. It could have been designed for use by Shackletons for it is flat and without looming hills, the highest point being a mere 250 feet above the sea.

At 0548 hours on 9 December 1958, VP254, captained by Flight Lieutenant Walter Boutell, lifted into the Singapore sky when it took off from Labuan. The aircraft carried its normal crew of two pilots, a flight engineer, two navigators and five signallers with an extra passenger, the acting Deputy Police Commissioner of North Borneo. The Shackleton was on a routine anti-piracy patrol.

Soon after take-off, ground control diverted the aeroplane. A report had come in that stated there were fisherman stranded on an atoll some 227 miles north of Labuan. Several people thought that they could be the crew of the Australian schooner *Ian Crouch*. This vessel, with a crew of eleven Australians under a British skipper, went missing on its maiden voyage from Hong

Kong to Australia. Later enquiries established that the men on the atoll were simply Formosan fishermen.

At 0710hrs, the captain radioed to confirm that the Shackleton had located the atoll, seen the survivors and diverted a fishing junk to take them on board. This vessel eventually turned out to be another Formosan boat, serial YF890, which had been searching for them. Its rapid departure for Formosa subsequently caused some confusion to those involved in the search with dark suggestions that the fishermen had been kidnapped.

A further report from the Shackleton followed at 1143. The rescue operation was proceeding well and the aircraft would resume its original task in a further fifteen minutes. Twelve minutes later, at 1157 hours, VP254 made a brief position report. After that nothing came save the ominous silence that suggests something has gone wrong.

An alert went to the duty Search and Rescue crew at 1615 hours. With no more news available, they went off to do an emergency beacon search along the intended track of VP254. Around midnight, two Shackletons growled off to reach the presumed search area at first light. Throughout that day, four Shackletons, three Hastings, one Sunderland and one Valetta looked for the missing aircraft. Many of the aircraft carried volunteer observers. Extra eyes always help. They had no success.

The Shackletons and the Hastings continued the hunt the next day. Six Valettas joined them, as did two Bristol Freighters from the Royal New Zealand Air Force along with two Albatross aircraft from the US Air Force. The probable effects of wind, tide and currents were calculated to amend the search area and give a greater chance of success. The searchers flew in ever-widening circles to maximise their chances of triumph to no avail. There was little question that the eleven souls on board had perished.

The Shackleton had vanished in the area of the Spratley Islands in the South China Sea. On the sixth day after VP254, coded 'Bravo' in 205 Squadron, went missing, Flight Lieutenant John Elias, who would eventually gather the largest number of hours flown in the Growler at 12,297, flew over Sin Cowe Island. Below them, he and his crew saw large white letters created from sand. They read 'B 205'. Close to them was a wooden cross. It was a clear reference to the missing aircraft although the island seemed to be without life.

The next day, on 16 December 1958, the Royal New Zealand Navy frigate *Rotoiti* reached the island to put a landing party ashore. The medical officer of the ship later stated:

On the 15th we were told to go to Sin Cowe island on which a cross had been noted by a searching aircraft. Approximately at 1300 hours on the 16th December we sighted the island. The captain decided to send a whaler ashore and ordered me as medical officer to exhume the body or bodies. The crew of the whaler comprised five oarsmen, and an executive officer as coxswain. A Royal Air Force aircraft guided us through the reefs by dropping smoke floats.

After landing on the beach we first made a search of the island. There were no signs of any life or aircraft wreckage. There were signs of previous occupation evidenced by open tins and beer bottles. These were of American origin, and had been there for some time. We found a grave in the centre of the island surmounted by a large wooden cross. Painted on the back of the cross was the following inscription: 1355 9th December 1958. In front of the cross was painted number 205 and RAF colours. At the foot of the grave were placed two Chinese rice bowls.

We proceeded to open the grave and found a rough wooden coffin. We took this out and opened it and found one body in a fair degree of decomposition. The body was clothed in what appeared to be underpants and vest. The only obvious injury was a large wound in left lower leg. In my opinion this wound if not treated would have caused death by bleeding. Also in the coffin was a Royal Air Force cap and khaki stockings. There was a watch on the left wrist. We removed the body from the coffin and wrapped it in blankets and canvas and placed it in the whaler. We closed the grave and left the cross in position. We took a final look around the island and then returned to the ship. Next morning the body was taken from the ship by helicopter from HMS *Albion*.

The single body proved to be the remains of the flight engineer. Flight Sergeant David Dancy was a Bomber Command veteran who became a warrant officer during the War, a rank in which he won the Distinguished Flying Cross for his gallantry

Following this episode, *Albion* made her own enquiries. Officers from the ship went to the Chinese Nationalist island of Itu Aba on 18 December 1958. There they interviewed the captain of a fishing vessel who had witnessed the crash. His evidence confirmed that nobody had survived although they had found one body floating in the water. They took this to Sin Cowe Island to bury with dignity. The letters they saw on the side of the Shackleton were reproduced on the cross they erected and written on the sand to attract the attention of searching aircraft. Managed without the aid of an interpreter, the HMS *Albion* team agreed that the captain's vessel, registered in Taiwan, was the *San Foren*. This later became the *Ray Fu Chen* while the captain was identified as Gan Chung-Huang. In later weeks, he received formal thanks and a cash reward for his efforts.

Dancy's body and the wooden cross were moved by HMS *Albion* to Labuan. Dancy was reburied there in Ulu Pandan cemetery. The cross was re-erected at St George's Church at RAF Changi.

The mandatory Board of Inquiry into the crash and loss of life, as was so often the case, found itself with very little hard data. Evidence presented suggested that a minor inspection schedule just before the accident had not carried out a compass swing, a procedure to check that the magnetic compass gives a true reading. The Board dismissed this as a possible cause, icily stating that 'there is no possibility that this contributed in any way to the accident'. They stressed that the omission was a technical infringement only. No major component had been disturbed during the inspection schedule and the compass was not due for swinging.

The familiar phrase as to the cause of the accident duly appeared:

As there is insufficient evidence to positively determine the cause of the accident the Board is unable to determine the responsibility for it. The Board considers it most likely that the accident was caused by an error of judgement by one of the two pilots.

This could be read as a veiled suggestion that a turn had been tried too close to the sea.

Air Chief Marshal Sir Edward Chilton became Air Officer Commanding-in-Chief of Coastal Command in July 1959. He went to flying boat training in 1926 on completion of his Cranwell pilot instruction. There were then no specialised navigators as such. Pilots found their way around with basic map reading, which relied heavily on roads and railway lines. Before the Second World War, the only part of the Air Force that studied and used air navigation techniques came from those involved in maritime reconnaissance. He took a succession of posts that involved navigation duties or maritime experience and which culminated in his appointment as commander of Coastal Command.

As David Greenway points out:

When Air Chief Marshal Sir Edward Chilton was AOC-in-C Coastal Command, he wrote a booklet called 'The Coastal Command Captain'. It was full of the wonderful things he thought Coastal Command captains should be doing and even included a diary of events which he expected these amazing heroes to follow. From memory it went something like this:

0600 Awoke. Had cold shower.
0615 Woke crew
0630 Went for run with crew
0700 Ablutions
0730 Breakfast with crew
and so on, etc., etc.,,

This booklet was issued to, I think, all the officer aircrew in his command who received it with horror-struck astonishment.

Chillie then followed this up with a note which said:

'You will all have read my booklet on 'The Coastal Command Captain' and thus seen how I expect these leaders to conduct their responsibilities. As follow-up, I intend to introduce a Coastal Command Captain's tie so that these fine men can be recognised in civilian clothes. Accordingly, I would like some suggestions as to the design of this tie.'

I think he only got one reply and that was from Paddy

Flynn, a somewhat bitter former Cranwell cadet and my captain on 206 Squadron. Paddy wrote, 'Sir, what a splendid suggestion. Could I suggest that we have the tie black so that we can wear it with uniform.'

Nothing more was heard on the topic.

Duncan Sandys and his 1957 Defence Policy had effectively stopped the development of new front-line military aircraft. This was amended within the next years. In February 1960, the Government decided that ground missiles designed to deter an enemy were too vulnerable to sneak attacks. Instead, aircraft and submarines would carry deterrent missiles, a decision that remained in force for a measly two months. At that point, the development of submarine-based weapons was abandoned in favour of the new V-bombers armed with US missiles.

Although manned aircraft would continue in service, the writing on the wall was clear enough. Technology was inching forward surely to replace old-fashioned labour-intensive skills.

It made little practical difference to Shackleton crews. They had developed a strong camaraderie, partly brought about by the number who flew in each aeroplane and realised that it could only be an effective fighting unit if everybody worked together, irrespective of individual rank. Perverse pride took over. It took dedication to operate an aircraft, directly descended from a famed wartime forerunner, with obsolescent equipment on board allied to four deafening piston engines. Both those who flew and those who groomed the aeroplane on the ground became accustomed to the comments made by the rest of the Air Force along the lines of whether they operated an aeroplane or the box in which it came.

On top of their maritime duties, for which even more equipment was shuffled into the fuselage, there were also trips in which either good fortune or injury, even death, could result as Bernie Donders describes:

Once upon a time, many years ago, in 1959 to be precise, I was called in by my commanding officer on No 120 Squadron at RAF Kinloss to be told that I was going to be the captain of one of three Avro Shackletons to fly to the

Caribbean on a goodwill tour. After the initial adrenaline surge, the excitement started to abate, we got down to some serious planning. This was supplemented by a briefing from an Air Ministry gentleman who explained that there had been a request from British Honduras, now the state of Belize, for air support. At the time, Guatemala had been threatening to take action over its border dispute with British Honduras. This request was given consideration by the Ministry but the decision was that it was not practical to send a detachment of Hawker Hunters or English Electric Canberras so the Shackleton Mk3 was chosen.

Action involving Guatemala had one vital difference to that against various discontented terrorists. The potential enemy had an air force:

The 120 Squadron crews were a little bemused in that as a maritime reconnaissance aircraft the Shack could hardly act as a great threat to any Guatemalan Air Force aircraft. I remember that at one point during the briefing, one of the pilots asked what fighter aircraft the Guatemalans possessed and we were told 'old WWII P51 Mustang fighter'. It was pointed out that the Shackleton Mk3 had no rear facing armament which could deal with an attack from behind so the question was what action should we take if such an event, though very unlikely, occurred. The response was that we should fire off our photoflash cartridges behind us in the hope that the enemy would go away. Nothing changes to British military equipment provision, does it? The general opinion was that the Shackleton had been chosen because three aircraft with their Rolls-Royce Griffon engines would provide enough noise to scare anyone!

Despite the possibility of fighting in the air in actions reminiscent of the Second World War, a pleasurable compensation also beckoned:

We were told that, combined with the trip to Belize then the capital of British Honduras, we were to carry out a goodwill

120

tour of the Caribbean Islands in an exercise called Calypso Stream.

So on the 25 April 1959 the boss, Wing Commander Freddie Reed, 'A' Flight Commander, Squadron Leader Jim Wightwick and myself left Kinloss in our aircraft on the first stage of our adventure. The first night was spent at the tropical paradise of RAF St Mawgan in Cornwall. Well, compared to the weather at Kinloss it always seemed warm there. The following day we headed for the American base at Lajes in the Azores from where, after another night stop we proceeded across the Atlantic to Kindley USAF base in Bermuda. After a couple of nights there, being well looked after and supplied with copious amounts of rum-based cocktail we set off once more, this time to Palisadoes Airport in Jamaica. Here we were warmly welcomed and entertained by the Kingston RAF Association members and given a lot of publicity in the local paper, the *Daily Gleaner*. We stayed for four days during which time we publicised ourselves by about three hours of formation flying over the Island. On the 30 April the detachment flew from Jamaica to Belize.

This time, as an aircraft captain I was given the honour of being entertained in the Governor's Residence. We would have daily conferences with the Governor, Police Chief, and other dignitaries so for a while I felt rather like 'Our Man in Havana'. During the time we were there we did our best to make a lot of noise in formation around the British Honduras/Guatemalan border. At the end of these sorties we split up and were given carte blanche to fly anywhere we wished and as low as we liked – a pilot's dream if ever there was one! Searches for gun-running ships in the area were also flown but with no positive results of course.

There was one incident that happened during our stay which amused me. We were having lunch in the mess of the British Army regiment, when we noticed that the Duty Officer always sat on his own at the window by the entrance door. When the reason for this practice was queried the answer given was 'He is watching out for Queen Victoria.'

Apparently, in the nineteenth century the good lady had arrived at the mess unexpectedly and she 'was not amused' at her reception. Ever since that day a determined effort had been made not to let it happen ever again!

No matter how big or how small a trouble might be, Shackletons had become accustomed to being called upon to face down potential wrongdoers. They would continue to do so in the years ahead.

CHAPTER EIGHT

Bernie Donders in the Caribbean completed his part in the goodwill tour that followed on from the British Honduras and Guatemala episode in 1959. After displays in Trinidad, the three aircraft went to Bermuda. En route, the detachment commander, Freddie Reed, suffered engine failure. His aircraft could not go on so he suggested, in the polite manner that the Royal Air Force prefers, that Bernie gave up his aeroplane and crew so that the wing commander could head back to Britain. Bernie and a skeleton crew could ferry home the sick Shackleton after repair. Disappointed, even aghast at the thought of spending a couple more days in the sun, Bernie forced himself to agree.

The remaining two crews left the next day. Bernie and four companions settled down to relax for a peaceful two or three days. A signal duly arrived to tell Bernie that a replacement Griffon would be loaded on to a Coastal Command Meteorological Flight Hastings at Aldergrove and would shortly arrive. Soon afterwards, Base Operations at Kindley Field advised that the Hastings had left the UK to head for the Azores. The following day Bernie received a copy of a signal from the Hastings captain to Coastal Command. The aircraft could not leave Lajes because of strong adverse head winds that would severely reduce its range of 1,690 miles. Immediate improvement in the winds was unlikely.

Bernie and his scratch crew promptly accepted an invitation from a Bermudian family to move into their capacious house for the rest of their enforced stay. They took up the offer for they had all suffered enough with the toilet arrangements in the US Bachelor Officers' Quarters at the American base.

After a couple of days, another signal arrived. There was no suggestion that the westerly winds would abate so a new route had been agreed. The Hastings would now fly to Gander in Newfoundland. Another signal followed. The Hastings had reached Canada. Unfortunately, one of its four Bristol Hercules engines had failed on the way. The aeroplane was grounded until a replacement came from Britain.

A fresh engine reached Gander for the Hastings after some days of waiting. The original aircraft finally took off for Bermuda with the Griffon. On arrival, the ground crew worked furiously to fix the sick Shackleton so that it was able to take an air test on the morning of 21 May. The aeroplane was fine. Bernie and his crew forced themselves to leave the holiday island, reaching home by 22 May 1959.

No matter what the remainder of the service endured, Coastal Command still had a vital job to do. If war came, enemy submarines had to be found and killed. The service still required the aircraft even though they had achieved a venerable air. Men were still needed. Coastal Command had become almost the only option for former fighter pilots and other aircrew to continue flying. Many felt, with good reason, that they were essentially traditionalists with their piston-engined aeroplanes.

Despite the 1957 plans, which apparently decided that manned aircraft were no longer a prime requirement, the Royal Air Force continued to offer long-term careers for aviators, albeit in reduced numbers. No matter what the politicians might tell themselves, the military services were uncomfortably aware that future conflicts would not be confined to enormous missiles with devastating warheads deployed in a global war. Plenty of more traditional conflicts awaited.

Eventually Parliamentarians and legislators in civilian clothes in Whitehall realised some conventional ability had to be retained. There was the crushing disadvantage that all arms spending increased yearly because of progressively more expensive research costs. It seemed that a weapon no sooner entered service than it was outdated.

Coastal Command continued to recruit although indications were that a hostile submarine was unlikely to play an identical role to that of its predecessors in two world wars. The USS *Nautilus*, nuclear-powered and known to be large and fast, had been commissioned into service in September 1954. The Soviet Navy would not lag behind their greatest rivals. Political and military minds accepted the depressing knowledge that such craft could stay submerged at deep level for long periods many miles from a target.

Solid fuel technology already promised the imminent production of a new and deadly weapon that could be launched underwater. The submarine-launched ballistic missile need not bother itself with merchant ships no matter how valuable their cargo. It need only hit the port where a merchant ship would unload. Not even determined Scousers could operate in a radioactive Liverpool.

This depressing scenario applied only in the absolute worst case. In anything less than all-out global war, maritime reconnaissance would still be necessary and the only British aeroplane able to deliver that was the Shackleton.

For Bernie Donders, the MR3 Shackleton produced one of its better efforts with a faulty nosewheel. During a training flight on 16 October 1959, in Shackleton WR988, the nosewheel adamantly refused to lock in the down position even when the emergency system was called into play. Bernie was not a person who gave up easily. If he could manage it, that nosewheel would come down. He rocked the aircraft. He stalled the aircraft. No success. Talks with ground control led to more procedures as well as technical advice. Nothing worked. Locking the nosewheel was way beyond anybody's abilities.

Without a fully serviceable undercarriage, landing WR988 would not be the easiest of operations. As the light died in the sky, Bernie agreed to make an emergency landing. The fire section would lay down a foam path to inhibit any sparks from the slithering metal fuselage causing damage. Bernie briefed the crew and made his approach. His skill produced a landing with minimal damage. No crew members suffered injury.

Examination showed that a broken hydraulic jack common to

both the normal and the emergency hydraulic systems caused the problem.

A couple of days later, a relieved captain and a cheerful crew had a drink together. Bernie was a trifle perturbed when the flight engineer mentioned that he had been studying the crash-landing procedures since the incident. Bernie had not, the engineer said sombrely, followed the book. The instructions made it clear that when the aircraft came to rest, the captain should order, 'Out! Out!' and not 'For ★★★★'s sake, get out quick!'

Despite this terrible lapse, Bernie was duly awarded the distinction of a meritorious green endorsement in his flying logbook on the orders of the Air Officer Commanding of Coastal Command's Number 18 Group.

Apart from any direct entrants from National Service, already under notice of abolition, and direct entry applicants from civilian life, one important source of first-rate military pilots existed close to Sleaford in Lincolnshire. The Royal Air Force College at Cranwell enjoyed a superb reputation. Cranwell's three-year courses produced professional officers destined for the higher reaches of the service. The training period, identical to that needed for a degree, gave pinstripe-suited dwellers in Whitehall a pretext to call the College 'Britain's University of the Air'. Less impressed or more envious mortals who actually wore RAF uniform occasionally called it Sleaford Technical College. Bill Howard was one graduate:

At the end of July 1960 I had just completed three years of training at the Royal Air Force College Cranwell. During the first year we had carried out some pretty basic navigational training in the Vickers Valetta, a rotund lumbering twin-piston-engined machine, affectionately known as 'The Pig'. This was not particularly meant to be derogatory but was born of its similarity to a nursing pig because of the long row of equally-spaced hemispherical astrodomes along the top of the fuselage.

In year two we started our pilot training in earnest on the Piston Provost. This machine was designed for basic training from its outset by the now long defunct Percival Aircraft Company and as such was perfect for the job. Powered by the

Alvis Company (now also sadly defunct) seven-cylinder Leonides radial engine driving a three-bladed variable pitch propeller, it had enough power to keep you out of trouble and not too much to put you into same. The fixed tail-dragger undercarriage challenged one's landing skills while avoiding the risk of wheels-up landings at this early stage of the learning curve. Docile in the stall, it was quite exciting in the spin but was reputed to recover itself if, in a state of rising panic, the student let go of the controls completely in anticipation of having to bale out.

Trainees needed to master the Provost before they could move on to a new and generally exciting phase of training – in jet aircraft. The performance was in stark contrast to that of piston-engined training aircraft:

After 150 hours we progressed to the De Havilland (yes, you've got it – also defunct!) Vampire T11. Pressurised and powered by 3,000 lbs of thrust from a Goblin single-stage centrifugal jet turbine engine, this training development of a fighter opened up a whole new world for us, taking us above the pleasant but limited unpressurised realms below 10,000 feet to exciting new ethereal dominions from where we could gaze down on lesser mortals from 40,000 feet.

After three years and with 300 hours under our belts, we finally gained our coveted RAF Pilots' Wings, convinced to a man that we were now truly God's gift to aviation.

We duly received our postings. The sharpest went to Fighter Command, the pedestrian to Transport Command, the 'career-men' to Bomber Command and the remaining assorted ne'er-do-wells, rabble-rousers and mavericks to what was known as the RAF's 'Cinderella', Coastal Command.

Bill Howard found himself in the latter group and went to Kinloss. The Marine Operational Training Unit had its own method of causing consternation amongst new students:

I drove from the Home Counties to RAF Kinloss on the Moray Firth with a fellow ex-Cranwell mate. The road system, vehicles and general pace of life were more leisurely and it took us three days. We finally arrived at our destination, which was the home of the Maritime Operational Training Unit and also the base for 120 Squadron. They had shiny new Mk3 Shackletons – the one with the nosewheel, wing-tip fuel tanks and some minor concessions to noise insulation. On MOTU, however, we were to enjoy the numerous idiosyncrasies of the more ungainly tailwheel model, the T4 version of the Mk I.

This was to be something completely different after the high-speed, high flying, single-jet Vampire. We moved with great trepidation, and with no intermediate stepping stone like the twin-piston Varsity trainer of later years, straight on to the mighty cacophonous Avro (yes – also gone) Shackleton, propelled at near sea level and in sedate and stately elegance by 10,000 horsepower from four superbly engineered Rolls-Royce V-12 Griffons.

MOTU had undergone some changes, all beneficial, since its early days. Maritime operational flying needed significant standards of efficiency, both individual and collective, from aircraft crews. To augment training, MOTU had built a Maritime Crew Procedure Trainer to take students through the tactical scene they were likely to meet when flying on operations.

The ground-bound trainer began existence, rather as all Chadwick's real aeroplanes had done, as a copious series of sketches and calculations on the backs of old envelopes. A prototype showed a number of weaknesses which were duly corrected before the sketches became production drawings.

RAF Maintenance Units produced most of the metalwork. Civilian contractors made some particular gearboxes although their drawings gave no indication of wiring or components or the purpose of the box. Finished shells returned for final work by a specially formed Kinloss project team.

Four cubicles, all independent of each other, made up the trainer. They were intended to carry out independent exercises on demand with a control console to co-ordinate them. The console originated all wireless messages and verbal radio contacts and produced a whole variety of anti-submarine scenarios. It was also possible to display the position of the pretend aircraft. This allowed the controller in the console to pass radar information by voice radio or run convoy support exercises in the guise of a tactical commander.

The console controller could change the scenario at will as he could hear the trainee's intercom exchanges. The exercise could easily be modified to reflect any situation within the squad. The Crew Procedure Trainer saved the expense of actually flying the Shackleton on many occasions and specifically allowed much more practical training, especially for air signallers.

For Bill Howard, converting to the maritime reconnaissance field in the Shackleton was a memorable time:

The course started with ground school. After numerous of these throughout my service and civilian aviation career, I can honestly say that this was the finest course I have ever undertaken. 'Comprehensive' seems an inadequate term to describe it. Before I even laid a hand on the 'Old Grey Lady' I felt that I knew her intimately in, of course, the nicest possible way! We also covered ancillary subjects like weaponry and ballistics, ship recognition, underwater sonics, radar and radio in all their myriad aspects, photography, search and rescue, survival . . . and catering – yes, catering – don't laugh. When you are airborne for upward of twelve noisy, vibrating hours, the timely arrival of a pint mug of condensed-milk-laced tea and a generous helping of 'honkers stew' can be an essential and truly spirit-lifting experience, believe me. In Coastal Command, crews stood or fell according to their catering abilities.

By the end of the ground school, I had definitely warmed to this idea of a life in Coastal. Who would want to sit watching an autopilot at 40,000 feet in a VC10 en route to Bahrain, or rush around for an hour at zero feet in a Hunter, nervously watching the fuel gauges unwind, or strap on a Vulcan for a one-way trip to Moscow with a megaton bucket of sunshine? No, a life ranging the oceans of the world, with stopovers in exotic out-of-the-way places in the company of nine other reprobates, was becoming more appealing by the day.

The Royal Air Force had firmly dismissed attempts during the previous decade to pass Coastal Command to the Royal Navy.

The two-man Fairey Gannet, powered by a single double Mamba engine, which gave it contra-rotating propellers, had joined the Fleet in 1953. Designed to fly from aircraft carriers, its original role was to hunt submarines. Advocates for the Fleet Air Arm insisted it was a natural complement to the Shackleton. The corollary was that both aircraft should be under one single authority. In due course, the Gannet's anti-submarine role fell away but an airborne early warning version, the Gannet AEW 3, with some extremely smart radar came into service in March 1960. Operating from carrier squadrons way out at sea, it could peer far into the distance.

The Royal Navy and Coastal Command were not entirely at daggers drawn. Both appreciated the other. Indeed, 206 Squadron at St Mawgan designated the Royal Naval Air Station at Culdrose, known as HMS *Seahawk* to those stationed there, some twenty miles distant, as a war base. This role was tested during exercises, which sometimes led to interesting incidents.

During exercises, which always seemed to begin in the small hours, some six Shackletons would roar off into the night. They would take ground crew with them for Culdrose in the expectation that a ruthless enemy would soon bomb St Mawgan. The remaining ground crew had the delightful job of packing their gear, useful spares and general impedimenta before they too headed for Culdrose. Their odyssey of a journey sometimes included the need to take fuel for the Shackletons in a large, near one thousand gallon bowser with a mind of its own about the Cornish hills and slopes between the two airfields.

There were few enough Shackleton squadrons that could avoid such preparations for a possible war. They were in the same quandary as every other front-line fighter or bomber squadron. Rural communities grew accustomed to the sudden arrival of martial aeroplanes at the local peaceful aerodrome.

Bill Howard continued his conversion training at Kinloss. He was well aware that Shackleton landings, particularly by pilots new to the type, were generally considered to be worth watching as anything could happen. Tailwheel landings in any type of heavy aircraft generally call for an arrival in the approved three-point attitude at a pace that allows the aeroplane to settle front- and tailwheels together in a graceful manner. With the

Shackleton, an arrival that put the main wheels on the tarmac first was usually a sign of too much speed. The aeroplane's centre of gravity behind the mainwheels persuaded the tail to move down and meet the runway smartly. The wings' new angle of attack produced more lift that encouraged the big balloon tyres and the springy shock absorbers to send the aircraft skywards once more. The bounce could be truly dazzling.

Nothing was gained if the reverse took place. If a pilot was a little slow and let the tailwheel touch first, the crew heard an almighty thump as the mainwheels crunched down on tarmac, swiftly followed by a jolting of their teeth.

For learners, already dismayed by the result of their handling, the intervention by their instructor made matters even more frightful. A mighty application of Griffon power would send the Shackleton skywards in earnest. The student would be told, not always gently, that he could try again. Bill Howard soon grasped why old pilots, especially those on Shackletons, often quoted the adage that 'it's not the landing that matters – it's knowing what to do when it goes wrong.'

The day finally arrived for the eagerly anticipated first familiarisation flight on the great beast. The T4 sported a bluff Perspex 'nose and chin' radome, giving a good forward view unlike the Mk2 with its longer nose. This presented a more attractive appearance, albeit with distinct visibility problems, particularly in a cross-wind landing. The T4 also had a fixed tailwheel. After an extensive walk-round exterior check during which we pulled and pushed on various bits and pieces to ensure that they moved as they should and did not show any inclination to detach themselves, we clambered aboard via a ladder up to the rear door, then forward through the fuselage humping ourselves, parachute bags and other personal kit over the two mighty wing spar housings to finally reach the pilots' seats which occupied a rather airy, elevated position either side of the access route to the nose area.

Once inside the aircraft your senses were assailed by sights and smells which were to remain for ever in the memory. The smell of leather and oil and cooking, racks of flares and smoke markers, the arcane paraphernalia of the navigators' station, the colourful knobs on the archaic but beloved 1154/55 W/T radio set, the bewildering array of dials and switches on the engineer's panel and alongside this, the lethal-looking Very pistol with its array of chunky and equally lethal-looking codes signal cartridges.

I clambered up into my seat.

Bill Howard quickly discovered a small fault that impinged upon his suitability as a Shackleton pilot:

First problem. At a diminutive five feet six inches, I couldn't see out. Thus started what was to become an essential feature of my pre-flight preparation for the rest of my long career on the Shack – the plundering of protesting crew members' seats for extra cushions to give me the necessary boost, not only to see outside but to reach the rudder pedals. There next followed a comprehensive series of pre-flight checks and we were ready to start.

Engine starting was a combined effort by the pilot and flight engineer, with the other essential element, the ground electrical power being monitored by the unfailing ground crew.

Finally seated and able to see out, Bill was ready for the next phase. Flight engineer and pilot worked in unison. The captain operated the throttles and sorted out the magnetos. The flight engineer chose the master fuel cocks, primed the engines and finally worked the starter motors. Bill continues:

On the T4 the master fuel cocks were located at an angle behind the left-hand pilot's seat, in easy reach of the engineer, a feature that later gave rise to an exciting moment in my life. Engines were started in a particular order – 3/4/2/1 or starboard inner/starboard outer/port inner/port outer. This was to minimise the risk to life and limb of the ground crew if they had to intervene with a fire extinguisher to deal with a fire on start-up. For example, if the starboard inner caught fire, their approach to deal with it from behind the whirling propellers would be seriously endangered if the outer were already running.

Bill Howard, like almost every other Shackleton pilot in existence, found the Griffon engine something of a wonderful beast. This opinion, valid enough from one point of view, did not totally convince the men on the ground whose job was to keep the Shackleton flying. The politest description of the Griffon for them was that it was noisy, a sentiment with which aircrew beginning to suffer from high-tone deafness agreed, that it was thirsty and, above all, temperamental. Griffons generally needed a top overhaul after 400 flying hours. On squadrons, every day saw the replacement of a Griffon. It was not the engine most loved by the ground crew despite its many virtues.

Senior engineers who made policy dearly wished to replace the Griffon but there was no immediately available substitute. Avro planned an MR4 Shackleton which would have two Nomads in place of the outer Griffons while a projected MR5 would carry four. The Nomad was an intricate diesel engine connected to a turbine that recovered power from the exhaust system. In essence it was two engines. Mounted on the Shackleton, they would have given still longer endurance combined with an amazingly low fuel consumption. Their installation would have required an almost entirely new fuel and cooling system. Nobody asked the crews for their thoughts.

As it turned out, test bed installations by both Avro and Napier proved ineffectual. The project was abandoned although some technical experts wondered if the American Wright Cyclone engine would serve. Nothing came of that idea either.

The admiration of the Griffons by those who needed them for flight in the Shackleton is another testament to the dedication and hard work of the ground crew. Bill Howard had no qualms about the power plants as he prepared for his first airborne venture in the Avro aeroplane:

With all four now started and running sweetly as only Griffons can run, and with all after-start checks completed, it is time to taxi. The brakes on the Mk1 and Mk2 Shacks were pneumatic. Two engine-driven pumps provided a just adequate supply as long as you were not heavy handed (Mk1) or booted (Mk2) with the brakes. That said, for a novice pilot, the Mk1 was a particular nightmare to taxi. The brakes operated by a combination of hand levers on the control yoke and progressive foot movement of the rudder pedals to achieve a turn while braking. This meant of course that the rudders had to be unlocked during taxiing and were thus free to be swung about by strong gusty winds. This latter put unwanted and unexpected inputs into the rudder pedals with subsequent wildly erratic braking. Unplanned excursions off the taxiway were not unusual.

Braking was just one part of the flying ordeal presented by the Shackleton:

Take-off was a particularly spine-tingling experience. The great handful of throttles were positively eased forward to the attendant and unforgettable rising growl of those beautiful Griffons. Early problems of maintaining direction soon diminished and disappeared as rudder effectiveness increased with the airflow. At around 60 knots, a positive forward push on the control column brought up the tail to be followed by a rearward heave at around 100 knots and she became airborne. Finally another positive check forward prevented the nose rearing up as the old girl realised she was finally free and in her element. A very physical performance.

This first familiarisation flight involved general handling, steep turns and stalls – that sort of thing – ending up with a demonstration approach and landing. This last gave me my first nagging doubts about whether my earlier enthusiasm for the job would last. With mounting concern I observed the sheer physical demands of keeping this beast on an even keel on what was a rather gusty approach. Great handfuls of throttle and massive control yoke deflections seemed to be the order of the day. We arrived over the threshold with much further stirring and trampling of the controls before finally settling on three points. All this I observed with considerable alarm. How was I ever going to master this mighty machine? Maybe this would spell the end of my brief flying career. Maybe, after all, I wasn't God's gift to aviation.

Bill Howard still had much to learn on a course that was insistent on detail. Large aeroplanes with piston engines need care and attention from everybody concerned be they aircrew or ground crew:

Asymmetric handling in the event of an engine failure was an important part of the training. Two particular events remain clear in my memory. One exercise involved the establishment of one's personal 'critical speed' in a worst-case scenario with two engines failed on one side. At altitude, two appropriate adjacent engines were actually shut down with the propellers feathered. So, here we are with a couple of engines out on one side and the speed decreasing. To maintain direction requires a bootful of rudder to counteract the asymmetric engine thrust. The loss of two engines means the aircraft needs extra power from the remaining two. More power, more asymmetry, more rudder, more drag, more speed loss, more power – you get the idea? In fact you eventually run out of ideas and directional control. The point at which that occurs is your 'critical speed'. So the message is, if you want to keep yourself and your crew alive, always give yourself a handsome safety margin above it by taking whatever alternative actions you can to conserve speed.

Having completed the exercise aloft, my intrepid instructor then elected to demonstrate a landing with the two engines shut down. We descended into the Kinloss circuit and turned downwind. At this stage he was giving a calm, typical QFI (Qualified Flying Instructor) delivery . . . 'so here we are, old son, no problems . . . nicely positioned . . . speed OK . . . power just right . . . half flap selected . . . blah, blah, blah . . . ' As we turned on to the base leg, the undercarriage went down, the power went up, the speed went down as did the amount of smooth QFI chat, whilst the heavy breathing went up. As we turned on to the final approach things appeared to be getting quite interesting. The QFI had by now ceased to offer any vestige of running dialogue and the heavy breathing over the intercom even blocked out the roar of the two Griffons as they fought a losing battle against gravity. Indeed he appeared almost prone in his seat, trying to achieve sufficient rudder control.

I glanced nervously back at the flight engineer, rigid in his seat and gripping his desk, his eyes out like chapel hat-pegs. At 300 feet any thought of full flap was forgotten and the undershoot area looked a distinct possibility as a diversion alternative. We scraped over the threshold and the Old Grey Lady thumped on to the tarmac with a protesting shriek from the tyres and a vicious swing towards the 'live' engines as the throttles were closed. Much pedalling on the rudders and we finally ground to a halt.

A long, long pause ensued while the breathing subsided. And then . . . 'So there you are, no problems on two engines really . . . right ho, old son, after landing checks, please!'

When completing the long litany of checks, I was tempted to slip in an additional one of 'underpants' but thought better of it.

Away from its activities at the Kinloss MOTU, Coastal Command carried on with a bewildering pattern of work. Not that everything was deadly serious even when stations and units became involved in the regular routine of the Royal Air Force. As David Greenway recalls, life still had funny moments:

It was at St Mawgan one day when the first eleven decided to have a grope in the ether. The crew comprised OC Flying Wing, the Wing QFI, the Wing Nav and another Nav from Operations, the Wing Engineer, the Wing AEO and an assortment of Siggies from Ops, all of whom had, at some stage been trained on the Shack. At one stage during the flight there was a really purple exchange on the intercom which went something like this:

'Captain to crew. We are going to do some pilot bombing. Beam, stand by with a couple of flame floats.'

'Beam, roger.'

'OK, beam,' said the captain a minute later, 'flame floats now, now, now.'

And the voice from the beam came back, 'But I thought you only said TWO flame floats.'

It was at St Mawgan as well when I was on parade when the AOC-in-C was inspecting the station. As normal on these occasions, the great man stopped to talk to a very much bemedalled SAC.

'How long have you been in the Air Force, Airman?'

'Six months, sir.'

'Well, where did you get all those medals?'

'I was in the Navy before, sir,' replied the airman.

'Ah,' observed the C-in-C, 'we don't get many sailors in the Air Force.'

'No sir,' agreed the SAC, 'they're mostly in the Navy.'

Needless to say, the C-in-C's face was an absolute picture.

Annual inspections by the Air Officer Commanding-in-Chief were a burden to be borne with equanimity. A natural desire to show everything in the best condition from buildings, trucks, aircraft to the men and women, led to occasional madness and disasters as Stuart Law recalls:

There were times in the RAF when you had to put up with inspections by various high-ranking officers. For these occasions we lowly ground crew were tasked with making our aircraft look sort of good! When you realise we are talking of Shackletons then the expression silk purse/sows ear comes to mind. However, we washed off the oil stains, scrubbed at the exhaust marks, cleaned the windows, slapped a bit of paint on here and there, lined the props, put covers on the wheels, made sure all the aircraft were facing the same way. At the same time others would be making sure the buildings were clean and tidy, all the ground equipment was painted in the hope someone would say 'strewth that looks good.' At the end of all these preparations off we went for a beer hoping nothing nasty happened before morning.

On this particular occasion something did happen.

During the night Malta was hit by the gentle winds of a Sirocco, a delicate little breeze all the way from North Africa, full of Saharan sand, most of which ended up on top of our fleet of six or seven Shacks. When we reported in for the morning shift we 'erks' were greeted by the sight of various NCOs and the odd officer rushing around trying to locate brooms. They didn't succeed. Not that it mattered because no one came near enough to inspect.

137

As Bill Howard inched towards the end of his MOTU course, more incidents came to enliven his life. It would seem to a disinterested onlooker that his whole course was bedevilled by mishaps but this is untrue. A traveller using the train each day only remembers the one time in a whole year when an interloper took extreme exception to another passenger using a mobile telephone. The same reaction occurs in aviation. Routine flights with no excitements do not jar the memory and they are the vast majority. But not everything can be conveniently forgotten:

> Remember those fuel master cocks behind the pilot's seat? Well, the memorable flight on this occasion was my Progress Flight with the MOTU boss. Everything had gone quite well up to take-off and I was anticipating a practice engine failure as we got airborne. The procedure for failure simulation was for the QFI in the right-hand seat to surreptitiously slip his right hand between the cockpit window and the side of the flight engineer's panel, extending one, two, three or four fingers depending on which engine he wished the engineer to cut. The engineer gripped the fingers to signal his understanding and the appropriate idling cut-off switch was operated.

The pilot knew at once that he had a problem. The aircraft swung. If an outer engine was chosen, the swing was more marked. In both cases, the pilot needed a fast response. He had to put pressure on the rudder to maintain direction and identify the engine that no longer could idle. This was not always the easiest of tasks unless he had noted a momentary reaction on the engine gauges. Given the automatic propeller controls which compensated for such events, the indicators rapidly regained their normal settings.

Once the engine was identified, the pilot closed the appropriate throttle and feathered the propeller. The shutdown was finally in the hands of the flight engineer who closed the fuel master cock for the engine. Bill Howard's experience showed that occasionally not everything went to plan:

> Off we roared down the Kinloss westerly runway to lift up over Findhorn Bay. All OK so far. 'Undercarriage Up!'

Suddenly the half-expected failure and a marked swing to starboard. A bootful of left rudder to compensate. 'Dead leg – dead side!' The simple rule. If you boot on rudder with one leg, the other leg is doing nothing. It's a 'dead' leg and indicates the side of the failure. 'Checking number four'. Ease back the throttle, no increase in asymmetry so that engine is 'dead'. 'Feathering Four!' and the prop winds down to a standstill. I was about to call for the checklist when suddenly the aircraft, climbing only sluggishly with the undercarriage still retracting, lurched to the left and the airspeed decreased alarmingly. It was not readily apparent to me what had happened but not so where the QFI was concerned. The language was blue as he informed the flight engineer that he had switched off the master cock for the port outer instead of the starboard outer. He had a command of obscene invective which was unparalleled in my experience and I marvelled at the length of time it was maintained without any repetitions.

Meanwhile we had a problem, staggering away over Findhorn Bay on only two engines. The QFI took control and a brief moment of reasoned calm returned whilst throttles were appropriately set to ensure safe restarts. Back on four engines, we turned downwind, the Progress Check was postponed and we landed. Post-flight, a one-sided interview between the boss and the engineer continued behind closed doors. I sloped off to the Mess for an early beer.

Being able to handle the Shackleton was one achievement. Coastal Command needed more. The aeroplane flying in its operational role demanded skill and precision:

After completing the basic handling stuff, which included being turned loose with another student and a long suffering rear crew to carry out circuits and landings, we moved on to the operational training which proved heady stuff. We carried out pilot bombing from 100 feet on static and moving targets, dropped ex-WW 2 depth charges – awesomely spectacular, dropped Lindholme gear – the standard SAR kit comprising a large dinghy and two equipment containers. We photographed ships, we tracked submarines, simulated torpedo attacks and hurled assorted pyrotechnics and flares into the Scottish seas and heavens. Best of all we got to fly together as a crew of ten. A mixture of officers and NCOs. It was a fine blend of varied experience and probably the very best training ground for a young, wet-behind-the-ears Pilot Officer. If you had ever imagined you were God's gift to aviation, you were soon advised otherwise.

The culmination of the course was a twelve-hour sortie out to the west of Ireland and then due south – to Gibraltar and the exotic delights of La Linea over which it is perhaps politic to draw a veil.

Postings finally came through and I found myself going across the sea to Ballykelly, to 204 Squadron with its MR2 Shackletons. Ah, the joy of directional toe-brakes and a rudder lock. Taxiing would be a breeze! Oh yes. And the fuel master cocks were repositioned too – on to the pilots' panel, well clear of any flight engineer's errant fingers.

'Cinderella' Service? Well, I was certainly having a ball and would continue to do so throughout my long partnership with the Old Grey Lady.

Peter Armstrong, who had joined Ballykelly's 210 Squadron as a flight lieutenant pilot in February 1961 remembers the station well:

The Squadron unit establishment was 6 Shackleton MR2 aircraft. The bulk of our tasks were anti-submarine operations and air/sea Search and Rescue. We also carried out mail drops to the Atlantic weather ships, shadowed Russian 'Elint' (Electronic Intelligence) trawlers and a variety of training exercises. My crew in early 1961 was the first in the Command to have an AEO captain appointed.

At that time No 203 Squadron with 6 unit establishment MR3 Shackletons was also based at Ballykelly as was 204 Squadron with six MR2 aircraft. The Air Sea Warfare Development Unit (ASWDU) had two Mk2 aircraft. The station also played host to a variety of NATO aircraft attending Joint Anti-Submarine courses at JASS and a war dispersal detachment of three nuclear capable Vulcan aircraft. RAF

Ballykelly was unique in that, as a result of runway lengthening, the Belfast to Londonderry railway line ran across the main runway. Under normal conditions trains had priority over aircraft. In the event of an aircraft emergency landing, the ATC tower had the ability to control railway signals in both directions and halt trains. As far as I know it was the only ATC tower to have a set of railway signalling bell telegraphs and levers installed! Incidentally, the nearest railway station, Limavady Junction, was a request stop; you needed to let the driver know before the train left Belfast!

Transport Command had started to receive modern aeroplanes that had a pretence of long range. As with any aircraft, the further it flew non-stop the more fuel it needed to carry. More fuel pumped into on-board tanks meant fewer passengers or less cargo. Only a desperate operational reason allowed overloading an aeroplane with roundels on its wings.

Shackletons continued to fly all over the globe either as troop transports or freight carriers when the need arose or, more often, as 'Shacklebombers', a new nickname that the Old Lady acquired through her ventures into active service. Incidents and damage occurred although no lives were lost. Engine fire warnings appeared without reason. WB818, a Mk1 had a taxiing accident at Gan in May 1961. It went eventually to Seletar for storage before being taken off charge in April 1962. At Ballykelly, a three-engined approach and landing on 20 April 1961 went rather badly. WR968, a Mk2, left the runway and caught fire. It was reduced to scrap and struck off charge the same day. An MR1, VP294, a former Grapple participant that had served with MOTU during its ten years of service crash-landed at Gan on 15 May 1962. Write-off resulted.

Active service still lay in wait for Shackletons in new and exciting theatres of conflict. 1961 had seen 37 Squadron employed in the Radfan, dropping supplies and leaflets over the area in the Aden Protectorate. During that time of commotion, 37 Squadron may have been the subject of the tale told of the young and junior Army officer who led his men out on patrol from their base in an old hill fort. He neglected to leave behind a guard. On returning, the soldiers discovered that their precious

141

fort was in the hands of a bunch of the very rebels they opposed. A Shackleton in the area duly received a plea for help. If the aircraft knocked down the gate of the fort, the soldiers could resume their domicile. The subaltern had a clear belief in the crew's pin-point bombing ability. The crew were not so convinced. They accordingly flew over the target and dropped three one-thousand pound bombs. They certainly opened the gate but managed also to totally destroy the walls on all sides. Only the corners remained standing.

Pleased with their efforts, the Shackleton crew were cheered when the subaltern's voice eventually came into the headphones.

'Thank you, gentlemen,' the courteous and cultured voice remarked, 'thank you very much but that wasn't quite what I had in mind.'

Shackleton aircraft went to Bahrain in 1961 to help deter Iraq from an invasion of Kuwait. If trouble lurked anywhere or was merely suspected of doing so, Shackleton aircraft and crews were ready to fly. Even to the extent of demolishing forts.

CHAPTER NINE

Coastal Command suffered from a general civilian belief that they enjoyed a serene life. The British public admired fast fighters and bombers with strange wings but were not sure about aircraft that looked as if they were more at home in a war with Marlene Dietrich crooning lyrics in husky German and Bernard Miles escaping from enemy territory to fly again with a gallant bomber force.

Shackletons did not spend hours over the oceans at sedate heights as they did square searches with serene Rate 1 turns. On exercises, any new crew member who contemplated a tranquil tour found himself rapidly disabused of the thought. When practising convoy protection at night for example, a radar contact with a submarine – always an enemy despite its Royal Navy identity – followed by a sharp and urgent command of 'Action Stations! Action Stations!' was the precursor to a rapid series of moves. Down went the first buoy followed by markers and active sonobuoys. Griffons snarling, the aircraft flew successive steep turns around the target. Dazzling star shells cracked out to illuminate the sea below, usually showing frothing water if the submarine captain decided to go deep and become a 'disappearing contact' as the official jargon had it.

What was worse for the fledgling was that such encounters were not isolated events but returned with irksome regularity.

Consolation came only with the realisation that the target did not fire back with live ammunition as some forty tons of Shackleton powered by near enough nine thousand horses made a bombing approach.

Peter Armstrong had moved across the Ballykelly airfield from 210 Squadron to join 204 Squadron as the junior commander of 'B' Flight. This gave him promotion to squadron leader. Life proved as interesting with his new team exactly as it had in his previous post:

As with 210 Squadron, 204 Squadron carried out all sorts of tasks in addition to anti-submarine and air/sea rescue, Russian surface and submarine surveillance shadowing and training detachments to both Malta and Gibraltar. One of the Squadron's most notable tasks was a detachment of three aircraft with supporting ground crew for about two months to Jamaica early in 1962 to ferry hurricane relief supplies between several Caribbean islands. I well remember their arrival back in March 1962 with bomb bay panniers full of oranges – a present from the RAF Association Jamaica branch! I also remember the uproar when Customs found several dutiable items hidden in some aircraft. Such was the morale in the Kipper Fleet at that time that when 'the Boss' assembled all the detachment the perpetrators came forward. While the illicit items were confiscated no other action was taken.

It was in April 1962, shortly after the return of the Jamaica detachment (and perhaps as a reward for being left at Ballykelly with the remaining two aircraft), that I was tasked as Detachment Commander/Aircraft Captain to take Shackleton Mk2 (WL739) carrying a spare Rolls-Royce Griffon engine in the bomb bay between RAF Ballykelly and the USN Barbers Point air base on Oahu in the Hawaiian Islands near Pearl Harbor.

We were informed that a Mk3 Shackleton was visiting maritime air bases across the USA to carry out demonstration flights of the new, active sonobuoy system. In 1962 the main tracking devices used by the RAF to track, localise and attack submerged submarines was a mixture of active and passive fairly short-range sonobuoys, usually dropped as a pattern of three. The active sonobuoy was quite a new device and I believe it was hoped to get some sales to the USA. Unfortunately, the demonstration Mk3 had an engine failure. Carriage by Shackleton seemed the quickest way to get a replacement engine to them.

The route chosen for the Shackleton was a familiar one. As long as nothing went amiss, the journey was simple:

Our route out was via Lajes in the Azores, USAF Kindley Field in Bermuda, USN Base Corpus Christi in Texas, then over the mountains on oxygen to US Navy North Island, San Diego. Finally, we would make a long, almost thirteen-hour ocean leg to USN Barbers Point, Oahu in the Hawaiian islands. During this final outbound leg we 'lost' an engine a few hours after passing our 'point of no return'. Each transit leg had been followed by a minimum twelve-hour stop to re-fuel, have a meal and eight hours sleep and flight plan for the next leg.

We received and fitted a 'new' engine flown out civil air after about ten days and set off on our return journey. Our first leg, to exploit strong easterly tail winds, was to the USN Alameda air base on the side of San Francisco Bay. Once again on the following day we had to use oxygen while crossing the mountains en route to USN Corpus Christi. Unfortunately, one main wheel tyre deflated during what should have been an overnight stop, and we were grounded for the Easter weekend and the following week. After fitting a new main-wheel, which had been flown out, the next leg to Kindley air base in Bermuda was uneventful. The following day we set off for the Azores. At the end of this transit we found that a hydraulic leak had developed and the undercarriage had to be 'blown' down. As we were all now very keen to get back to base, our flight engineer made up and fitted a stainless steel replacement hydraulic pipe in the USAF base workshops. This worked perfectly during our final seven-hour flight back to Ballykelly. The total flying time was just over 103 hours.

By 1962 the Shackleton was effectively the only front-line air-craft in service with the Royal Air Force that relied on piston engines. This made it ideal not only for its trooping role but as a provider of air experience flights for air cadets, adult members of the volunteer Royal Observer Corps (ROC), the occasional local dignitary of advanced years and others. Flying civilians in operational jet aircraft usually needed at least the semblance of a medical examination. For most people at that time, before holiday packages with cheap flights to far away seaside towns had been invented, a trip in an aeroplane was more to be cherished than endured. Air cadets and ROC personnel particularly welcomed the opportunity. It brought them closer in spirit to the men who were prepared to fly and fight for their living.

Unlikely accidents still happened. Number 224 Squadron lost a member when he fell out of a beam window on Shackleton WG533 as it ground its way over the Straits of Gibraltar on 12 August 1962. Maritime patrol aircraft crew rarely needed parachutes so they were not worn.

One air cadet, a member of his school's force, was Derek Vanstone who is now a bookseller, unsurprisingly specialising in aviation books. He describes his trip in a 201 Squadron Shackleton:

In the summer of 1962 I was one of 18 boys from the RAF section of the Combined Cadet Force at my school, Hele's Grammar at Exeter, who attended a one-week camp at RAF St Mawgan. The highlight of this camp for us, as with any of them, was the chance to fly in at least one type of aircraft.

I think there were then two squadrons based at St Mawgan, both equipped with the Mk3 Shackleton. Much to our delight, especially as this was the nearest thing to a Lancaster bomber, we were all promised a flight in this type. These were to last from seven to ten hours. One lucky cadet would be selected for a twenty-four-hour patrol. If I remember correctly he only managed about half of that time because the aircraft returned with an engine problem, much to the delight of the rest of us!

At that time I had only flown in two types; a Chipmunk (about six hours total in air-experience flights, including aerobatics, from Exeter) and one hour in an Anson whilst at a camp at RAF Wyton. Commercial flying in those days was

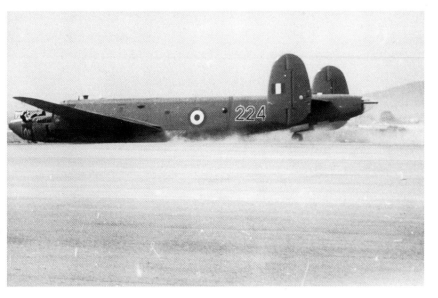

A 224 Squadron Shackleton WL792 comes to grief at the
1957 Battle of Britain Display in Gibraltar.

Photograph: Trevor Dobson

Caution! Navigator at work. Geordie Marsden of 120 Squadron plots his way across the world, circa 1952, surrounded by the tools of his trade.
Photograph: Geordie Marsden

Trevor Dobson, an armourer with 224 Squadron in Gibraltar, takes time off from being an extra in the film *The Silent Enemy* to display some 1000lb bombs, part of the Shackleton's war load, 1957. Destined for Shackleton WL792, which took part in the film, the aeroplane made a belly landing during the Battle of Britain display the following month as shown in plates 1 and 2. *Photograph: Trevor Dobson*

Ron Smith, a flight engineer with 38 Squadron, sits in the sun at Sharjah, filling in some essential paperwork! *Photograph: Douglas Winsome, 1963*

Bernie Donders takes a bow. His Shackleton MR3, remarkably undamaged, after a landing during which the nosewheel stayed resolutely in the 'up' position, 1959. *Photograph: David Greenway*

Not the most efficient method. Aviation fuel arrives for the Masirah Shackletons by local dhow, 1958. *Photograph: Mike Reed*

24 Shackletons flew over Buckingham Palace on 31st May 1956 as part of the official commemoration of the Sovereign's birthday. This photograph shows the last aeroplane in a bumpy flight that was hard work for the pilots. The formation came from squadrons based in Ulster at Ballykelly and Aldergrove and from the two Cornish airfields at St Eval and St Mawgan.
Photograph courtesy of a Shackleton crew member in the Flypast

Replacing a Griffon engine is sweaty work. Ground Crew at Sharjah have a hot time, 1963. *Photograph: Tom Holland*

The captain's office. *Photograph: Roy Davies*

Flight engineer's haven. *Photograph: Roy Davies*

The Big and the Small. A ground crew engineer is dwarfed by the Mk2
Shackleton, circa 1957. *Photograph: Stuart Law*

Not an officer in sight! An all NCO crew in front of their Shackleton MR1, 1956. *Photograph: Jim Humphreys*

Shackleton Mark 3 prototype WR970 on an early test flight, 1955.
Courtesy of Private Archive

59 days to Majunga. Crofty, 5th from right in white hat, 1958.
Photograph: Mike Norris

Last Shackleton crew at RAF Kinloss, 1971. *Woodward Collection*

not within the pocket of working-class families (we travelled everywhere by bus) so I considered myself very lucky.

Derek did not have to wait long for his chance to fly in an operational aircraft. This would be rather different to his earlier jaunts:

A couple of days after arrival my turn for a flight arrived. With one other cadet, I was told to report to the crew room for a briefing. We had to draw parachutes from the store first. No problem, I had worn parachutes in the Chipmunks and had been shown how to use them. The main briefing was over when we arrived. We were simply told by the pilot that we would be doing some 'mandatory' training flying, a term that has stuck in my mind ever since. I don't think I understood the word at the time! Being a mere cadet and rather shy I did not dare to ask any questions.

We then walked out to the aircraft and climbed aboard. A Flight Sergeant, the flight engineer, instructed us to dump our parachutes on the floor in the corner as we would not be flying high enough for them to be of any use in an emergency. So much for all the parachute instruction! He then told us to sit on the floor in what was, I think, the galley area, with our backs against the rear wing spar. There were no other seats available for us and this would be the safest point if we crashed on take-off! No doubt he took great pleasure in trying to frighten young cadets but we thought it was a great laugh.

Take-off was quite spectacular, mostly because of the noise and vibration. It was certainly more entertaining than the Chipmunks (apart from aerobatics) or Anson. We slowly climbed to about 1,000 feet or so and my first recollection is of seeing the huge china clay quarries that are a feature of Cornwall. We then headed out over the Bristol Channel for the first part of the training programme, which was to do some practice SARAH homings. I think some poor soul had been detailed to sit on a cliff on the north Cornish coast with a beacon so that the crew could each have a turn at finding him. This was interesting especially as I had – and still have – a keen interest in anything electronic or radio as we were able to watch the systems men operate the location devices, read the traces on the screen and hear the tones of the beacon. It also gave us time to get our ears acclimatised to the NOISE and VIBRATION! No ear muffs in those days.

Shackleton crews took care of their guests, even the young ones. When the SARAH exercise finished, the cadets were presented with mugs of coffee. Another treat came along:

I was invited to stand in the cockpit between pilot and co-pilot near the entrance to the bomb aimer's position, having climbed over the two wing spars, mug of coffee in hand! Wonderful! Having never flown in an aircraft of this size the views of the engines and wings were fascinating. The pilot demonstrated turns without spilling our coffee. This, of course, was of great interest to someone planning to become an aeronautical engineer, as was the view from the cockpit window where the flexing of the wing structure could be clearly witnessed as we turned. Next was a climb down to the bomb aimer's position with spectacular views! This was really exciting and I wished I could have stayed longer but there was another cadet to consider.

Lunch-time approached and meals had been heated in the galley so, with my cadet colleague I went to the galley to eat my first ever airborne meal. I'm unable to remember the meal though and I think I enjoyed it, but I guess a seventeen-year-old will eat anything!

The meal was probably yet another variety of honkers stew. The very finest version never allowed any one flavour to be the foremost. One signaller did claim to season the meal with occasional mint sweets to impart a distinctive taste but no proof has survived:

The next thing I recall is that we were told to sit down behind the wing spar again for a landing. This was a little disappointing as we had only been airborne for about three hours. I don't think we were told why we were landing. As we came over the threshold I recall seeing Victor bombers

148

painted in anti-flash white parked near the end of the runway. They were probably on diversionary stand-by as it was at the height of the Cold War, but we were told nothing about this. The next few minutes remain a total mystery, as we reached the end of the runway and then back-tracked for another take-off after about ten minutes! Here we go again we thought as we roared down the runway, now nearly totally DEAF. I recall empty crockery (no paper plates but the real thing) crashing about as we accelerated. What? G-Force in a Shackleton! Those mighty Griffons I guess.

Things now began to get really interesting. We flew out over the English Channel and started to circle the Eddystone Lighthouse some thirteen miles south-east of Polperro and which was then still manually operated. My fellow cadet was sitting in a seat near the blister window on the left side and I was standing, leaning over the back, when, much to our amazement, we were joined by a Sea Vixen on our wingtip. Wow, not only flying in the nearest thing to a Lancaster bomber but in formation with a Sea Vixen – doing his best to fly slowly enough! Friendly waves were exchanged all round.

Derek soon learned that the encounter was not simply chance:

Apparently we had an RAF photographer on board to do a photo shoot (maybe we picked him up on our brief return). We circled the lighthouse several times to allow the photographer to take his pictures with the Eddystone Lighthouse and the sea as a back-drop. This was unbelievable to a shy young air cadet! The view was fantastic and I have experienced nothing like it since. The weather was fine and the sea calm. Finally the Sea Vixen broke formation and dived down towards the sea to return to land base or carrier. Oh, I wish I had had a camera with me. Better than stooging around the Atlantic on a long boring patrol in my view. What a tale to tell my school friends who were not in the CCF!

But more was still to come! We turned towards Plymouth and at very low level flew towards Plymouth Sound and the city. We looked at each other aghast – Plymouth Hoe was higher than us! A big red and white lighthouse stands on the

149

Hoe. Royal Navy ships of all shapes and sizes (we had a navy in those days) flashed beneath us and then, with a heave on the 'stick', we rose above the city centre. My legs buckled with the G force (all of 1.5 I'm sure!) because I was still standing behind the seat and only a strong grip on the back of the seat stopped me from kneeling. Did the pilot forget we were on board! Wow again! This was surely a flight to remember.

The low-level flight over Plymouth was part of the crew's preparation for an important event later in the week. Her Majesty the Queen was to open a new civic centre to replace the one that had been obliterated during a wartime air raid twenty years earlier. After the ceremony, the sovereign would be honoured by a fly-past by the local squadron:

On return, two very grateful, somewhat overwhelmed and now very DEAF air cadets thanked the crew for an enjoyable flight (of about six hours in total) and returned to our billet to recount our tales to the rest. I don't think they believed us!

I have flown into St Mawgan since on a commercial flight but the Shackleton flight still remains one of the most memorable incidents in my life, even after forty-seven years. I have of course seen them flying, up to the retirement of the older Mk2 in the early nineties, and I had the pleasure of a personal tour around the Mk3 at the Newark museum some years ago, where it was silent and sad and seemed much smaller inside than I remember from my flight. The smells were just the same though and the memory could still replace the silence with the roars of the Griffons and the vibration of the airframe.

The middle of 1962 saw the first small crack in the iron policy of the Royal Air Force that women could not serve as aircrew. Transport Command quietly announced that air quartermasters would receive aircrew status and flying pay. Qualification would provide the rank of sergeant and a flying brevet bearing the letters 'QM'. The category was open to both sexes.

The previous decade had seen a line drawn under some of the more dismal problems of colonial rule. Cyprus had moved towards an independence agreement which took notice of UK interests in the Cold War. Archbishop Makarios had been elected as the future president in 1959 and the island became a sovereign country on 16 August 1960. The British military continued to serve there in what were officially Sovereign Base Areas. The British Government had further agreed with Kenyan representatives that independence would arrive within a handful of years. A number of other territories shuffled their feet and wondered if they could twist British arms for concessions, warranted or otherwise.

Shackleton servicing teams had grown well accustomed to infuriating habits from the big aeroplane. Periodically a particular aircraft would continue to show the same defect even after the offending parts were replaced and the troublesome piece consigned to the rubbish bin. One snag that was easily put right was recurrent tailwheel shimmy. This was usually remedied by a helping of oil which topped up the damper. One Shackleton from 205 Squadron, serving a long way from home at Changi, refused to conform. The shimmy declined to behave. In fact it grew steadily worse. Checks revealed no problem. Replacing tailwheel parts had no effect. The only solution was, it was eventually agreed, a new rear fuselage. This arrived, complete with a fitting party, in the fullness of time.

Replacing the old rear with the fresh piece took some weeks but it was eventually completed. A smart-looking Shackleton rolled on to the Changi runway for a test. The aeroplane acquired some interested passengers for the two senior officers on the technical side decided to go along for the ride. This would let them judge how well the new fuselage functioned.

The captain decided that caution was sensible. He determined to first of all do a fast run down the runway to ensure that the tail had no qualms about rising. He would brake and taxi back for the proper take-off. Away roared the Shackleton. The tail lifted in the approved manner after an exceedingly short run. The pilot closed the throttles and began to brake. Noise beyond belief filled the fuselage. The aircraft shook, vibrated violently as it twisted across the runway from side to side. The pilot fought to keep it on the tarmac. The aeroplane, finally under control, was declared rogue. It received one final flight authorisation. It was cleared for a single ferry journey to Seletar to be scrapped.

It was in the Far East that another knotty problem to exercise the minds of Whitehall began. Known casually at the time as the Brunei Rebellion it proved in truth to be the precursor of a more painful confrontation between Sukarno's Indonesia and the collection of independent states that formed Malaysia.

The United Kingdom had proposed in 1959 a scenario, much of which was less than welcome to some of the indigenous population, in which Malaya, Singapore, Sarawak and Sabah jointly created the Malaysian Federation. The inclusion of Sarawak upset many of its Chinese population and others who were already looking upon left-wing and communist policies with favour. Intelligence reports reached Whitehall and the Malayan authorities. They said flatly that 'Brunei is potentially in a dangerously revolutionary condition.' Despite this unambiguous report from an impeccable source, no preventative action took place. Full independence from the United Kingdom for the new Federation of Malaysia was a mere nine months distant so any bad blood between the Sultan and his subjects should be handled gently.

On 8 December 1962 armed rebels calling themselves the North Borneo National Army attacked Seria, the oil town on the Brunei coast. The *New York Times* duly told its readers on 10 December 1962 that:

> British troops battled in Brunei today to crush a rebellion avowedly aimed at wresting that oil-rich sultanate and the adjacent crown colonies of Sarawak and North Borneo from Britain's control. Broadcasts said the rebels were losing, but the general situation was described as serious.

The Associated Press feed told its newspaper subscribers, amongst them the splendidly named *Ocala Star-Banner* that Britain 'had airlifted hard-fighting Gurkha troops to this tropical sultanate to help crush a revolt for independence from Britain'. Troop numbers were tossed into the report, which did bear some resemblance to the truth. British newspapers published stories filed by their local correspondents that were closer to reality.

Even more accurate are the Forms 540, the Operational

Records form of the Royal Air Force. They deservedly noted the function of various squadrons although the Shackleton itself took something of a back seat after the initial agitation. On 9 December 1962 the Forms 540 for 205 Squadron, based at Changi, record that two Shackletons, each with thirty-three Gurkha infantry on board, landed at Labuan that day. The aircraft kept their engines running as the soldiers, stationed in Malaya, disembarked at high speed and immediately created defensive positions. The Shackletons left for they had more work to do. During the mere fortnight's life of the rebellion, the Shackletons assisted by ferrying reinforcements and patrolling coastal areas.

Despite much speculation in the British press, President Sukarno's Indonesia always denied that it was involved with the uprising although a spokesman duly alleged that 'the people's upheaval in North Borneo is a struggle for independence and happiness'. British observers who learned that Indonesians burned effigies of 'British imperialists' in Jakarta's Freedom Square were not so sure.

The next years saw Britain involved in several areas of the world. Shackletons were not always to the forefront in such campaigns although there were enough disturbances to sometimes make the routine of looking for enemy submarines seem almost peaceful. The time scale usually overlaps but memories stay separate.

Douglas Wilson, the signaller who began his flying career with 220 Squadron before serving on the Valiant returned to Shackletons after seven years away. The Valiant had become prey to main-spar failure weaknesses. In 1963, after another spell at Kinloss, his life took a new turn:

At the end of the course I was posted to 38 Squadron at Luqa, Malta on Mk2 Shacks, for the start of three hectic but thoroughly enjoyable years. The beauty of 38 Squadron was that it wasn't exactly Coastal Command but belonged loosely to Near East Command, Cyprus; so it didn't feel itself obliged to follow too strictly the Coastal Command way of doing things. i.e. 'There's two ways of doing things – the easy way – and the Coastal Command way.

153

Shortly after I arrived in Malta I was detached to Gibraltar for a two-week exercise. People often say that they remember quite distinctly where they were when J. F. Kennedy was assassinated. I don't remember too clearly because my flight sergeant had just come through and we had been celebrating my crown downtown. We were told the news when we got back to the Mess.

Drinking toasts to the new crown that went above three stripes in a Maltese bar did not save Doug from real work:

My three years in Malta consisted of a series of detachments – Cyprus for the first year. Trouble had blown up again between the Greek and the Turkish communities. 38 Squadron's job was to patrol between the North of Cyprus and the Turkish coast to keep an eye out for Turkish invasion forces and in the event of an invasion to fly service families out to El Adem in Libya. This was in the days of King Idris. For anyone in doubt about Turkish invasion we initially flew close to Mersin and Iskenderun and there were barges in these ports ready to take on troops. After many arguments and threats about international waters, prudence took over and we withdrew to a twenty nautical mile limit. The main problem with these detachments, apart from wife and new-born baby left in Malta, was that we were on permanent stand-by and generally under curfew, so couldn't get around this beautiful island.

Cyprus was only part of the ongoing story for 38 Squadron:

The next year saw the squadron detached to the Middle East. 37 Squadron in Aden was actually only a flight of four aircraft – half a Squadron. 38 Squadron was tasked with augmenting Middle East operations, mainly from Sharjah. The tasking was anti-gun running. Dhows were taking arms from the north part of the Gulf down to Oman and the Yemen and Aden. They mostly ran at night, without any lights and often manoeuvred to try and escape the pursuing aircraft. So it was a case of setting up patrol, homing on by radar and attempting to establish if the ship was carrying arms or illicit cargo. We also operated out of Salalah in South Oman. This was a desert strip. The job here was to fly low up the wadis in support of the Sultan's Own Forces against rebels infiltrating from the north. On first surveying the terrain we assumed that nobody could drive across the 'Mountains of the Moon' or the shifting sands of the Empty Quarter – but we found tracks and an abandoned Ford Power wagon that proved that they did. When we sighted anything suspicious we called in Piston Provosts of the Sultan's Own Air Force, generally abbreviated to SOAF.

Neither aircraft nor the men who crewed them went completely without a break from Salalah. Airstrips in the desert sound romantic but they do inhibit normal living for both aircraft and crews:

We went to RAF Khormaksar in Aden occasionally for a break and to catch up on servicing and laundry – in that climate you quickly reach a point where the smell of your own flying suit offends even you. But at that time Aden was on a knife edge with terrorist activities and it really was no rest. Salalah on the other hand, where attack was much more of a threat, was a great deal better. Of course, there were no families at Salalah. Recreation consisted of turning out all the lights at night and sitting out in the patio (scrub land) with a crate of beer and watching the Sputniks pass across the sky. If you had a day off you went down to the beach at Raysut accompanied by a band of heavily armed askaris and preceded by a vehicle called the 'wobbly wheel' designed to set off any land mines in the road. We lived initially in tents out on the bundu, but after having everything blown away during a dust storm, the fire engine was moved out of its bay and all the NCOs slept in the fire bay.

In general, at that time, Coastal Command personnel got the worst accommodation going, the best transit accommodation being reserved for transport and bomber crews. The biggest drawback to being up-country was that the bathing water was salt water and the only advantage of going down to Aden was to bathe in fresh or, rather, desalinated water.

Despite assurances that 38 Squadron would not be disbanded and would remain at Luqa, these counted for little when need arose. Maltese independence sparked a move to Halfar, still on the island, but the runway was deemed to be insufficient length for a Shackleton at all-up weight. The Squadron kept flying and training to a minimum until disbandment followed.

The Indonesian problem surfaced once more to the great satisfaction of those who had prophesied such an event. Most of the offensive air action became the province of the Canberras from various squadrons. Shackletons took part during a variety of detachments. The first was a twelve-day stint from 19 May 1964. The aircraft and crews concentrated on the task for which they were designed and trained. They patrolled over the water in a seemingly never-ending chain of survey patrols. One small triumph came when the crews discovered that Indonesian fishing boats did not care for a low-level pass by a Shackleton. The Griffons produced sufficient air disturbance to turn over light boats.

That aside, squadrons from Britain sent out aircraft to support the resident Number 205 Squadron. They flew regular reconnaissance patrols from Labuan, taking the opportunity to study various Soviet naval vessels that turned up as well as Indonesian ships. The presence of the Shackletons undoubtedly deterred any Indonesian attempt to use its diesel submarines which had been supplied by the Soviet Union as, indeed, had many of its surface ships.

The discord between Indonesia and Britain did lead to a fine example of sang-froid although the story sadly has nothing to do with the Royal Air Force but much to do with the British Army. The British military attaché, in Jakarta was a monocled officer, Lieutenant Colonel William Becke. Faced by a crowd of rioters who wanted to burn down the British Embassy, he instructed a subordinate to march in front of the building, back and forth, back and forth, playing his bagpipes.

In the scuffles that followed, Bill Becke's monocle was smashed. His coolness was possibly exceeded by that of the Ambassador himself. Andrew Gilchrist was equally imperturbable. He remarked at the very height of the riot that it was a considerable shame that the Indonesian nation had not adopted the game of cricket. The rioters, in shying stones through Embassy windows, were displaying an enviable and impressive power and accuracy.

Although flights to foreign lands held a whiff of adventure, Coastal Command Shackleton crews had several things to keep them busy on a normal day. Amongst their duties, which were never neglected, was the one that lived with the simple name of Search and Rescue. On the night of 17 November 1963 at just after 2100 hours, the duty SAR aircraft from 201 Squadron at St Mawgan left to find a ship in misfortune.

A Dutch motor vessel, the 571 ton *Kilo*, with ten crew, on its way from Liverpool to Rotterdam ran into tremendous bother when she met heavy seas off southern Ireland. One barrel of her securely stowed deck cargo punctured and caught fire. She had seventy tons of sodium stored in ninety drums on deck. More of them came alight as no crew members could reach the cargo and heave the blazing drums overboard. The ship burned. This was a major problem even if the hold cargo, a consignment of amyl-acetone and whisky, was ignored. The ship started to take the ocean on board. This worsened the problem, for sodium and water are like flames and petrol. The mixture on deck started to provide an orange fireworks display as drums exploded, hurling metal into the air like berserk mortars. The *Kilo* was in grave danger of going down. The crew could not launch their lifeboats and abandon ship. The high seas put paid to that idea.

They fastened themselves below decks while the skipper changed the ship's heading. The wind was blowing the flames back on to the bridge but the *Kilo* needed the wind behind her. The nearest safe port was Milford Haven, an oil terminal with tankers at every jetty. Their captains would have been more than dismayed if a fiery ship with flaming projectiles had joined them. Her skipper decided to head up the Bristol Channel in a bid for sanctuary.

The Shackleton dealt with a cloud base between 800 and 1,000 feet with a south-westerly wind between 40 to 45 knots, gusting to 70 knots. Immediate visibility was good for the sea was white with phosphorescent foam that gave the SAR crew the chance to see the mountainous waves below. These were like monstrous blocks of flats, their sky-reaching tops separated by a mere half mile.

North-west of Lundy Island, the searchers found the furiously blazing *Kilo*. Her captain had put on all the power he could muster. The fierce tailwind helped the vessel hare through the water. Despite their best efforts, the SAR crew could not attract the attention of neighbouring vessels to change course and help the stricken craft. The untamed flames on the Dutch boat took no notice of the constant dousing they received from the ocean. *Kilo* was consistently submerged by mountainous waves. Each time she threw off the water during the next half mile and continued onward like a gallant terrier.

The Mumbles RNLI lifeboat, the *William Gammon* hit the waves at 0320 on the morning of 18 November. Her coxswain, Lionel (which he loathed) Derek Scott, the youngest in the RNLI at twenty-six, later recalled that it was 'one of those black holes of a winter's night when everyone is in bed with a pillow pulled over their heads not wanting to know about the outside world. I had a telephone call to say there was a ship on fire. It was blowing a Force 11, 70 miles an hour plus. If you thought of standing on top of a motor car doing 70 miles an hour, well, that's about an equivalent.'

Several lifeboats had put to sea on receipt of the emergency call. None had a possibility of catching the *Kilo* for she outran them. Only the Mumbles boat had any hope of success although her passage was continually thwarted by enormous waves as she met them head-on. Derek Scott steered a wide circle to swoop up the fronts of the long, curling waves and surf down their backs. Although he made progress, he had no real idea of the *Kilo's* position:

> I heard a Shackleton low above us. How he found us goodness knows, but like the guardian angel he was, he pointed us in the right direction, changing the pitch of his engines, waggling his wings and heading towards the vessel. We had been taught this on courses I attended with the RAF.

The Shackleton dropped flares to guide the lifeboat which twice failed to get alongside the stricken vessel. Scott managed it at the third attempt for the *Kilo's* master decided to make for Mumbles Bay. With the lifeboat keeping station, the Dutch vessel beached at 0450. Three quarters of an hour later, as flames neared the inflammable cargo in the hold, William Gannon took off the crew.

Torrential rain did its best to douse the flames while the tide eventually refloated the ship. The skipper and his chief engineer returned to their vessel to dock it at Swansea. The faithful Mumbles lifeboat went with them, accompanied by the unwavering Shackleton.

The aircraft returned to St Mawgan when *Kilo* docked safely. The signal flares had done their job even though there was no direct speech between the two rescue craft. The SAR Shackleton touched down at 0610 hours despite winds that gusted from 50 knots to 75 knots whilst simultaneously swinging through 30 degrees.

Derek Scott received the RNLI Silver Medal, the first of two that he won in a long career, further supplemented by the Bronze Award. The Shackleton crew knew that another job would inevitably come along in the near future.

The brochure for a Christmas cruise on *Lakonia* tempted fate. The Ormos Shipping Company, known far better as the Greek Line, offered a voyage under a warm sun, free from cares and worries:

HAVE YOUR HOLIDAY WITH ALL
RISK ELIMINATED.
ENJOY A HOLIDAY YOU WILL REMEMBER
FOR THE REST OF YOUR LIFE

With an inducement like that, 646 passengers, only twenty-one of them non-Britons, booked tickets for a relaxing journey that left Southampton for Madeira on 19 December 1963. The 376-strong ship's crew were mainly Greek with a handful of German sailors. The captain was Mathios Zarbis, fifty-three years old and well accustomed to the sea. Passengers and crew brought the on-board total to 1,022 souls.

Lakonia, already thirty-three years old, was originally a Dutch passenger craft named *Johan van Oldenbarnevelt*. The ship was pressed into British service for trooping duty during the war. When hostilities ended she returned to civilian life but eventually proved unprofitable. Her owners sold her in March 1963 to the Greek Line. They organised a further refit, albeit minor, which brought up her weight over 20,000 tons. The decks and public areas received new names and the swimming pool was enlarged. Passenger accommodation received twelve extra cabins and comfort increased with the addition of complete air conditioning throughout the ship. In a final gesture to grandeur, the hull was painted white.

The ship's first voyage under her new name on 24 April 1963 was a substantial success and she proved tremendously popular. The Greek Line accordingly planned a programme of twenty-seven cruises in 1964. *Lakonia* received a minor upgrade from 9 December to 13 December 1963 prior to her Christmas cruise. The yard installed a new pneumatic fuel injection system, redecorated the cabins and remodelled the kitchen and pantry. She also had a safety review. *Lakonia* carried twenty-four lifeboats which could take 1,455 people. She had an automatic fire alarm system as well as specialised fire-fighting equipment. Every person on board had a lifejacket available and a further 400 were stowed on the deck. The crew had conducted a boat drill before the ship was put back into service while British authorities gave her an inspection twenty-four hours prior to the start of her voyage to Madeira. *Lakonia* did have, naturally, a Greek certificate of seaworthiness. As a final gesture, passengers all took part in a boat drill on 20 December.

The initial days were typical of a cruise designed for well-off passengers. Three honeymoon couples were amongst the British contingent as were five London taxi drivers taking a holiday break. Passengers played deck tennis or shuffleboard by day with the promised enjoyment of good food and dances in the evening. The cruise lived up to the brochure's promise of 'absolute freedom from worry and responsibility'.

At about 2300 on 22 December, one of the ship's stewards noticed smoke, thick and soupy, trickling from under the closed door of the hairdressing salon. He checked further and faced a wall of flame as he tried to enter the area. The blaze shot into the hallway, spreading and making for the staterooms. He and another crew member emptied extinguishers on the near-inferno to no avail. The fire had already gained hold.

The two reported to the ship's purser. Alarms sounded too softly for most passengers to hear them. The few that did so simply assumed that a waiter was being summoned to another cabin. On the bridge, the alarm pinpointed the location of the blaze.

Most passengers were enjoying themselves in fancy dress at a 'Tramps' Ball' in the Lakonia Room as the ship's ballroom was grandly identified. Some smelt smoke but assumed it was from cigars – it was, after all, a cruise for the more prosperous. The ship itself was about 180 miles north of its first port of call, Madeira.

Captain Zarbis tried to announce the alarm and give fire instructions on the ship's intercom system without success. The fire had already put it out of action. The weak alarms also stopped so passengers in their cabins below simply assumed that it had been a fire drill or test for the crew.

Smoke started to enter the ballroom at about 2330. The music died away. Crew members appeared to usher the tramps to the boat deck where they were joined by the passengers who had preferred the ship's cinema to dressing as down-and-outs.

The radio operator sent out the ship's first call for help. The upper deck was already on fire. Passengers who had been asleep in their cabins had problems in escaping. Many ignored the crew's instructions to wait in the main dining room for the route to it went through the spreading flames.

At midnight, the radio room transmitted another SOS and sent another at twenty-two minutes past midnight. The latter asked for immediate help. The captain had ordered everybody to abandon the ship. Moments later, the radio room was on fire. No more messages would leave the burning *Lakonia*.

The calls for help did not vanish into an unlistening ether. A US Coast Guard station alerted ships within one hundred miles of the *Lakonia* by a new Atlantic Merchant Vessel Report computer. At Lajes, the USAF's 57th Air Rescue Station sent four C54 Skymaster rescue aircraft, complete with paramedics, to the scene. Each aircraft carried life rafts, blankets, food and survival packs.

From Gibraltar, an SAR Shackleton, WL757 of 224 Squadron headed for the scene. It took three hours to get to the disaster, roughly 500 miles west of Gibraltar. The crew saw the burning *Lakonia* from sixty miles away for she burned along her whole length. David Leppard, the captain, then a flight lieutenant, recalled:

We were in the area for about six hours, circling the blazing ship. When we arrived the *Lakonia* was burning fiercely. Four other ships were within three miles of her. We saw many empty lifeboats from which people had obviously been picked up. There were also a number of full lifeboats. Others were clinging to rafts. Between 50 and 150 survivors were jumping into the sea from the ship's stern. We dropped survival gear, Mae Wests and dinghies to them. So did the American aircraft. When we had exhausted all our gear we marked individual survivors and groups with smoke canisters so that they could be picked up by launches.

The survivors at the stern took about an hour to get off. We saw no children but there were many women. It looked as though all the ship's boats had already gone, but it is difficult to say because the port side was completely obscured by smoke. We kept hearing minor explosions but it didn't sound as if the ship was breaking up. A different coloured smoke would puff up occasionally, probably indicating that a boiler had burst. There was flotsam, deck-chairs and seats in the water. Flames were coming through the side of the ship and through the deck. We flew alongside and looked through the portholes. It was a real inferno inside.

She had a ten-degree list to starboard when we left but she seemed fully afloat. There was one person on board when we eventually left. He was in uniform with a white cap. He did not seem to want to leave. It looked like the captain.

About six hours later, another Shackleton from Gibraltar arrived on the scene, along with a Mk3 from St Mawgan. The empty lifeboats were not once full of passengers. Three were lost in the deck fire and the rest were of very little use. Some had no rudders, others had rusty chains that would not lower the boat to the sea. When they did launch, mishaps were not unknown. The second boat to go banged against the ship's hull, tipped over and spilled its passengers into the water. Many had no plugs for the bung-holes in the boat. The occupants had to rip off clothing in an attempt to stop the water coming in.

Exploding boilers extended the fire which had stretched to every part of the ship. Rescue vessels soon arrived, the first one being the Argentinian *Salta*. She took on board the majority of the survivors. More ships came along including HMS *Centaur*.

In all, 33 crew and 95 passengers died out of the 1,022 on board. Many survivors had severe injuries. Some passengers alleged crew cowardice and the looting of passenger belongings from cabins as well as language difficulties between English and Greek speakers. Most crew tried extremely hard both to fight the fire and save passengers. The number of survivors is testament to their efforts.

On 24 December, tugs attached towropes despite severe difficulties. They made for Gibraltar through unsettled seas. The weather worsened. Five days later, at about noon, the end came. *Lakonia* heeled over to her starboard and went under with a huge splash. She sank south-west of Lisbon.

The Greek Merchant Marine Ministry board of inquiry decided that *Lakonia* should not have passed safety inspections before sailing. Lifeboat davits were rusted and lockers with life-saving equipment in them did not open. Drain holes in many lifeboats were without stoppers, forcing their occupants to constantly bail water. The lifeboat drill a week before the voyage was inadequate. Only five boats were lowered when all should have been tested. Additionally, the 'Abandon Ship' order came too late while deck operations had no supervision by responsible officers. Crewmen, with a few noteworthy exceptions, made no effort to rescue sleeping passengers from cabins below deck. Captain Zarbis, his first officer and the ship's security officer were charged with gross negligence. Another five faced accusations of simple negligence. The cause of the fire was attributed to a short circuit.

Coastal Command crews were well accustomed to death's grim facets. They had always been ready to save lives, irrespective of nationality. Dave Leppard was one who wondered if he and his crew had done enough. He was reassured by a letter he received from a survivor, a lady who had been with her husband in a lifeboat when he died, probably of a heart attack. She contemplated ending her life by sliding into the water herself when, as she wrote, 'I saw this Lancaster coming towards us'. As it dropped a smoke float to mark the lifeboat's position, she saw the squadron number on the fuselage. A few days earlier, she and her husband had spent half a day in Gibraltar Bay on board the *Lakonia* and watched a 224 Squadron aircraft on circuits and bumps around the Rock. 'Although I knew that my husband had died in the fire,' she wrote, 'the sight of your aircraft flying overhead with 224 on the side gave me strength to go on. I knew the RAF would save us.'

As it happened, Dave Leppard gave HMS *Centaur* a fix and they picked up the lady in distress. Light blue and dark blue had worked together once again.

CHAPTER TEN

A South African Shackleton crashed in August 1963. Severe icing caused its pilot to lose control. All thirteen on board died when it ploughed, inverted, into Cape Province's mountains at Wemmershoek.

One of 120 Squadron's aircraft, XF710, a MR3, had its own brush with disaster on 10 January 1964 near Culloden. The aeroplane and its crew were scheduled for a Long Range Operational Flying Exercise (LROFE). The aircraft had full fuel tanks, a complete SAR package and its war load. Although heavy, this was well within the aeroplane's abilities. Two Griffons were noted as producing excessive exhaust smoke. This was nothing special. The routine was simply to examine precise oil replenishment data for both engines from previous flights. These were both well within acceptable limits. Extra care demanded a check to ensure the engines did not lack output. This involved a full Reference RPM check. A plug change cured a magneto drop of more than 400 RPM on Number 2 engine. XF710 ultimately became airborne at 2316 hours.

After a normal take-off, the aircraft climbed steadily to its planned operating height at over 7,000 feet. With no warning, a solid thump came from the starboard side. The flight engineer's instruments showed a drop to 2200 RPM for No 3 engine accompanied by a distinct yaw to the right. The engineer, John

Mepham, reported that No 3 Griffon was ablaze just as its propellers oversped to 3300 RPM. The fire extinguishers for the burning engine failed to tackle the flames.

The destruction of the engine was unbelievably fast. The cowlings 'melted before my eyes like tissue paper' the engineer later reported. The port side of the engine became exposed. The fireproof bulkhead to the rear of the engine failed to do its job, allowing the de-icer fluid tank to explode. This in turn laid bare the wing mainspar region which became wholesale flames that melted the wing top panels over an ample area so that they peeled back in the slipstream.

The flight deck crew had not been idle as their aeroplane fell apart. John Gladstone the captain, known throughout the Kipper Fleet as 'Pop', raised the nose of the Shackleton in the standard procedure to control an overspeeding propeller but to no avail. He turned the aircraft on a course back to Kinloss. The second pilot, Jimmy Lee, and the radio operator, Bill Hickman, carried out the radio distress procedures. John Gladstone decided to dive partly in the hope that it would put out the fire, partly to be able to land if a chance presented itself. The fire continued to eat at the mainspar but worse was to come. The top engine bearer tubes for the blazing engine burned through. The complete power plant disappeared downwards and to the aircraft rear. It took the starboard fin and rudder and part of the tailplane with it. The engine splashed into the Moray Firth from where it was later recovered.

John Gladstone needed Jimmy Lee's help on the controls. Although the port engines were working well, one right-hand one had vanished in toto and its partner was suffering. Its controls, located behind its companion, had burned through. Number Four engine went into idle. It also caught fire. Attempts to close it down completely failed. Gladstone asked the flight engineer to go forward to reset his altimeter. Both pilots needed all their strength to jointly keep the wings somewhere near level. Gladstone saw the ground in the light of the flames before the engineer finished his task. The flight engineer scrambled back to his seat moments before the Shackleton hit the ground, bounced and finally slid to a stop yards in front of the village dance hall at Culloden.

The whole crew got out, either through the top hatch or the rear exit. They ultimately ended up in the dance hall where they sat in the kitchen, drank gallons of tea and contemplated how good fortune sometimes arrived when least expected.

The guilty engine, once hauled out of the Moray Firth, was carefully examined. A small hole in a piston had allowed combustion gases to burn the small end of its connecting rod. The liberated rod flailed and cut through the crankcase and the propeller oil pipes. This caused the overspeed and the fire. At 2400 RPM, a Griffon piston goes up and down, up and down, up and down forty times every single second. This allows the crew very little leeway if something goes wrong.

On 31 March 1964, the *London Gazette* carried the following citation in its Supplement:

> Flight Lieutenant Gladstone was captain of a Shackleton air-craft detailed to carry out a night patrol over the Atlantic. Ten minutes after take-off from Kinloss and at 8,000 feet over the mountains west of Inverness the starboard inner engine showed signs of failure and almost immediately caught fire. Within seconds the fire assumed major proportions and spread to the wing, in spite of the efforts of the captain and crew to control it. Flight Lieutenant Gladstone turned back towards Kinloss but the fire had become so intense that the starboard inner engine fell out and the starboard outer engine also caught fire. He was by this time no longer able fully to control the aircraft and knew that a crash landing was inevitable.
>
> On emerging from a thin layer of cloud he saw that he was heading straight for the town of Inverness at a height of only 1,000 feet. Flight Lieutenant Gladstone's main concern was to avoid the built-up area and so prevent the aircraft or parts of the burning wing from falling on civilians. He fought to maintain control and in the face of almost impossible odds, succeeded in clearing the town and bringing the aircraft down in a small field just before the starboard wing disinte-grated. After the crash he supervised the evacuation of his crew from the aircraft, which was by this time a total wreck and blazing furiously. He also directed them in clearing

people from the few nearby houses and also stationed men to control the crowd which had collected. Finally, on arrival of the civil fire brigades he ensured that they were briefed on the position of the fuel tanks and pyrotechnics in the wreckage so that all possible steps could be taken to avoid injury to the firemen. Throughout the incident Flight Lieutenant Gladstone displayed courage, skill and devotion to duty of the highest order. In a situation of the gravest danger all emergency and crash drills were correctly carried out. His calmness, leadership and gallant behaviour undoubtedly saved the lives of his crew of ten and prevented loss of civilian lives and property.

John Gladstone received a bar to the Air Force Cross awarded to him some years previously.

Sundry Shackleton crewmen of reasonable longevity noted that their annual medical picked up hearing deterioration in one ear. Audiogram tests showed that in many cases, the eardrum was damaged. The Air Ministry immediately took the attitude that there was no proof that any hearing loss was permanent. Most of the sufferers continued to fly. Years after the event, they learned from Whitehall that deafness is a concomitant of growing old. No proof that their 'Shackleton Ear' was related to hours spent in the company of growling Griffons was acceptable.

There were fears the honkers stew would vanish from the joys of maritime reconnaissance flying. Catering supplies appeared to have exhausted the stocks of gloomy-coloured tins that bore a large arrow with a date that recalled the invasion of Normandy. One crew, admittedly flying a Royal Aircraft Establishment Shackleton, found their ration pack provided at a European station was made up of meat, instant mashed potato and peas. The march of progress that provided instant pre-packed meals in supermarkets was tiptoeing into service thinking. Frozen meals and ingredients began to creep to centre stage. They needed mere reheating in the galley but fish and chips or steak and kidney pie represented a definite step upwards. Some galley slaves nonetheless judged that the traditional mixture of ingredients would continue to produce delicious results.

Fears in Coastal Command that the Shackleton Mk3 was too

heavy on take-off for the power provided from its Griffons led to an experimental redesign at Coventry and Woodford. The Mk3 crews subscribed to a general view that the MR1 could potentially fly up to 24,000 feet or stay in the air for twenty-four hours. The MR2 enjoyed much the same achievement but improvement after improvement gave the MR3 an eventual all-up weight of 108,000 lbs. Not even the Griffon could be guaranteed to haul that off the 6,000 feet long runways that were standard at the time. More thrust was essential, particularly for take-off.

The plan proposed to boost the Shackletons was a scheme to install Viper jet engines in the outboard engine nacelles. These would provide more thrust to help the heavier aircraft off the ground. The Vipers, originally developed for use with the Jet Provost, were to run for just two minutes, enough time to heave the Shackleton off the tarmac. Calculations showed that at around 100 knots, the Viper gave roughly the same thrust as the 'up-and-down' engine. The totally bizarre aspect was that the Viper, a jet engine would have to use Avgas, known in common parlance as petrol, the fuel that powered the Griffon. Jet engines do not take kindly to that mixture; piston motors are similarly annoyed if fed Avtur, a superior form of paraffin, generally known as kerosene. To make mistakes less likely, military Avgas bowsers are finished in cheerful yellow while Avtur tankers are a smart green. The engineers agreed that the Viper would need an overhaul every few hours if fed Avgas.

Shackleton pilots had become accustomed to wearily gazing at the Operating Data Manual to calculate take-off performance. This was a reasonably complex procedure which involved the use of six or more graphs thoughtfully reproduced in the manual, depending on the weather and possible use of water methanol.

Shackletons still turned up where warring factions threatened each other with more than just words. David Greenway remembers:

In late December 1963, 38 Squadron was sent on an emergency detachment from Malta to Cyprus. The Turks and the Greeks were posturing again so we were sent out to keep the two sides apart and generally sort out the problem. Now this was something of a surprise to us because we had no idea that HQ NEAF actually knew that they had Shacks under command. I think they must have noted us dropping in one day to pick up some desert boots or Kokkinelli or something from Akrotiri so, from then on, we were marked men.

Anyway, we all hurtled over there and, after some argy-bargy and not inconsiderable negotiations, Ieuan Thomas (OC 38) explaining the complexities of the Shack to the Air Staff and how it could best be operated, we were sent to patrol the Northern Line. Memories play tricks, but I think they wanted to start with three Shacks airborne all the time so that we could ensure that no ship crossed the magic 200 mile long line. They were somewhat taken aback when Ieuan said that actually we could do that task with only one aircraft at a time. 'No,' they insisted. 'It must be three aircraft.' You may imagine our consternation when Ieuan told us of this exchange. He actually floored them with the statement, 'We've got radar you know!' They should have stuck to desert boots.

The Squadron stuck to its guns. That was probably a good thing. Three Shackletons flying around all the time with growling Griffons would probably have deafened the donkeys so beloved of local farmers:

We started the grind of one aircraft airborne all the time which nicely cranked up the hours for us. We all got over 100 a month quite easily and managed to fly off the annual squadron hours in the first three months – so they gave us a fresh allocation! Actually, we didn't man the line all the time, but we compromised on two Shack twelve-hour sorties per day, taking off at midday and midnight. It was a matter of pride that the oncoming aircraft lifted off as you were crossing the threshold and Akrotiri started to set their clocks by us.

It was desperately boring stuff with absolutely no movement by either side, so we took turns at each other's role in the aircraft. I mean you could see for bleeding miles and the coast to the north and to the south stood out clearly, so it was difficult to keep interested. I remember one siggy who took over as nav for a couple of hours, chasing the GPI arrow around the chart. 'Just keep a check on where we are and mark our position every so often,' was his brief. When the nav returned from his kip, there was the siggy soldiering on, head down over the nav table, carefully carrying out his duties. And there, on the chart was a mass of round blobs – no times, no lines joining the blobs, no nothing; just chicken pox! Wonderful!

The inclination to emphasise the importance of the employment led to another minor hitch:

Such was the importance of those on the ground that every message we sent had to be passed to the highest in the land. One night one patrol captain reported that he had just been buzzed by a couple of what he assumed to be Turkish F84 aircraft. 'Roger, stand by,' was the reply. Eventually, after some twenty minutes or so while the relevant cocktail party was found, the message came back, 'Message from SASO. Stay on patrol and remain icy calm.' Thereafter, every message we sent was suffixed, 'Remaining icy calm.'

In the beginning, 56 Squadron came out with their Lightnings and generally messed around, making a fearful noise as they tried to regain control at about 12,000 feet after take-off. Their detachment coincided with 73 Squadron, one of the resident Canberra squadrons, being presented with a Squadron Standard. To mark this auspicious occasion, it was decided that some form of fly-past was required and there was, therefore, a degree of plotting in the bar (where else?) as to what form this should take. There was the usual sort of thing with drawings on pieces of paper and comments such as, 'Well, we could try Canberra, Canberra, Canberra. Then Lightning, Lightning, Lightning, Lightning . . . ' At which point, one of us would creep up with a wax pencil and put a huge cross on their drawing with the cry, 'And a Shack in the box!'

This extremely helpful suggestion failed to impress the fast jet pilots and, if truth be told, the Canberra jockeys were not enthusiastic at the thought of ancient-looking aeroplanes thundering over the saluting base:

> After many attempts to join the formation with 'A Shack in the box,' we were told to poke off. The outcome, needless to say, was a rather indifferent formation fly-past. And the highlight of the day? A truly outstanding display flown at very low level by a Shackleton which quite stole the show. But what did they expect?
>
> Eventually, 56 were replaced by 111 Squadron, so we threw a party to welcome them, thereby creating a problem because we had bought the mess out of champagne! During the party, I sidled up to George Black (OC Tremblers) and said that I hoped that 111 Squadron wasn't as chicken as 56 was. As intended, this was like a red rag to a bull. 'What do you mean?' asked George. 'Well,' I said, 'Hank Martin refused to fly in formation with us.' 'What speed can you give us?' he asked. And when I told him 220 knots, he said, 'Right. Friday morning, OK?' I turned to Ieuan Thomas and sought his clearance. 'Yes,' he said. 'I'll be in the nose!'
>
> And so it was set. We took off some two hours before 111 Squadron in order to get some decent breakfast in us before the big event. Typically, Tremblers took off straight up, rounding off at 12,000 feet. I have no idea why they did this, but it sure used up a lot of gas. Our breakfast was infinitely preferable. And then George Black brought his 4-ship in to formate on us. It was actually great fun watching them trying to join up because the Mk 6 Lightning had automatic flap which popped out at 240 knots. Thus, as they slowed down to join up, out went the flap and up they went! After several attempts, George got fed up with this, so he raced past and slowed down some 300 yards ahead of us, regained control and then reversed into position!

The Shackletons accomplished their own particular wish during their time at the Sovereign Base Area:

> We managed two fly-pasts of Akrotiri, specifically over the loyal ground crew of 38, one in vic and one in echelon,

before the Lightnings had to go back for fuel. We remained airborne as it was time for a bit more excellent nosh from the galley. But it was a fun thing to do and we managed to get some air-to-air photographs. I never discovered if anyone took any photographs from the ground so it would be nice to hear if anyone did – and to see the results, please!

Eventually others got to hear of the good time we were having in Cyprus and so Coastal Command asked if they could join in. We had some wonderful reunions, meeting up with other deaf people we hadn't seen for some time. Eventually, the precision antics of the wonderful Shackleton got too much for the station and, one evening, I was accosted by the SATCO. 'You Shack chaps piss me off. You're so boring. I mean you line up on the centre line at twenty miles and just grind it in. Why can't you do something racy like a run in and break?' Once again I turned to Ieuan Thomas and sought his clearance and he agreed that I too could run in and break the next time I landed at Akrotiri.

That did not come about in quite the manner expected. Dave Greenway had to return to Malta and missed the immediate opportunity. Not all was lost, though:

When I next flew to Cyprus, I was bringing a newly refur-bished aircraft (WL758) so this was something of a shake-down for it. I was given clearance for my run in and break and so we came in at speed. I eased the beast over to port and applied something less than the same G as one would during a follow-up attack on a submarine as we turned towards the downwind leg. There was the most colossal bang, accompanied by a louder-than-normal roar-ing noise, and the whole of the top hatch disintegrated! The hatch itself was fine; it was just the perspex which had gone and almost with Ron Brown, my engineer, who was stand-ing beside me. Amazing. Sadly, with the new aircraft now grounded awaiting spares, we were banned from doing run in and breaks but it was fun while it lasted. I am delighted to report that Ron is still around. When we met at Tidworth not long ago, we fell on each other like long-lost brothers.

We both think we haven't changed. We only have to shout a bit louder.

A further sign of changing times occurred in September 1964. Malta, self-governing soon after the Second World War, became a fully independent nation. They threw off the yoke of Whitehall. The island had not, like many other colonial territories, taken up arms against Britain for it was long used to the appearance of strangers from the most ancient days, from early Greeks, Phoenicians and Carthaginians to Byzantines, Arabs, to the mediaeval Knights of St John and a brief sojourn by Bonaparte's troops. Britain legally acquired Malta at the end of the Napoleonic Wars. Her men spent their pay locally with some abandon, a practice they continued until they finally left the island.

It was thus no surprise when the very first Maltese Independence Day on 21 September 1964 featured a fly-past by 38 Squadron (and others) as David Greenway once more remembers:

. . . enjoyed our involvement in the Malta independence celebrations although it turned out to be very hard work. The RAF elected to organise a fly-past of all the types on the island so we set to to practise as far as we could. It very quickly became clear that there was no way the jet pukes could keep up with us, so they had their own formation with a different holding pattern to ours. The trick, of course, was to try to get the formations to coincide over the dais at the appointed hour. Rehearsals were nigh on impossible and we sweated buckets trying to formate on our flight commander, who had just come to 38 from a tour on Sabres. He was completely unable to fly a level turn so we were constantly heaving and straining to stay in formation with the speed varying from a perilous 120 knots to over 200 knots. My co-pilot had been a very experienced Maritime Air Instructor when I went through MOTU in 1959, so he was hardly inexperienced now. In the end we worked out that the only possible chance we had was for one of us to work the controls while the other worked the throttles. He was amused to see me heaving and straining to keep up but, when he took the controls, he couldn't believe what a problem it was. It was the only time I ever heard him swear – and he was a really mild-mannered, lovely chap.

A further pleasure came along almost by accident:

About a week before Independence Day, I was at a party at Xmxija (naturally) and was talking to a nice chap about nothing in particular when the subject of photography came up. It turned out that he was the cameraman for Pathé News and he was desperate to get some air-to-ground shots of Malta. Did I know anyone who might be able to help? Obviously we took him flying on the last rehearsal to shoot the fly-past from the air and the ground. He actually did a very good job and more than half of the independence film he took was of Shackletons – joining, turning, straight and level, in the break and heaven knows what else. It was very good PR. Perhaps the nicest thing was that we hit the fly-past dead on time. What with the different speeds, we were still over the dais by the time the jets had come and gone! They never stood a chance. Old age and treachery won again.

The first test flight of a Shackleton modified to carry two outboard Viper jet engines took place on 9 January 1965 when WR973 took off from Langar. No problems were reported and Coastal Command could look forward to the MR3 turning in fine performances once testing gave way to production. For Shackleton crews, Parliament produced more important information. An announcement, as well as the Defence Debate, in February 1965 were the keys. Denis Healey, the Minister of Defence, began by stating in his preamble that:

Last year's defence White Paper described major changes in the equipment programme of our forces covering at minimum cost their most urgent needs up to the middle 1970s and beyond . . . described . . . how we planned to change the role of our forces . . . reduce the budget . . . by 16 per cent.

He then covered a wide range which included the mandatory statement for all politicians that British forces were the finest in the world and would shortly receive the best equipment available. For the Royal Air Force, this included an upgrade in maritime patrol aircraft:

> So far as the equipment programme is concerned, our greatest effort has been devoted to new aircraft . . . We have already ordered our full requirement for the Maritime Comet, the HS801, and it will be the first jet specialist maritime reconnaissance aircraft in service anywhere in the world.

Flight magazine duly noted that it was a Parliamentary tradition to state year on year that the Shackleton would continue in service for another decade, a statement that left the manufacturers with the conundrum of incorporating the necessary age-stretching modifications and the crews to soldier on with an aeroplane that they long ago believed would soon be replaced.

The minister was too cagey to give a firm date for the arrival in service of the modified Comet 4C. Neither did he explain how the new aeroplane would manage the Shackleton's ground attack role. It would, though, allegedly have the ability to carry about sixty troops at a vastly better speed, over a longer range, and in greater comfort than the Shackleton. The introduction of the new aircraft, renamed Nimrod, would depend on how quickly the major fuselage redesign came to fruition. Nonetheless, the days of Shackleton maritime reconnaissance were clearly numbered if all went according to plan.

The Maritime Operational Training Unit at Kinloss decided that it should shift. If the Shackleton was destined for retirement, the station should be ready for any new challenge that came its way. So it was, in June 1965, MOTU packed its bags and moved. As Coastal Command never did things by halves, they transferred back to St Mawgan in Cornwall.

One student who went to the new location was Andy Collins. He recalls:

> When I was posted to the Maritime Operational Training Unit at RAF St Mawgan, it was a bit of a blow. This was the era of the Lightning and the three mighty, jet-powered V bombers and here I was going to an aircraft whose roots lay in the Avro

Manchesters and Lancasters of the 1940s. When my instructor at RAF Oakington heard that this was my destination, he told me that the Shackleton was a bit like an elephant; grey and wrinkly on the outside, and when one climbed in the back it was dark and smelly. The mental picture conjured up was not attractive but it was not wholly inaccurate. I only ever flew tail-wheel Shackletons not the newfangled nosewheeled ones with their hydraulic brakes and nosewheel steering.

Climbing up the short ladder which hooked over the sill of the door at the rear starboard side of the Shackleton, one was faced with the port look-out, or port beam, position. A comfy, swivelling, leather armchair faced a bubble window, which could be opened in flight to allow extraordinarily high quality photographs to be taken with the hand-held F134 cameras which we carried.

As with every Shackleton crew member before him, the internal layout impressed itself into Andy's brain. In common with every other pilot new to the Shackleton, the sheer size was initially a worry:

Handling an aircraft of this size and design on the ground was, at first, a bit of a challenge. It had no actual steering on the ground and directional control was via independent pneumatic brakes and by judicious use of outboard engine power. The trouble was that a large burst of power on an outboard engine to adjust one's direction of travel also produced an increase in speed, and the induced turn had to be countered with a further burst of power on the other side to stop the turn when on the appropriate heading, which produced more speed. Use of brakes, on the other hand, produced the opposite effect, so that one could end up pointing the right way but firmly stationary. To complicate matters further, over use of the brakes drained the pneumatic pressure alarmingly fast and when one heard the engineer's plaintive cry that air pressure was nearly zero, one had to stop wherever one was and run the inboard engines (which housed the pneumatic pumps) at fairly high RPM until the pressure built up again. There was definitely more art than science to it.

Fortunately there was a very large dispersal area at St Mawgan, so the QFIs could allow a fair bit of leeway to students in the early stages. A large part of one's first trip was spent on the ground! When one finally got moving, there still remained the problem of lack of forward visibility. The tail-wheel configuration meant that the long dome of the gunner's compartment obscured the view directly forward. A gentle weave was required to clear the path ahead. Manoeuvring the Mk2 on the ground was described as being like driving a double-decker bus backwards from the front of the top deck while looking through a letter box.

Douglas Wilson also arrived at St Mawgan as an instructor on the MOTU. Signallers and air electronics operators were vital in the work of maritime aircraft. New equipment, new procedures, new radar and sonics had combined to make their duties essential. Detecting underwater threats and menaces from unfriendly surface ships still had importance:

Towards the end of 1965 I was posted to St Mawgan as an Air Instructor. The Shack course was five months long. The first half was taken at the Ground School where the basic theory relating to the electronic equipment – radio, radar and acoustic sensors – was taught, together with Aircraft and Ship recognition, tactics, meteorology and the usual background knowledge required for a proficient job.

After the desk work came the real meat for which most students had joined. They moved on to the flying phase of their course:

During circuit training for the pilots the electronics team were introduced to the aircraft and its systems. After the crew were settled in, more and more exercises taught them how to use the equipment to full advantage. This developed their skills and techniques and ability to work as a team. Airmanship and working together cannot be taught in the classroom. They come with coaching and tutoring together with time and experience.

The aircraft was the Shackleton T4, a Mk1 re-rigged as a

flying classroom. In addition to the student crew, the staff crew consisted of a staff pilot (generally the aircraft captain), a staff navigator and two staff electronics instructors. The crew worked up during a series of maritime exercises, navigation exercises, acoustic exercises including Stage II training. They also had live training with a submarine where possible, cooperation with Naval units, numerous radar homings, ship photography, practice Search and Rescue techniques as well as emergency and fire drills. They never had a dull moment. All aspects were extensively debriefed after flight.

As the students approached graduation, they were introduced to another traditional perquisite for long-range aircraft operators:

Towards the end of the flying phase the crew were tasked with flying overseas. This was generally to Gibraltar or Cyprus. It was a bit of a jolly for both staff and students. It did have its practical side for it gave crews experience in flying outside the UK and operating from a foreign airfield. It also gave them a chance to bond socially as well as affording a break from their intensive workload.

At the end of the course the crew were checked out by a different set of instructors. This Crew Check provided an independent assessment of the ability of individual crew members and the overall function as a crew. This was not generally an enjoyable experience for the student crew. The check was very rarely a failure but in that event would be reflown with another set of instructors. Failure by an individual at some part in course was more common. Although the failure rate was relatively small, the standards were extremely high. The normal course of events on failure was to re-course the student to the next course and in most instances that worked out OK.

The Shackleton was reckoned to be a sick-making aircraft at the best of times. Air-sickness was fairly common. Fortunately, I was not a sufferer. Motion sickness when you first start flying is to be expected; most people get used to it. In some it seems to be partly due to a state of mind – you've heard so many tales of sickness on the Shack that you are predisposed to it before you even get on board. Some people are genuinely prone to air-sickness and for those that persevere and suffer whilst carrying out their jobs, I am entirely sympathetic. The T4 had a particular problem in that people who sit sideways on to the fuselage or have no window for visual reference are particularly prone. The mid-upper turret had been removed from the aircraft by this stage and the radar bench was aft of the galley and sideways facing. Strong smells also seem to bring on air-sickness and what with the usual stale smell of the aircraft and being situated between the galley and the Elsan toilet, the radar station was not well placed. Trying to instruct radar homings to a student with his head in a honk bag is not an easy task.

A further eight men died on 8 December 1965 when an MR3 from 201 Squadron smacked into the Moray Firth, eight miles north of Kinloss while on local flying practice. Once again, a lack of witnesses and the absence of flight record data led to the familiar conclusion that no definitive cause for the crash was established.

The Royal Navy sent divers with a supporting ship to the scene. Over the next days, they were able to recover several crew bodies. Five were buried at Kinloss Abbey Burial Ground, the remains resting side by side amongst dead soldiers, sailors and airmen from wars earlier in the century.

The Shackleton crew were far from the only British servicemen to die that year. Aden had taken a toll although that would soon revert to peace. Similarly, matters in Borneo had cost lives. The Government was nonetheless optimistic. There were, as always, some distant problems but nothing that could not be handled, especially as new equipment was on order.

Then Rhodesia, under the control of Ian Smith, unilaterally declared independence. The dispute went back to 1964 when two parts of the Federation of Rhodesia and Nyasaland became independent as black majority controlled states. Nyasaland changed its identity to Malawi while Northern Rhodesia became Zambia. Southern Rhodesia, firmly under the control of a white minority, decided it would now be Rhodesia, a move that was announced officially on 11 November 1965, a date chosen with some forethought. Remembrance Day still carried implications of sacrifice.

Reaction came from the United Nations which imposed a programme of voluntary sanctions on its members. This expected them not to recognise Rhodesian nationhood, to refuse it any assistance, to sever any economic ties and, most important of all, bar oil deliveries to the upstart. This resolution became the flimsy legal basis for British action. It gave Downing Street reason to believe that they would receive co-operation from other countries which had tankers going to Beira. This Mozambique port handled crude oil for Rhodesia. The country had no coastline so it should be simple enough to prevent vital fuel reaching the rebel state.

British politicians knew that outright military intervention against the Rhodesian government would alienate voters. The Government ruled out even a blockade of other exports for they believed that an oil boycott would be enough to bring down Smith. His support from his middle-class white population would rapidly decline if they could not even run their motorcars. Downing Street wanted, in truth, to re-assert colonial rule from London, a move that would enable Whitehall to eventually introduce black majority rule. The British discouraged any multilateral military action against Rhodesia or the extension of sanctions against Smith's backers in South Africa and Mozambique despite demands from many African states for such a move.

Sanctions, enforced by a blockade, would hold back international pressure but compel Rhodesia to come to terms. As often is the case when decisions appeal to politicians, intelligence sources were more dubious. In October 1965, the Joint Intelligence Committee flatly told the Government that even a full trade embargo would fail to cripple Rhodesia although they conceded that rigid and protracted economic pressure 'might in time induce the white electorate to throw out the rebel government.' Soon after this cold assessment, Britain's Prime Minister, Harold Wilson, assured his Jamaican counterpart that sanctions had started to bite. Smith would be finished within three months. He went further at a Commonwealth conference when he prophesied that Rhodesia's unilateral independence would be over 'within a matter of weeks rather than months.'

During February, the intelligence assessment received confirmation when the Government learned that road tankers were roaring across the Beit Bridge into Rhodesia from South Africa. This was, as intelligence observers knew, one of three routes for oil to Rhodesia. The other two were a rail link through Mozambique and the pipeline from Beira. The Umtali Refinery in Rhodesia could handle crude without a problem.

Harold Wilson was even less happy when the military advised him that unscrupulous shipping companies were able to send oil tankers into Beira without hindrance. Reports of 'pirate tankers' proliferated, much helped by excited newspapers and a calculating Rhodesia. They themselves let it be known that arrival of oil supplies proved they had won the economic war.

On 6 March 1966, a Fairey Gannet AEW3 aircraft from HMS *Ark Royal*, diverted from a voyage to the Far East, produced evidence that two oil tankers were heading for Beira. Intelligence swiftly established that they had been chartered by a shipping agent in South Africa to deliver oil for an unspecified customer. The Greek owner of one ship had a contract to provide sufficient oil that covered one year's usage by Rhodesia. Not that there was any proof of the final destination. However, news that six new oil storage tanks were under construction in Beira left the more thoughtful in little doubt.

The United Kingdom announced the establishment of a maritime blockade to prevent oil reaching the rebel state. The United Kingdom had both a Royal Navy and maritime reconnaissance aircraft. They could establish a ship's identity very quickly. The first moves were not promising. The most convenient airfield was found to be that of Salisbury. In Rhodesia. Much scurrying around found a timely location in French Madagascar. Unfortunately, French pique initially refused Britain's request to base three Shackletons there to patrol the Mozambique Channel. They relented after three days although the RAF had already made plans to base the aircraft at Mombasa in Kenya. They did, after all, have the range. By 19 March 1966, Shackletons were flying daily single-aircraft patrols. These complemented carrier sorties made by the Royal Navy but soon replaced then entirely. Harold Wilson believed that the Beira Patrol would rapidly settle the Rhodesian hash. Murmurs from the military, especially the Royal Navy, that the intervention was a further drain on resources could safely be ignored. Rhodesia would soon succumb. Time would tell.

Indeed it would.

CHAPTER ELEVEN

Viper engines began to appear on the Shackleton MR3. According to expert opinion they would outlive the Shackleton. The Vipers were only to be used for two minutes during the take-off. Limited use would cause fewer problems although a particular one did emerge rather rapidly. The combustion chamber became home to streaks of flame that burned the turbine nozzle vanes and the carrier rings. There was a simple cure to this turbine burning. The engine needed segmented cast nozzles to replace the 'tin' carrier rings and vanes. This could be attributed to the Viper using Avgas instead of Avtur.

The proposed cure received a firm refusal. The keepers of the Government's gold delighted in pointing out that 'it's only got to last two minutes each time, so it would be a waste of money,' a reply they trotted out even when a modification allowed the Viper to cruise for some four hours, the time it took to use up its oil. Technical ingenuity apparently meant very little to the suits who guarded the nation's wealth.

On 27 August 1966 Shackleton WR977 photographed a yachtsman setting out on a round the world voyage in the yacht *Gipsy Moth IV*. The same aeroplane became further involved the following year. Working with a T4 Shackleton, the aircraft homed in on Sir Francis Chichester on 25 May 1967. He was not best pleased. Flares headed towards the aeroplane from his

Very pistol, an action which caused the crew some bemusement. Being shot at, as one remarked, was nothing new but to have a British citizen wielding the weapon added a fresh dimension to the affair.

Meanwhile, despite reservations from the military, the British Government went ahead with its blockade of Rhodesia from March 1966. Morally this had some support but, as often happens when politicians propose and military officers dispose, a continuing strain on resources eventually told its own tale. Apart from the Shackleton contribution, other RAF people found themselves in some unlikely places such as Zambia where a Javelin detachment spent some time while Ian Smith decided whether or not to start a war.

A mere three Shackletons were originally employed from their makeshift home at Majunga, Madagascar. At first, each one flew missions that lasted twelve hours. They went at a good speed over the shipping lanes to the northern end of the Mozambique Channel before turning south to fifty miles south of Beira. The radar operators came into their own, covering a swathe about fifty miles each side of their course. If a contact came along, the Shackletons investigated further. The aircraft reported all tankers, giving the location, course and speed as well as their identity. They also had to give details of any bulk carriers in the area and declare any warships seen. They also had to notify any tanker previously declared suspect as well as vessels not on the list of innocent ships along with any tanker that was apparently heading for Beira, having previously declared for another port.

For the Shackleton crews, one of the more outlandish aspects of the business came with their communications problems. Majunga had not moved into the world of high quality radio. The Shackletons, with equally aged equipment, had to pass their reports via a relay station. This turned out to be Salisbury who delighted in helping the men who flew. They took the opportunity of passing on interesting pieces of information such as cricket scores and details of the current test match.

At first, the Shackletons each flew some four hundred hours per month but it shortly became clear that daily flights were an expensive luxury. The commitment dropped to one flight every three days for merchant shipping rapidly realised that entering the Mozambique Channel without a Shackleton observing them was a near impossibility. Royal Navy frigates alerted by the aircraft arrived to investigate their presence. The ship could be arrested if in breach of the UN resolution, which could lead to the seizure of cargo. In short, the game was not worth the hassle. But it went on.

Douglas Wilson soon found himself detached to Majunga with 38 Squadron:

'It will be all over by Christmas' – that favourite cry. It lasted years! The Navy were glad to see us as mail delivery had been a problem. Now they had a friendly Shackleton to drop a mail canister from the bomb bay. Woe betide you if you had no mail on board!

Initially crews lived downtown in the Hotel de France, but a visit by staff officers from Aden put paid to that. The hotel was condemned because of cockroaches. Nowhere south and east of Malta are you free of cockroaches! It was not within the remit of the staff officers to offer suitable alternative accommodation. The mayor offered his residence (La Maison du Maire) – at a price – and it was diplomatically accepted, even if it wasn't really suitable. One crew took over the Maison and the other crew rented the Apartment Archat. The ground crew, when they were not virtually living on the airfield, were housed in the Village Touristique, by the beach. It was a pleasant enough spot, but not ideal. It should be mentioned, that the ground crew worked very hard to keep the aircraft serviceable – especially the engine fitters, as we had a lot of engine failures, and lacked even the most basic equipment to carry out engine changes.

Madagascar was a real eye opener. So primitive at that time. So different. A mixed French, Arab, African and Indian culture.

The duty crew took off at sunrise (approx 6 am) and flew till dusk (approx sunset). Drop mail and then a radar search to locate shipping, homing in to identify, report to the Navy and then establish whether boarding would be required. The other crew was on stand-by until the duty crew had completed half its patrol time, in case the aircraft airborne went u/s. In all it was a fairly relaxed atmosphere – much different to Aden. When 38 Squadron disbanded the Majunga Patrol was taken over by other Squadrons from UK.

Although the Beira Patrol only took away three Shackletons, there were few enough aeroplanes consistently available for deployment, either in Britain or elsewhere. Conserving resources until the Nimrod appeared in service became an article of faith with Coastal Command. This occasionally led to unkind observations when newspapers learned, for instance, that a single Shackleton was available for Search and Rescue duties in the whole of the United Kingdom. The Ministry of Defence (Air) confirmed that only one Shackleton stood by in Britain, provided in turn by the units in Cornwall, Scotland and Ulster.

The helicopter had not yet become a ubiquitous presence over Britain's coastline but was steadily grabbing the role of fixed wing aircraft. Recovery from the perils of the ocean, though, was still largely down to lifeboats. They often needed an eye in the sky to find their quarry, be it a luxury yacht or a lad with an inflated motorcar inner tube.

Much comment came when a pleasure boat, the *Darlwin* vanished on a cruise from Fowey in Cornwall on a return trip to Falmouth in August 1966. She towed a skiff, some sixteen feet in length which was seen by an RAF helicopter drifting on its own near the Eddystone Lighthouse. The *Darlwin* had set off with a total of thirty-one people on board. She was sighted by fishermen outside Fowey at 1620 hours, after which she vanished in worsening weather. Several bodies and scraps of wreckage were found after a few days in searches which absorbed not only the rescue services but some private efforts.

Flight commented that the event showed a disturbing state of affairs. It underlined, in their view, the inadequacy of Coastal Command's resources in crews and aircraft. The aircraft shortage was worsened by the 'extensive modernisation programmes for Mk2 Shackletons, now in full swing, and for Mk3s, which programme is nearly over.'

Shackletons continued to fly in their intended role as submarine hunters and rescue aircraft. The Nimrod might be a planned replacement but, in the interim, the job had to be done even with limited resources.

Even with the aid of Vipers, performance was not always wonderful on the Shackleton MR3. Douglas Wilson heard, as did many, of the sad tale of a Shackleton MR3 that was forced to divert to Lisbon with engine problems. The pilot, fearing that he would land in the water, lit the Vipers and was, allegedly, barely able to clear the Salazar Bridge on the approach. The details were rather more horrifying.

Ballykelly's 203 Squadron had a MR3 aircraft on detachment to Cyprus and, as Christmas approached, it was time for the Shackleton to return home. With ten aircrew and nine ground crew, the spares packs and some of the personal belongings in the bomb bay weighed a fair amount. As any MR3 had a tendency to be tail heavy, the nose compartment, well forward of the centre of gravity, became the home for the remaining personal belongings and, it being that time of year, several sacks of oranges from Kolossi Plantation, close to RAF Akrotiri.

The trip to Ballykelly had a scheduled time of three days. Night stops were planned for Luqa and Gibraltar. The aeroplane set off on 11 December with everything slotting neatly into place until the Luqa to Gibraltar leg when the Shackleton spent sixty minutes flying through a demanding sandstorm. This was not the only tiny drawback. At Gibraltar the refuelling crew pumped in too much petrol which put the Shackleton roughly 3,500 lbs above planned take-off weight. The captain, Mike Bondesio, made a painstaking ODM calculation. He decided to carry on as he had plenty of available runway.

Vibration rattled through the Shackleton after they had been airborne for two and a half hours. The airspeed dropped by some twenty knots as Number One engine suffered a translation unit failure. Sparks flew in all directions. The captain shut down the engine. The Shackleton, about miles miles to the north-west of Lisbon, began an immediate diversion. The story eventually appeared in the *London Gazette* citation for Mike Bondesio's Air Force Cross, published on 16 February 1968:

On 13 December 1967, Flight Lieutenant Bondesio was captain of a Shackleton aircraft flying from Gibraltar to Ballykelly.

The aircraft carried a crew of ten and nine passengers. At 0953 hours at one thousand feet above the sea and almost 90 nautical miles north-west of Lisbon, a fault developed in the propeller of number one engine. The engine was shut down but the propeller would not feather and continued to wind-mill slowly. Fuel was jettisoned and a diversion to Lisbon initiated.

At 1010 hours, when still about 45 nautical miles from Lisbon, number four engine developed a severe oil leak which demanded that this second engine be shut down. During the feathering process full power on the two remaining sound engines did not prevent the aircraft losing height to five hundred feet.

Flight Lieutenant Bondesio now faced a very serious situation. He prepared his crew and passengers for ditching and declared a full emergency to Lisbon control. To keep the aircraft out of the sea the port auxiliary jet engine, normally used only to augment take-off power, was started and run at full power. The use of this engine prohibited further jettisoning of fuel and the aircraft power to weight ratio remained critical. Flight Lieutenant Bondesio was unable to start the starboard jet engine because the leaking oil from the adjacent number four engine presented a severe fire risk. With two piston engines and one jet engine all running in excess of accepted operational limits it was possible to hold height at five hundred feet at about 150 knots in straight and level flight. Nothing more than a shallow turn could be made without loss of height and speed.

Flight Lieutenant Bondesio nursed the aircraft in this configuration to the entrance to Lisbon harbour where the visibility dropped to one and a half miles in smoke haze. At such a low altitude the airfield approach instruments in the aircraft were unhelpful and no ground radar assistance was available. Following the coastline towards Lisbon airport, Flight Lieutenant Bondesio was suddenly confronted with the towers and span of the Salazar Bridge which links the north and south banks of the estuary. Unable to clear the bridge the aircraft was gently edged seawards again in an unsuccessful attempt to gain height. At this point the crew of a civil aircraft flying locally became aware of the Shackleton's predicament and closed the crippled aircraft in an attempt to shepherd it into Lisbon airport.

Crossing the coast the Shackleton encountered some thermal uplift enabling enough height to be gained for the aircraft to clear the outskirts of the city. At about two miles the runway came into view roughly aligned with the aircraft track. The aircraft landed safely at 1036 hours. Throughout this very serious emergency Flight Lieutenant Bondesio showed great coolness and presence of mind. For twenty-six minutes, under great strain, he fought to keep his heavy and unmanoeuvrable aircraft out of the sea. By his superb airmanship and by his courage and determination, he brought nineteen lives safely through a very perilous predicament and prevented the loss of a valuable operational aircraft. He displayed the greatest qualities of leadership and captaincy and his exemplary handling of a very dangerous situation was in accordance with the finest traditions of the Royal Air Force.

It came as a nasty shock when a spate of accidents hit the Shackleton force in November and December 1967, followed by another in April 1968. Charles Montgomery, a Shackleton pilot who became a squadron leader, possessed a professional interest in these incidents, which arrived in such close succession. He flew some 3,000 hours on the Growler. His first assessment deals with an accident that involved Shackleton WL786. This MR2 was over the Indian Ocean near Lhokkruet on 5 November 1967 when an overspeeding propeller had fatal consequences:

In the beautiful summer of 1966, Flight Lieutenant Hugh Blake was a young captain on 120 Squadron, based at RAF Kinloss in Morayshire, North Scotland. The Indonesian Confrontation was still going on, so the resident Shack squadron in Singapore, 205, was reinforced by the UK based squadrons in rotation. Four of 120's seven crews were in Singapore, then, in October, the three crews remaining at Kinloss flew to Singapore to replace three of the other crews. One crew, all bachelors, stayed in Singapore for the four months of the detachment.

In August of that year, Hugh acquired a new co-pilot, twenty-one-year-old Flying Officer Charlie Montgomery, who was straight out of training. They got on really well, with Hugh a first class pilot and tactician teaching Charlie the ropes. In October they flew to Singapore for the remaining two months of 120 Squadron's detachment to RAF Changi. In those days Changi was the RAF Transport and Maritime base, with fighters at RAF Tengah and short-range transport and helicopters at RAF Seletar. Singapore International Airport was at Paya Lebar, being replaced by Changi International Airport in 1981.

The life for the RAF personnel in Singapore was an enviable one. The Changi Officers' Club offered sailing, swimming and fishing, with great food and even boasted its own resident band. Indian, Malay and Chinese cuisines were abundant in Changi Village as well as in the city. The flying was great, with detachments to Hong Kong, Labuan, Kuching, Butterworth (Penang), the Indian Ocean islands, Australia and New Zealand. An overseas allowance supplemented the normal salaries with duty free shopping enabling the servicemen and women to return to the UK at the end of their tours with the latest hi-fi kit and many other goods. The standards of service in the Messes was outstanding for all ranks and the married families had large houses with servants to cook, clean and look after their children. It was a hard working but idyllic existence for those fortunate enough to be stationed there.

After a great detachment, which included flying to Hong Kong for a few days, Hugh and his crew flew one of the Shacks back to Kinloss, with night stops at RAF Gan, an island in the southern Maldives, RAF Masirah at the mouth of the Gulf of Oman, RAF Akrotiri in Cyprus and RAF North Front in Gibraltar.

After Christmas leave, Hugh and his crew were back into the squadron routine of training and Search and Rescue stand-by. Then a message came from Coastal Command requesting a captain and co-pilot for a full tour with 205 Squadron in Singapore. Musing on their recent two months in Singapore, Hugh and Charlie volunteered immediately.

However, the bosses decreed that Charlie had not spent enough time on his first tour and so was not eligible. Hugh won the captain's posting and another 120 Squadron co-pilot, a young married Flying Officer known as 'Bubbles' Bungay scored the co-pilot posting.

Hugh, Bubbles and their families duly flew out to Singapore. After converting to the Mk2 with its tailwheel, which is far more difficult to handle on landing than the nosewheel equipped Mk3, Hugh and Bubbles were crewed together.

One of 205 Squadron's duties was to provide Search and Rescue cover at RAF Gan, a staging post for transport aircraft flying between the Middle East and the Far East stations. A crew with their Shackleton would spend two weeks on the duty in Gan, being at one-hour readiness for all aircraft movements in the area, then to be relieved by another crew. On 5 November 1967, Hugh and Bubbles had finished their stint in Gan and were flying their Shack home to Changi for some well-earned time off with their families. On board were the normal crew of ten, plus one passenger.

Some five hours into the flight, the awful, unmistakable noise of an overspeeding propeller was heard. On an outboard engine, control of the propeller RPM had been lost. There could be several causes for that, but in each case the drill was to raise the nose to load the prop, whilst closing the throttle and lowering the RPM control lever for the affected engine. In this case nothing worked. The prop had become a windmilling disc, generating a massive amount of drag, accompanied by enormous vibration and noise. The Shack was losing altitude and ditching was now inevitable.

As the pilots were fighting for control of the aircraft, the engine tore itself from its mountings and fell away, taking a large part of the outboard section of the wing and the associated aileron control surface with it. Hugh had to ditch the Shack with only partial control of the aircraft available to him. When the Shack hit the water, Hugh, Bubbles and five other crew were killed in the impact. There were four initial survivors. They managed to launch a multi-seat dinghy and get into it. Sadly, one of the crew who survived the impact and made it into the dinghy, died from a massive heart attack. The survivors were later rescued by ship.

The accident was the first in a series of four fatal accidents that would hit the Shackleton fleet over the next five months. The second mishap came along just a fortnight later on 19 November 1967 when an MR3 with the serial WR976 went into the sea some miles from Newquay in Cornwall during a low-level exercise. Charlie Montgomery continues:

The Shackleton MR3, with a maximum All Up Weight of 105,000 lbs was some 7,000 lbs heavier than the MR2. The fuselage was deeper, to accommodate the nosewheel assembly and it had an external fuel tank on each wingtip. The MR3 was also fitted with a stall warning system. This was a simple device, a small spring-loaded flap protruding beneath the port wing, close to the leading edge. In straight and level flight, the stall warning flap would be kept flush with the wing by the airflow. The Angle of Attack (AoA) is the angle at which the wing meets the relative airflow. As the aircraft approached the stalling AoA, the separation point of the airflow near the wing leading edge would move forward, the spring would overcome the reduced airflow and the stall warning would be activated, operating a 'stick shaker' on both pilots' control columns.

The normal margin for stall warning activation in this system was 10 knots Indicated Air Speed (IAS) but this was greatly reduced in a turn, reducing to zero warning at 60 degrees angle of bank.

In mid November a joint anti-submarine exercise was held in the south-western approaches, off the Cornish coast. The target submarine was HMS *Onyx*, an Oberon class submarine at that time just about the quietest class of 'boat' in the world. HMS *Brighton*, a Type 12 anti-submarine frigate was amongst the naval forces taking part in the exercise.

Squadron Leader Brian Letchford was a Category A Captain on 120 Squadron. Maritime aircrew were categorised A – Exceptional, B – Above Average, C – Operational and D – Provisional, i.e. newly qualified and still under training.

Brian's crew were detached to RAF St Mawgan in Cornwall for the duration of the exercise. This crew normally carried two co-pilots. There was an extra pilot on the squadron, and as Brian was the 'A' Flight commander, his onerous office duties meant that he could not spend as much time with his crew as the other captains. One of the co-pilots was Flight Lieutenant Jacques David, a French Canadian who had joined the RAF. Jacques did not go with Brian's crew on the exercise detachment.

Earlier in the year, Flying Officer Charlie Montgomery had volunteered to be the RAF Kinloss Air Cadet Liaison Officer. Kinloss hosted Easter and Summer Camps for Air Training Corps Cadets in the Highland Region. Flights in Chipmunk piston-engined trainers were an exciting feature for the cadets. In those days, all RAF pilots were trained *ab initio* on the Jet Provost, so Charlie had never flown a single-engined piston aircraft. Whilst his crew were enjoying two weeks' leave, Charlie was sent to the Edinburgh University Air Squadron to be checked out on the Chipmunk. His instructor was Flight Lieutenant Sir Angus Clydesdale, later the Duke of Hamilton. As a result of this two-week detachment, Charlie had some leave owing so the boss told him to take a week off. Charlie and two other Shackleton mates went to the Cairngorms for a week and Jacques took Charlie's place on his crew at Kinloss under the command of Flight Lieutenant Ken Whittome:

On the Sunday morning, Ken and his crew were scrambled on a Search and Rescue mission for a stricken trawler. As they were thundering down Runway 26 at Kinloss, a wireless message came through changing their task. They were now diverted to the south-western approaches to search for survivors from a Shackleton which had crashed at sea. Jacques did not know it just then, but it was his own crew that had gone down.

During the exercise, Brian's crew were tasked to provide Close Air Support to HMS *Brighton*. They were patrolling at low level, below 1,000 feet, when one of the crew spotted the tell-tale 'feather' from a submarine periscope. The call of

'Snort, Snort, nine o'clock two miles!' led to the command of 'Action Stations!' and the flying pilot turned sharply towards the target. The turn was entered with excessive vigour and the aircraft stalled, losing most of the lift from the wings. Recovery from the stall, especially an accelerated stall with a wing drop, uses up some altitude. In this case the aircraft was too low to effect a full recovery, and hit the water.

Most of the crew were killed at impact. One air electronics operator had a miraculous escape. The accident happened very quickly, so he had no time to strap in. As he was thrown forward, he instinctively curled up into the foetal position, with his arms clasping his legs. His next recollection was waking up in the sick bay of HMS *Brighton*. He must have been thrown from the aircraft where the fuselage broke up just behind the cockpit. Whether he pulled the toggle to inflate his lifejacket, or the toggle caught on something as he was thrown out, will never be known. He was pulled from the water, unconscious, but with a fully inflated lifejacket, by the crew of HMS *Brighton*.

Sadly, amongst the victims of this accident was Flight Lieutenant Denis Filion, a Royal Canadian Air Force (RCAF) navigator on an exchange tour with the RAF. Denis was a very fit, outgoing sportsman who spent many a weekend enjoying the varied sports activities in the Cairngorms, with his wife Laura and their four children. The very next day, a RCAF aircraft arrived at Kinloss with Laura's brother, who was also a serving RCAF officer, and her sister-in-law, with the whole crew placed at Laura's disposal for as long as she needed.

There are two melancholy corollaries to this accident. The 120 Squadron 'B' Flight Commander at the time was Squadron Leader John Vere-Sharp, irreverently known amongst the junior officers as 'Hyphen the Terrible'. John left the RAF in 1968, moved to Oxfordshire and married Brian Letchford's widow, Ronnie. One night, John died silently in his sleep – he was in his early forties. Ronnie was widowed twice in the space of a few short years.

Whenever a serving member of the armed forces died, an effects officer was appointed to help the bereaved family with their immediate needs and to deal with all the administrative procedures that have to be completed. The effects officer was normally a junior officer from the deceased's unit. Sergeant John Gent was a young, newly married air electronics operator who died in this accident. Flying Officer Charlie Montgomery was appointed as his effects officer, which was a fairly daunting task for a young pilot lacking in desk skills, but he was given a comprehensive briefing by the Kinloss Secretarial Branch. When the appointment was announced, Flight Sergeant Dave Harris from 206 Squadron called to see Charlie, explaining that he and his wife were close friends of the Gents and he would like to help in any way possible. That was a godsend to Charlie. He dealt with all the paperwork and Dave carried it all back and forth, thereby sparing the young widow the added strain of dealing with a complete stranger. After a few weeks, Mrs Gent left Kinloss to go to her family in England. On Wednesday 20 December, Charlie was the Kinloss Orderly Officer. His rounds included visiting the Operations Centre. As he neared the door, he met Dave Harris, who had just finished a preliminary briefing for a flight the following day. Charlie thanked him for his considerable help, warmly shook Dave's hand and they went their separate ways.

Flight Sergeant Harris died the following day 21 December 1967 when Shackleton MR3 with the serial number XF702 in which he served crashed in Scotland at Creag Bhan in the Cairngorm Mountains. Charlie Montgomery again had personal connections:

> Aircraft icing is a potential killer. If ice builds up on the airframe it can have several dire effects. It adds to the weight of the aircraft and adversely affects performance, especially in the climb. A build-up of ice on the wings can lead to a severe reduction in the lift produced. Ice on the tailplane can cause a rearward shift in the aircraft's Centre of Gravity (C of G.) If it is great enough, it can cause the nose to pitch up which causes lift loss and can stall the wing. Ice can also inhibit the effectiveness of the control surfaces and the propellers.

In piston engines ice can cause restriction or blockage in the air inlets that lead to the carburettor or fuel injector. At the very least this causes a loss of engine performance if not complete power failure.

Shackletons had a primitive anti-icing system which fed de-icing fluid to the wing and tailplane leading edges through wooden slats. The system was so ineffective as to be almost useless.

That Thursday was a day of muted celebration at Kinloss. Ken Whittome was running the Children's Christmas Party in the Officers' Mess, assisted by two other members of his off duty crew; Hector Thistlewood, an experienced navigator who had the rare distinction of holding a Commercial Pilot's Licence, and their co-pilot Charlie Montgomery. The widows of the 120 Squadron accident, with their effects officers, were completing the formalities of handing back their Married Quarters prior to collecting their children from the party and heading south to their families for Christmas.

Later in the evening, the 'Living In' officers would gather in the Mess for their Christmas dinner. Flying Officer Steve Roncoroni was a young bachelor pilot on 206 Squadron. His regular crew was commanded by Squadron Leader Mike 'Boots' McCallum. Mike and his crew were slotted for a live anti-submarine exercise in the Londonderry Exercise Areas to the west of Scotland. It would be a flight of over ten hours, landing back at Kinloss late that night. Flying Officer Terry Swinney was a young married pilot on 206. Some days before, Terry had seen the squadron flying programme and volunteered to fly in Steve's place, so that Steve could attend the Christmas dinner with all the other bachelors, of whom there were over twenty. Steve readily accepted Terry's gracious offer, knowing that the party in the Officers' Mess would be a marvellous affair with fresh Highland game as well as the traditional Christmas fare, good wines and great company.

Mike received a comprehensive weather brief, warning of a weak cold front between 5 and 6 degrees west which would produce mainly moderate icing conditions, but that over the hills it could become severe. The Freezing Level was forecast to be between 7,500 and 8,000 feet. It was later found to be lower, at 6,000 feet. The aircraft Stall Warning system had been adjusted after its previous flight, and was flagged as requiring an air test to prove its reliability. In addition to the normal crew of ten, there was an additional co-pilot and two passengers. One was the Kinloss Wing air electronics officer, the other a secretarial officer from HQ 1 Group.

The aircraft took off from Kinloss at 1230 local time and climbed as cleared by air traffic control (ATC) to 8,000 feet. The crew could have chosen to fly the long way round the north Scottish coast at a lower level, safely clear of ice, but it would have added more than an hour each way to the transit time. At 1258 they reported their position to ATC as seventy-eight miles from Kinloss, in the area of Loch Quoich, at the eastern end of the Knoydart Peninsula. These positions and times showed a lower than expected groundspeed. At 1259 the crew called Scottish ATC Centre to request clearance to cross the airway to the west of Scotland. Some five minutes after that call, the aircraft departed controlled flight and within less than a minute had dived into the ground.

Analysis of the aircraft instruments showed that it had rolled to over 180 degrees, that is, inverted. The RAF Board of Inquiry recorded that 'the aircraft impacted in a near vertical attitude (within 20 degrees) on a heading of approximately 350 Magnetic.' The crash site was ninety-four miles from Kinloss and it took the Kinloss Mountain Rescue Team three hours to get there, over very rough terrain.

In the Officers' Mess, at about 1630, Ken Whittome was called to the phone in the Reception Hall. He returned to the party room completely ashen, his joviality gone, called his helpers and said, 'Please do not ask any questions, I'll fill you in later, but these children must leave immediately.'

The children in question were those whose fathers had died in the 120 Squadron crash, just one month before. Together with their mothers, they were driven away from Kinloss before they could hear the appalling news. The rest of the children were taken home soon afterwards, and Ken led his helpers to the bar, by which time the awful details had become known.

Steve Roncoroni came into the Mess and was given the first of many large malt whiskies. He was inconsolable and wept unashamedly, not alone in that. The crew he had flown with for almost a year had all perished, yet by a quirk of fate he had not been with them that day. He could not forgive himself for accepting Terry's offer to fly in his stead, grieving for Terry and feeling distraught about his young widow. Three fatal accidents had taken some thirty lives in barely six weeks, with twenty from Kinloss. The Mess filled up, large quantities of alcohol were consumed, but, strangely, nobody could get drunk.

There was one more fatal accident to come in the next few months. Some wondered if the age and consistent flying that the Shackleton had endured was somehow responsible for the spate of accidents but it was, in truth, no more than a statistical freak. In simple parlance, Shackletons flew a considerable number of hours. Given that faults can occur with less than modern machinery, the wonder is that there were so few accidents. If the number of mishaps is related to the numbers of hours flown, the percentage rate is low enough to stand comparison with almost any other operational aeroplane.

Charlie Montgomery, who became an airline captain after his RAF service, relates the tale of Shackleton MR2 WB833 from Ballykelly's 204 Squadron that crashed on 19 April 1968 at the Mull of Kintyre:

After human factors, Controlled Flight Into Terrain (CFIT) was the penultimate untamed killer in aviation. It falls into two broad categories and occurs mostly at night or in reduced visibility. The most common fault is navigational error. The aircraft was not where the crew thought it was when it hit the ground. Less often, the aircraft is correctly on track but descends to an inappropriately low altitude. Today's sophisticated modern equipment has all but eliminated these errors as well as ones that lead to mid-air collisions.

Area 'Juliet' was an exercise area between the Mull of Kintyre on the west coast of Scotland and the east coast of Ireland. It was not a good training area because there was always some commercial shipping in transit through the area.

For some time the coastline of Kintyre, and in particular the area around the Mull, has been known to pilots as a dangerous area to fly at low level because of the freak weather conditions that frequently affect the coastline. The first recorded military air accident on the Mull was in 1941, when an Armstrong Whitworth Whitley from 502 Squadron crashed on the west slope of Beinn na Lice, no more than one tenth of a kilometre from the site of a Neptune crash in 1956. Since then until now, there have been nineteen recorded air accidents in the vicinity of the Mull and over a hundred and twenty lives have been lost in this remote corner of Scotland, making it one of the most notorious areas in the whole of the UK for air accidents.

The worst accident happened on 2 June 1994, when an RAF Chinook helicopter carrying a crew of four plus twenty-five senior intelligence officers from the British Forces and the Royal Ulster Constabulary crashed into a hill, killing all on board. The most recent fatal accident (in April 2005 as far as this article is concerned) involved a Loganair Britten Norman Islander, which crashed into the sea whilst attempting an approach to Campbeltown-Machriahanish Airport. The pilot and his one passenger were both killed. The aircraft was acting as an air ambulance. The sole passenger was a paramedic with the Scottish Ambulance Service.

On 19 April 1968, Squadron Leader Clive Haggett and his crew from 204 Squadron at RAF Ballykelly, were involved in a live anti-submarine exercise in Area Juliet. They took off at 0730 to exercise with the submarine HMS *Onyx* south of the Mull of Kintyre. The weather was bad with worse to come and a cloud base of around 400 feet with sea mist. During the exercise the aircraft was heard to overfly the coastal strip twice while turning to engage the submarine. On the second approach it hit a hillside at about 400 feet altitude at 1030. There were no survivors among the crew of eleven. Seven of the crew were buried in the graveyard of the Tamlaghtfinlagan Parish Church, which borders the airfield at Ballykelly, joining the graves of many others who had died on operations during the SecondWorld War.

There were two co-pilots on the crew. One of them,

Flying Officer Mike Creedon, had recently joined 204 Squadron to start his second tour of duty on the Shackleton. He was under training, converting to the Mk2 as his previous tour had been on the Mk3 with 120 Squadron.

There we have four fatal accidents in the space of less than six months. Of the ten pilots killed, two were serving on 120 Squadron at the time and three others had just left 120 Squadron on posting to their second tours.

The Under-Secretary of State for Defence for the Royal Air Force, Merlyn Rees, was questioned in Parliament about the accidents. After expressing his sympathy, he stated in respect of the 19 April accident that no evidence had been found that suggested any mechanical malfunction or failure. He then referred to the other accidents and declared that no common factor linked them to each other or to the most recent accident. Charlie Montgomery comments:

> The Secretary of State was almost right. What the RAF hierarchy failed to admit, but every junior officer and NCO on the Shackleton Fleet worked out for themselves, was that there was a common factor in the second, third and fourth crash. The captains were all Squadron Leader Flight Commanders. They had onerous and time-consuming administrative ground duties which precluded them spending as much time training with their crews as the other squadron captains. They were less current in flying practice than the other squadron pilots and tried too hard to display that 'press on' spirit where sometimes discretion would have been more appropriate.

The accidents did not finish the Shackleton's career in the Royal Air Force. Accidents happen to the best of people. The Shackleton had plenty of flying yet to come.

CHAPTER TWELVE

The contents of the Defence White Paper of 1968 had been widely leaked. The Labour Government found itself short of money for defence needs, a not unusual situation for either party when in power. The White Paper attempted to stay within a notional £2 billion cash limit. Amongst other measures, it proposed withdrawal of the British military from Singapore and Malaysia and from what was known as the Persian Gulf. This would be completed by the end of 1971. Future construction of aircraft carriers was eliminated. The fixed-wing elements of the Fleet Air Arm would transfer to the Royal Air Force when the current carriers ceased to operate after withdrawal from the Far East.

Although replacement of Shackletons by the Nimrod MR was confirmed, it was no 'one-for-one' exchange. A single Nimrod was able to cover the work done by three Shackletons. Coastal Command would disappear. Renamed 18 Maritime Group, it would join the new Strike Command. This latter would first come into force on 1 April 1968 with the merging of Bomber and Fighter Commands. Other Commands would also vanish. Airfields and supporting stations would close. The Royal Air Force, in common with the other armed services, would steadily contract.

Other changes came about. Centralised servicing took ground

crew away from being 'on the line'. They lost membership of a nominated squadron with its emotional attachment to particular aircraft and their aircrew. They were concentrated into the Handling and Rectification Flight. At the same time, the available aircraft were also pooled. Shackletons allocated to a specific squadron became a luxurious indulgence. The Aircraft Servicing Flight did remain and even retained its own hangar space. RAF Ballykelly, in common with most RAF units, had both advantages and drawbacks for those stationed there. Not every aircraft necessarily spent many days away from home. Stations which had no runway could, in the opinions of many, qualify as the most boring places in the world. Some could not even bring themselves to mention phrases along the lines of 'posted to Group headquarters'. The sprawling empire of the new Strike Command at RAF High Wycombe was not a location that appealed to everyone.

Andy Collins has his own opinion of Ballykelly, as he reveals:

The very name of Ballykelly conjures up a picture of little green Irish leprechauns. Certainly an impression of greenness remains to those who were fortunate enough to serve at that remote station; and certainly any RAF base that had a railway line running across the main runway demonstrated a fair degree of Irishness; the leprechauns were not so much in evidence, except perhaps to those whose Saturday evening may have been spent sampling that most Irish of all beverages, poteen!

The greenness of the country can be fairly attributed to the amount of rain dumped on it by the winds that blew straight off the wastes of the North Atlantic. It was said that if you could see Ben Twitch (the local name for the mountain that dominated the eastern horizon from the camp) then it was going to rain; if you could not see Ben Twitch then it was raining. The high annual rainfall and the airfield's level ground only a few feet above sea level made all unpaved surfaces a morass. They were only kept as dry as they were by the continued efforts of a pumping station which drained the water back into Loch Foyle, so that it could once again seep into the heavy Irish soil in a never ending circular battle.

One of Ballykelly's perennial surprises to new arrivals was the local railway. This had a special place in aircrew hearts:

> The railway line that cut across the main runway was the main Belfast to Londonderry line. Trains, naturally, had right of way over aircraft. On many occasions frustrated crews returning from a ten-hour Shackleton sortie would be told to overshoot to allow a train to pass. This could be particularly frustrating in poor weather, for it meant another instrument approach, which at Shackleton speeds was always a protracted business. It was made more difficult at Ballykelly because the main instrument runway had – inevitably – been built in line with Ben Twitch, the highest peak within miles. The approach therefore had to be down a 4-degree glide path, instead of the 3 degrees normally used. Even in clear conditions there would be some delay while the air traffic Land Rover went out to check that no hooligans had thrown bottles or empty beer cans from the passing train. As a final frustration, the line crossed the runway at exactly the point where, with a little bit of float, the landing Shackleton would touch down. Being a tailwheel aircraft, the Shackleton was always somewhat demanding to land. The slight elevation of the railway line was just enough to kick the aircraft back into the air just as one was about to congratulate oneself on cracking another good landing.
>
> There was an alternative to landing on the runway with the railway line. That involved the short runway. If a touchdown was even slightly late causing the pilot to have another go, the aircraft had to fly up the main road from the airfield to the village. This caused considerable adverse comment from those immediately beneath the flight path.

Ballykelly itself was another relic of the late conflict. The demands of a world war had brought about expansion in all the armed forces. Aeroplanes and men both needed space and RAF stations spread across vast acres:

> Ballykelly itself was a wartime station so many of the buildings dated from that era. Certainly the Officers' Mess and the huts

that were accommodation for the single officers appeared to be made largely of cardboard. There was, however, one modern building. This was the pride of Engineering Wing – a brand new 'Gaydon' hangar. This hangar was so beautiful that Shackletons were not generally allowed to use it in case they dripped oil and hydraulic fluid all over the lovely floor. Access to the hangar was further discouraged by the fact that to get to it from the airfield, aircraft had to be towed or taxied over a very narrow bridge. As Shackletons were the main users of the airfield, the real purpose of building the hangar was never truly apparent. Whatever it was, it was the kiss of death to the station, for within two years of its completion, the airfield was closed and was handed over to the Army.

Outside the station lay the attractions of Northern Ireland, which, despite the weather, or perhaps because of it, was very beautiful. The village of Ballykelly was only small, its greatest appeal being the Droppin' Well pub, later destroyed in a fit of pique by the IRA. Further afield lay the town of Limavady and the City of Londonderry. Station personnel tended to do their shopping in these two towns, but most of the social life was found within the station. This was doubtless in part because of the threat from terrorism, but largely it was because the social life within the station was good. Saturday nights in the Messes tended to be noisy and happy affairs. But sometimes on Sundays it was pleasant to drive across the border into county Donegal for lunch at one of the many country inns for which Eire is justly famous.

The Droppin' Well was the target of a bomb blast on December 1982. Eleven soldiers and six civilians died. After reconstruction, the name so fondly remembered by the Royal Air Force disappeared. The public house was renamed Riverside Bar. Andy Collins continues:

Many stories, almost all of them wholly untrue are told of the serviceman encountering the Irish attitude to life. Perhaps the most untrue of them all is that of the young airman enjoying a drive through Eire who calls at a country garage to fill up with petrol. The garage owner chats about the weather and other important topics as the fuel flows slowly into the car. Then as the airman is about to pay the bill, he is offered 'a drop of the hard stuff' by the friendly proprietor. Our hero, with proper views on drinking and driving, declines the offer with thanks. The proprietor becomes quite insistent, and finally reaches into his booth and pulls out a shotgun. He points this at the airman, who makes a rapid reappraisal of his puritanical views, and accepts the proffered glass of poteen and drinks it.

'That,' he gasps with streaming eyes, 'is absolutely disgusting. It is the worst drink I have ever tasted.'

'Yes', agrees the Irishman, 'it is pretty rough. Now you hold the gun.'

Many of the aircrew and ground crew will remember most clearly the time they spent away from the unit. Ballykelly was a station with many overseas commitments. It was not unusual for those associated directly with flying to spend half their life away from home. There were permanent detachments to the Persian Gulf and to Madagascar, and many short deployments to Norway, to the Mediterranean and even further afield.

Shackletons were no longer in production. Avro, along with a host of other manufacturers that had retained their individual names as part of the pre-war Hawker Siddeley Aircraft Group, dispensed with their individuality in July 1963. Central Government was broadly supportive of a simplified system consisting of two aircraft production companies, British Aerospace and Hawker Siddeley Aviation. New British types gave way in many areas over the following years to the products of largely US manufacturers.

In practice, if a Shackleton had a mishap and became 'Cat 5' (unfit for further use), the squadrons on the base had a quandary to solve. One less aircraft usually required the remainder to work harder. Slowly, brutally, inevitably, the number of Shackletons available decreased. Ground crews became adept at cannibalising any aircraft deemed unable to fly again.

Not only Shackleton numbers dwindled. Crew members also fell away as tour and service ends were reached. The MOTU at St Mawgan continued to train pilots for the Shackleton, which was, according to some sources, almost a museum exhibit. Mike Smith came to the aircraft late in its career but standards were still observed:

A posting to Shackletons from flying training was a not terribly popular compliment to those of us who were the arrogant over-confident product of the RAF flying training system. The aircraft could be a bit of a challenge and had to be flown close to the edge of its flight envelope in order to operate it effectively, so above average skill was required but the role was not exactly top of the glamour league.

The maritime world was a completely different Air Force to the Training Command from which we had come. This was the last enclave of the NCO aircrew, a strange unfamiliar breed, a proud, highly skilled bunch that do not suffer fools in any way, shape or form. Technically they had to say 'yes sir' in all situations but they could say it in a way that covered a whole spectrum of meanings! Normal rules applied to the sergeants who, like us, were straight out of training but the more senior flight sergeants and master aircrew had developed into a totally different breed.

Early in the ground school stage of the course we were in the coffee bar when one of the more senior NCOs called me by my first name – unthinkable breach of discipline only a month before – but fortunately I had enough savvy to go with the flow and see what the local rules were, everybody seemed to think it was normal so, strange as it was to me I accepted this new system.

It was more complicated than that.

A couple of days later, when I asked the same guy a question, he turned snapped to attention and crisply answered ending in 'Sir!' Totally confused, it took me a few moments to work out what had changed. The wing commander was standing behind me – so, first names at crew level but in front of the rest of the Air Force normal rules applied – complicated!

The Maritime Operational Training Unit had developed into a smooth and usually unworried training system. It was well accustomed to students and often quietly adopted action without telling the unfortunate occupant of a delicate position:

The Maritime Operational Training took about six months, during the first phase the flight deck crew (pilots and another new breed to me – the flight engineer) flew with a QFI who taught us to physically fly the old grey lady and once we had achieved a standard we were trusted to fly the thing as a 'captain' for a few circuits.

When I reached this magic moment I took off and all was normal until, as we were flying down wind, another Shack landed and burst a tyre coming to a halt on the cross runways, blocking both of them. Suddenly I had to be a captain and make decisions! I am quite sure that my very senior rear crew would have done whatever I said – as long as I said the right things! I set up for endurance flying and was told by the nav that we only had thirty-five minutes of fuel left before we had to divert to RAF Chivenor. At Chivenor the runway was about half the length I was used to, half the width of the St Mawgan runway and I would be landing into the setting sun. I informed the tower that we would stay for thirty-five minutes then divert. I was supremely confident that I could land the beast anywhere and was mildly disappointed when after fifteen minutes they had cleared the runway and, excitement over, we came in to land. On the plus side I had much more captaincy time than all my peers, a situation that brought me much joy.

What I did not find out until much later was that OC MOTU had not shared my confidence in my abilities and had told the engineers that they had twenty minutes to move the Shackleton off the runway (the initial estimate had been two hours) or he would take a bulldozer to it to make room for us!

Mike Smith, like many before him, now had to master the maritime reconnaissance syllabus that came after the problem of mastering the Avro design:

Now that we were fully qualified Shackleton 'First Pilots' we no longer had to be supervised by a QFI so for the remainder of the course we were mentored by a Maritime Instructor. This very experienced pilot's job was to, with the help of a staff navigator, AEO, AEOps and engineer, teach the whole crew of students to operate the aircraft. It was a huge syllabus: Area Reconnaissance, Ship Photography, Search and Rescue and the main role antisubmarine warfare were all covered.

Training flights were the introduction to the real work of maritime reconnaissance as well as search and rescue. They were not short affairs:

Flights lasted six to eight hours with the two student pilots doing shifts at the controls. When not flying we were expected to help in the galley and or take a visual look-out position. The day started as far as I remember one hour and fifteen minutes before take-off. The bus picked up the crew from the Officers' and Sergeants' Messes. Pilots went to the Met Office while the rest of the crew visited Ops to pick up codes and the classified manuals. The navs planned the flight. We then all met up for a full sortie brief before going to the aircraft about forty-five minutes before take off to 'wind up' the Old Grey Lady. The 'non-flying' pilot did the internal safety checks and took up residence in the co-pilot's seat. This was once we were on the squadron. At MOTU he found somewhere to sit while the MAI (Maritime Air Instructor) took the co-pilot's slot. The 'flying' pilot did the external examination, checking for gross errors, leaks, cracks and the like. There were often dribbles of fuel coming out but, as long as it was from the expansion pipes, that was OK. In fact crew members often used this supply of 'free' fuel to fill their Zippo lighters; you could always tell who had done this because the Zippo subsequently gave off plumes of black smoke when used.

The Shackleton's skin was held on by rivets. Part of the external inspection was to check for missing rivets. There were always some and as I recall the cut-off for acceptability was six. If there were more than six rivets missing between the two engines on either wing we would ask for replacements.

If all proved well, it was time to wind up the aeroplane and set off into the sky. Only the very worst of weather could stop the training sortie and this was rare indeed:

The start procedure was a real team effort. Firstly air traffic control had to give their permission, then the ground crew (by hand signal in those days), then the pilot had the throttle and ignition switches but the engineer had the start switch, primer (choke) and ignition cut-off switch. If the engineer over primed the engine would flood with fuel and once in the exhaust pipes it could catch fire. At this point the pilot would, speaking as calmly as possible, ask the engineer to cease priming and keep turning, the hope being that the plugs would clear of fuel, the engine would start and the fire would be blown out by the prop wash. One of the early lessons I learnt was that whatever disaster was befalling, the pilot must sound calm and confident to the point of boredom.

Once started, checks completed and look-outs in position we would taxi to a point where we could come into wind (with nothing behind us) and do engine runs to check that both magnetos were giving a spark. The drill was to bring one engine on each side up to 1600 revs and switch one magneto off at a time, if any engine lost more than 50 RPM you had problems.

It was whilst carrying out this procedure that a piece of Search and Rescue history was made. When taking over the duty of Search and Rescue the crew would sometimes have to do an aircraft prep start-up and go though all the checks and engine runs up to the point of take-off then return to dispersal and leave the aircraft primed to go. On this occasion the only convenient place to do the engine runs was on the runway threshold. Whilst carrying out the engine runs a scramble message came in and the pilot (quite recklessly) selected take-off flap, full power and brakes off and went. They fitted in the pre-take-off checks at 2,000 feet. As I said, a very reckless thing to do but the forty-five-second scramble time achieved is a record that will stand for all time for a multi-engine SAR aircraft.

Consideration of the Nimrod as a replacement for the Shackleton met something of a hurdle when the aircraft actually appeared, allegedly prepared to take over the role so well filled by the Old Lady. The Nimrod was at first found to be unsuitable for Search and Rescue duties because it was unable to drop Lindholme gear to anxious mariners. This was something of a setback although it was eventually resolved. Nonetheless, a sole example of the Shackleton continued on until 1972 in the role. At the same time, other Shackletons were earmarked for a new function which had not even been considered when the decision to take the aeroplane away from Air Sea Warfare was first mooted.

The Royal Navy could no longer provide a comprehensive airborne early warning system to protect the fleet against air attack. They had used carrier-borne Fairey Gannet AEW aircraft as airborne radar stations. The aeroplane had originally entered service in an anti-submarine capacity. Like the Shackleton, it enjoyed contra-rotating propellers although the Gannet was equipped with the Double Mamba turbine engine. Major teething troubles delayed the Gannet's entry into service with the Royal Navy. Parallel developments like the ASW helicopter made the Navy's need for a fixed-wing anti-submarine aircraft virtually superfluous. The Gannet handed over its anti-submarine role in 1960. It continued in an AEW role.

A new essentially US radar, APS20F, proved suitable and could be fitted to the Gannet, which required extensive modifications to carry the gear. With a crew of one pilot and two observers, it did excellent work. It finally entered service in March 1960 but a change of Government, with stern views on defence spending, led to the demise of the aircraft carrier from 1964 and onward.

As capital ships grew fewer, the number of flying Gannets decreased. Brains in the Air Ministry, concerned that the Red Air Force could perhaps exploit gaps in Britain's land radar, decided that the Gannet's radar joined to a large aircraft able to stay in the sky for many hours would be the answer to the quandary. The conundrum of finding a suitable aeroplane for such work was easily answered. A venerable, much admired, airframe was available.

As the carrier force fell apart, the Gannets were flown back to the UK to be scrapped. The reception airfield was Lossiemouth. The radars were rescued and fitted to a few Shackletons as the basis for a short-term land-based AEW force. There had been agreement between politicians, air marshals and admirals that the aircraft would act for both services. It became impolite to observe that the APS20 radar was creaking with age. It could not produce unfailingly excellent results on every occasion. On the plus side, it was astoundingly cheap.

Not every Shackleton trip, whether to sunny climes or Arctic wastes was full of joy and light as Mike Norris remembers:

I was serving on No 210 Squadron at RAF Ballykelly in 1968 when our crew was earmarked to go to Majunga for three months. We were to take over from 205 Squadron who had nobly given up a portion of their local overseas allowance to man the Patrol for the preceding six months. The 210 Squadron group consisted of two crews. We were to ferry out two Shackleton MR2 Phase III for the task. They were scheduled to remain in Majunga to support the operation through a couple of roulements (known in civilian terms as short tours of duty).

By 1968 Ballykelly had changed to centralised servicing with all the associated bits and pieces including the much maligned Task Control with responsibility for allocating airframes to tasks, among a miscellany of, doubtless, essential functions. Having recently lost our squadron ground crew to this relatively new organisation we treated it with great suspicion and not much love. We were informed that two aircraft were being specially prepared. When ready they would be allocated for the sole use of our crews, first to air test and then fly on a couple of training sorties to 'bed them down': all very convincing stuff, particularly to a first tour pilot officer second nav.

Well, things did not work out quite as planned. We were allocated WR955 'November'. It was not ready for air test on the due date. In fact it wasn't ready until four days before we were due to leave for Majunga. When we finally flew the air test, a number of faults became apparent. The bad news was that rectification would result in delay slightly beyond the planned departure date. I've no idea what happened next but clearly the powers that be decided that it was more important to depart Ballykelly on time than in a properly prepared airframe. The squawk box from Task Control squawked and told us to take the back-up aircraft, which we duly did. The back-up was, of course, any other Shackleton at Ballykelly serviceable to fly on the day. So we left for Majunga on time, to the minute, in WL800 'Juliet' on Friday 25 October 1968 trailing by thirty minutes 'The Boss' (BDG – those that need to know will know) flying with the other crew.

Although Mike and his companions did not realise it, they were about to undertake an odyssey that would have silenced Lemuel Gulliver and his chat about his Travels into Several Remote Nations of the World. Not all long ventures are confined to ships. RAF aircraft that went off to far places on journeys scheduled to stay in foreign countries always had an imprest. This was a cunning device by which one member of the party acted, in simple terms, as the accountant. On shorter trips, he would draw a fistful of money from the accountants and pay hotel bills, for example, throughout the trip. For larger expenditure he could sign the invoice for payment by the local British Embassy. The diplomats would also hand over real currency on request, a system that was always helpful in the days when British cheques did not always impress a shopkeeper in the remoter parts of the world. The imprest holder would also arrange for real money to pass to the officers in the group. The Air Ministry arranged monthly payments for officers to the two RAF Service Agents who were themselves banks. Such pay would have the imprest advances deducted once the paperwork reached headquarters. The agent system fell into disuse when the military salary system came into operation:

As always we climbed to a dizzying 1,000 feet, flew out via Inistrahull round Tory Island and intersected the 12 West meridian to fly outside Irish waters arriving in Gibraltar eight hours and fifteen minutes later for some well earned R&R. The following morning we flew to Malta again at 1,000 feet all the way for five hours and fifty minutes for a long week-end. In fact the weekend was prolonged by some difficulty over diplomatic clearance.

This was, for the most sensitive, the first tiny indication that events can always conspire against aircrew:

> We left Malta the following Wednesday, 30 October for RAF El Adem in Libya to refuel en route Djibouti. BDG had decided to fly with our crew on this leg and was not happy when oil began to appear all over the spinner of No 2. This was evidence of an inter-shaft leak. The propellers were feathered, the first of many on this trip.

A message went to Maritime Air Headquarters in the Mediterranean whose duty staff picked up the ball and ran with it. The Shackleton crew learned that a twin-boom Argosy would fly out immediately to El Adem with replacement propellers, crane and kit. Known in some circles as the 'Whistling Wheelbarrow' because of its prop-jet engines, the RAF noted the pointed radome on the nose of the bulbous fuselage. This gave the aeroplane its service nickname of the 'Whistling Tit'.

The Shackleton beat the Argosy to El Adem and endured a long wait. When the new propellers were finally in place, slight concern entered the crew's collective mind over their diplomatic clearance through Egypt and on to Djibouti. The Foreign Office negotiates special authorisation for military aircraft to fly over a whole range of foreign countries. The permissions are explicit with a range of conditions. The flight must be within particular times, at a specific height and follow an agreed route as well as other restrictions. Failure to comply with the clearance is a sure way to arrange an interview with hatchet-faced foreign policemen:

> We flew at medium levels (high for Shacks), and that was per-haps a factor in our troubles. We had been airborne for about five hours when our flight engineer started to kneel between the pilots, staring intently at the RPM counter for No 1 engine, and then at the temperature and oil pressure gauges.

214

Soon No 1 was feathered and we limped into Djibouti after nine hours and fifty minutes, mostly night, to add to the three hours and five minutes for the Malta to El Adem leg – a long day.

As always on these trips we carried a few ground crew. Luckily we had Corporal Croft the detachment engine fitter with us. He quickly saw that we needed a replacement for No1 engine and the message was passed up the line.

Even those unfamiliar with Djibouti would be able to guess that it is not the most upmarket spot on Earth. We, of course, were subject to constraints that were totally foreign to our colleagues flying transport aircraft. Our Coastal Command administrators, for instance, had, in their wisdom, decided that we would stay in service accommodation. At Djibouti, an outpost of the French Foreign Legion, service accommodation was not luxurious. The other aircraft was also in need of spares so both crews stayed together in adjoining rooms with space only for ten bunk beds. BDG had his own room, probably the cleaner's closet. The spares for the other crew's aircraft arrived after a few days and they set off for Mombasa and Majunga with BDG. For seven days we ate in a combined mess, food that owed more to Arab than French cuisine, happily washed down by rough red wine. Our spare time was spent on the beach followed by evenings playing battleships, uckers, hangman and all kinds of cards.

A replacement engine duly arrived to be fitted by Corporal Croft, ably assisted by his ground-crew colleagues and our flight engineer. We set off for a night transit flight round the Horn of Africa and off the coast of Somalia southwards to Mombasa on 6 November.

Life rarely gets simpler as the crew, now unaccompanied by another Shackleton, discovered:

We flew at or about 1,000 feet below controlled airspace in contact with Nairobi Flight Information Region, RAF Upavon and Cyprus Flight Watch. Even in those days Somalia was regarded as unfriendly so we stayed well clear of territorial waters and did not plan to use Mogadishu as a diversion.

215

Our options, should we have a serious problem, were either to return to Djibouti or press on to Mombasa. True to form after about five hours and past the point of no return the engineer adopted the prayer position between the pilots. Even I could see needles on instruments waggling around or pointing in the wrong direction. It seemed that we had a choice of which of three engines we should shut down. No 1 was duly shut down and about three hours' flying out of Mombasa No 3 was also feathered. We upgraded our PAN to MAYDAY. As we later learned, much of East Africa took an interest in our plight as the broadcast media made the most of an unusual story. Nos 2 and 4 engines were nursed all the way and we did restart No 1 engine for the landing at Mombasa after a flight of ten hours and twentyfive minutes with Sir Alex Ferguson's fabled 'squeaky bums' much in evidence. Crofty had a good look round and soon told a rather startled crew that despite shutting down Nos 1 and 3 in flight we'd need to replace Nos 2 and 4 engines. The problems with Nos 1 and 3 were solved from within the spares kept in the bomb bay pannier.

Some flights quickly reach their destination. Others try for world records of the longest time spent on a journey. Aeroplanes were designed to be the fastest means of travel between two points. On occasions, bicycles can beat them. Mike's story now proceeds with no interruptions:

There being no Foreign Legion base in Mombasa we checked in to the Nyali Beach Hotel on the eponymous beach to enjoy a comfortable break. Meanwhile, Coastal Command and Far East Air Force (FEAF) opened a debate to decide who should provide the two replacement engines. FEAF had operational control of the Majunga operation but we were some way short of Madagascar. We were not party to what might have been an esoteric and, possibly acerbic, discussion revolving around command and control, engineering and logistics.

In any event, after almost two weeks we were told that a 48 Squadron Hercules from Changi would deliver our replacement engines. Meanwhile, Corporal Croft, who was fast becoming a hero, had made enquiries about a crane to lift the afflicted engines out from, and their replacements in to, our aircraft. Wilkenair, the RAF's local agent, managed to locate a mobile crane, apparently the only suitable crane in that part of Kenya, in Mombasa docks. Our co-pilot's (the imprest holder) frequent visits to the British Consul in Mombasa to uplift funds did not go unnoticed in the corridors of power. We were moved out of the Nyali Beach Hotel and into the Joint Service Silversands Leave Centre a little further along Nyali Beach.

After delivery of our replacement engines, the crane was driven at snail's pace and at the cost of traffic chaos out to the airport where we found that the crane's legal maximum lifting limit was well below the 2,000 lbs weight of a Rolls-Royce Griffon 58. A short conversation took place between Croft and the crane operator, followed by a longer conversation between Corporal Croft, the crane driver and the imprest holder. The crane operator was suitably conciliated and work commenced. Eye witnesses describe the crane wheels bowing inwards as the weight of the engine was taken up – most couldn't bear to look. Crofty now hit an unexpected problem when he found that the diameter of the propeller shaft on one of the replacement engines was too large to permit the propeller reduction gear to be fitted. Clearly, the engine was fitted on to the aircraft before this became apparent so a lot of time and effort was wasted. Perhaps fortunately, in those days most service communication was by signal, in this case via the Consulate, which kept us at more than arm's length from the recipients of our bad news. I imagine that the signal revealing this latest problem might have caused some elevation in blood pressures. In any event, another engine had to be found and there was another hiatus while we waited for FEAF and Coastal Command to come to conclusions.

This time, a replacement eventually arrived from Ballykelly accompanied by a senior engineer officer from Northwood to 'investigate' our saga! He ordered an early start with the engine change and blew a gasket when he was told he would have to wait three days for the crane. When it finally arrived and work started he soon 'clocked' that the engine was far too heavy for the crane (even before 'elf and safety!). He could not believe that this was the only crane available and stormed off to 'sort this out'. The only way to get a suitable crane to Mombasa was to get one shipped in by sea from South Africa (Cape Town or Durban) or by road from Nairobi, which would take a week to ten days, not to mention the exorbitant cost! At this juncture he went away on the returning Herc with his tail between his legs but with some degree of understanding of the engineering conditions under which Crofty had been operating. I think his final judgement was that we had done well to get this far!

Finally, engine runs were completed satisfactorily. The flight engineer and Crofty reported that 'Juliet' was ready for an air test. A minimum crew with the doughty Croft on board put the aircraft through an extensive test flight on 11 December. We droned all around Mombasa for close to an hour and all was well, sweet as a nut. The final hiccup occurred next morning when our captain began to suffer from a painful ear condition diagnosed by the local RN doctor as 'coral ear'. He was grounded for at least seven days. Another signal to higher authority conveying the news that although the aircraft was now serviceable the captain was u/s probably caused some fluttering in the HQ Coastal Command dovecote. However, we were soon informed that a replacement captain was on his way from Ballykelly. He duly arrived on 14 December and after a short four hours and forty-five minutes hop we landed at Majunga on 15 December, fifty-two days after our departure from Ballykelly, having flown a total of forty-two hours and ten minutes while using eight engines and ten propellers. Our overall rate of advance was less than five miles an hour.

We stayed in Majunga a further six weeks flying eight 'Mizar' surveillance sorties totalling eighty hours and fifty minutes before returning to UK by Air Support Command Britannia. 'Juliet' stayed out in Majunga for another three months and as far as I can remember functioned satisfactorily before being flown back to Ballykelly through Africa without any delays. Naturally, there were some consequences.

218

I had arrived at the Apartment Desai, our accommodation in Majunga, to find that an old friend, then on 205 Sqaudron whose crew had been held back in Majunga until we were airborne from Mombasa had decided to use my bar book for all fifty-two days pending my arrival, some form of personal retribution for being late. I therefore had a built in handicap when it came to settling my Mess bill. One of our number, a careful Scot, asked our imprest holder to pay him his LOA by the day so that he would not spend beyond his means. He also featured in the Majunga telegraph as having turned down an AEOP conversion course (and pay increase) because he had just bought a new signaller's brevet.

We did not draw our full allowances while we were in the Nyali Beach Hotel but left enough in the imprest to cover our room bills. At the same time as our move to Silversands, there was a currency crisis and the banks were closed so that our co-pilot couldn't access the cash to settle the bill. The British Consulate stepped in to the breach, picked up the Nyali Beach tab and eventually recovered the money from the RAF. On our return to UK our imprest holder/co-pilot was the only one not to proceed on leave as he had to 'hot foot' to Northwood with the flight imprest as the station accounts officer wouldn't touch it with a barge pole. Subsequently Command decided that, since the bill had been settled from public funds, the Nyali Beach became service accommodation and we were, therefore, entitled to Local Overseas Allowance (LOA) not the higher rate Overseas Travel Allowance (OTA). The accounts officer at Ballykelly, naturally enough but unfairly, became the butt of our ire and wasn't top of the pops with the aphorism 'snatch' quickly built into his nickname. The outcome of all this was that we all had to cough up cash that we could ill afford. In the case of one of our number, the problem was compounded by a failure to remember that the healthy balance in his bank on return to Ballykelly should be offset against the large advances on his pay book in Majunga. When the imprest was finally balanced he had depleted the bank balance and the RAF stopped paying him for two months. His normal salary was £85 16s 10d. The first month he got 16s 10d, the next month £5 16s

10d. The third month he had to clear the overdraft that enabled him to survive the previous two. It was a lean time for him and the rest of us.

As a footnote to the story, the Coastal Command Categorisation Board (CCCB) visited the squadron immediately on our return to Ballykelly, prior to our taking post-detachment leave. By and large they weren't renowned for their flexibility or understanding, illustrated when all of the squadron's co-pilots were taken up together for a check ride with the famously unsympathetic CCCB pilot and most lost their categories. BDG wasn't too impressed. My brave first nav locked himself inside a flying clothing locker for the duration and, therefore, amid the general carnage, managed to hang on to his category.

Roger Ward found himself playing a part in more ordinary duties. Detachments to faraway places were all very well, but the Shackleton squadrons had a vital job to do. The Cold War did not simply fold up its blankets and sneak away:

The oddest detachment was what we called the Magical Mystery Tour. I'm not sure when but [it was] probably about February or March 1970. Every year when the Soviet fleet comes out from Murmansk ports, Shacks were sent up to Norway or Iceland to follow them usually at very short notice. We ground crews were given just a few hours to get things together and board a C130 to follow the four Shackletons (I think) or, given the difference in speed, overtake the Shack and get wherever it was we were heading before they arrived.

Surprise! Surprise! When we found ourselves in Malta, it was the Soviet Black Sea fleet that had entered the Mediterranean rather than the Murmansk fleet. The next few weeks were chaos; we had Shacks spread between Gibraltar and Cyprus, some broken down, often with the necessary spares in another part of the Med.

For Roger and every other ground technician, Shackletons divided themselves into categories – favourites and not-so-favourites. All three marks were in service at the same time and it really was the luck of the draw as to which one came along for attention:

Out of all the marks I worked on, T4, Mk2 and Mk3, my favourite Shackleton was the Mk2, maybe because it was the one on which I had most experience or gave me the best detachments.

My least favourite was the Mk3 with Viper jets on the outboard nacelles, mainly because the brackets holding the side panels on the nacelles were always cracking and it was a pain having to change them. They were good to fly in if they spotted a Soviet sub on the surface and hit the Vipers for a mock attack, especially if you were fast asleep down the back end and woke up to all the noise and flashes of the flares in time to see the conning tower disappearing under the waters of the North Sea.

One good thing about the Mk3 over the Mk2 was when you had to do a wheel change. The size and weight of the wheels of the earlier models made it a two or three man job, although I did manage to do a double wheel change on a Mk2 in Majunga once.

The pilot's pleasure at the hydraulic brake system on the Mk3 Shackleton sometimes caused problems for the ground crew – as, indeed, did other occasionally messy jobs:

One of the main differences between the Mk3 and the Mk1, Mk2 and T4 was the brake system. On the earlier Shacks it was pneumatic, while the Mk3 had hydraulic brakes. When doing a wheel change on a Mk3 it was always best to remember to lock up the brakes first. If you didn't, the brake discs fell and it was a hell of a job getting them back into position with the 'spider' tool for aligning the brake discs.

One terrible hazard on the T4 and Mk2 was when you had to empty the Elsan toilet bucket after a long flight. The way out of the rear door was just a simple ladder, made out of tubular metal, very easy to slip getting down when carrying a heavy object and naturally you are holding the bucket as far away from you as possible so you tend to be unbalanced. Unbalanced also describes the mood of anyone who has come a cropper carrying out this task. It only happened to me once, on MOTU not long after I arrived at Kinloss. It was not a problem on Mk3 as, being much higher, they usually used proper Giraffe access stairs or similar.

Another possible messy hazard for the unwary on earlier Shacks was emptying the Oil and Water Trap. This device removes oily contaminants from the pneumatic system. It is located on the outboard side of No 3 engine cowling just behind the firewall (I think). The idea is to very slowly undo the nut at the bottom of the cylindrical trap and catch the sludge into a container as it runs out, usually a paper cup or similar. It's awkward to get at and if it has not been done as frequently as it should it could be full and sometimes the sludge at the bottom is very thick. Once the thick sludge has oozed out and there is less resistance to the pressure the rest comes out with a whoosh, blowing everything that was in the cup back out, along with all the remaining sludge and depositing it all over the engine firewall, components, pipe work and face of the person doing the job – this is another thing that usually only happens once per person.

Refuelling can be hazardous in icy weather; it has to be done from the top of the wings, which can be very slippery, and angle of the wings on the Mk2 means it is easy to slide off the rear. The angle of the wings on the Mk3 is not as steep but you have further to fall. Also you have to get to the Mk3 wing tip tanks, tricky in wind and ice weather.

The end for Shackleton maritime reconnaissance aircraft inexorably approached. There were still detachments, there was still work to be done but time was running out. Strike Command swallowed Coastal on 28 November 1969. Number 18 Group added (Maritime) to its title and took over much of the administration of the Command. It did, after all, only have to manage until the last MR Shackleton went out of service.

CHAPTER THIRTEEN

As the last days of Shackleton service on maritime duties approached, most aircrew waited for news of their redeployment. In theory at any rate, they would not all be transferred to Nimrod flying which was generally reckoned to be a totally different experience to that of the Shackleton. The Nimrod flew higher and faster and was, it was cheerfully rumoured, a much more comfortable ride. Deafness was not by and large a concomitant of flying in the jet aircraft.

Shackleton aircrew, and some ground crew as well, made the most of their remaining months on the big piston-engined aeroplane. Andy Collins recalls:

In the days of the late nineteen sixties and early seventies when Coastal Command, and later 18 Group, had a truly world-wide role, Shackletons used to undertake some truly epic voyages around the globe. When one considers that the cruising speed of the Shackleton was about 160 kts (knots) it is hardly surprising that these journeys took some time. When one further considers that the Rolls-Royce Griffon engines were old and were working very hard, one can see why journeys that should have taken days often stretched into weeks.

The aircraft on the permanent detachments in Sharjah and in Majunga had to be returned to the UK from time to time for servicing. This involved travelling across large areas of Africa and the Middle East, and through the Mediterranean, to fly up the west coast of Europe to Ballykelly. This route was chosen because it was as far as possible over the sea, and did not involve crossing any mountains, or even serious hills. The Shack would not have coped. The route from Sharjah used to start painlessly enough, with a short two-hour hop to Bahrain. This got the crew into the ways of transit flying and allowed them to mix with the posher transport types who were always staging through Bahrain's Muharraq airport. Overnight accommodation was in the RAF's Britannia House – a sort of military Youth Hostel, but without the extravagant amenities.

The route was not one that sightseers or holidaymakers would have appreciated:

Morning would see the crew departing early to avoid the rush out of Muharraq. The day's flight of around seven hours would take them over very inhospitable desert to Khartoum, the capital of Sudan. With the Shackleton's notorious lack of power, it was necessary to fly at only a couple of thousand feet above the ground in the searing heat. An engine failure in this sort of country would have been very unpleasant, and certainly at the beginning of the flight when the aircraft was still laden with fuel the remaining engines would have served only to take one to the scene of the crash.

Khartoum itself was the driest place I have ever visited. At the front of the aircraft one was covered in sweat after landing, but by the time one had climbed down the aircraft steps at the rear, the almost total lack of humidity had dried one's flying suit off completely, leaving just a small white residue beneath the arms and in any other places where sweat had soaked in. At the junction of the Blue Nile and the White Nile, Khartoum was fairly prosperous, and the residents of the British Embassy lived a sort of latter day Raj existence. They were, however, very hospitable to us, though what they made of ten maritime aircrew who came and went overnight I dread to think.

The next day took us over the Libyan Desert towards Malta. The desert beneath us was no more hospitable than that of the previous day, but at least the last few of the nine hours of the journey were over the sea. Malta was always a welcome sight to the homeward bound crew, for here was the home of 203 Squadron, another Shackleton unit. One could count on meeting a few old friends, and bits of the aircraft that had gone unserviceable could now be repaired with the proper facilities. It was here or at the next stop, Gibraltar, that the aging aircraft tended to give up the ghost, refusing to move until an engine had been replaced. The crews were grateful to have got this far, for an earlier breakdown would have meant long delays awaiting renewed diplomatic clearance to overfly countries of often doubtful political stability.

The final legs back to Ballykelly were over the Mediterranean and the familiar waters of the North Atlantic. Normally our lords and masters would find a small surveillance task for us to do on the way, lest we forget what our role in life really was.

Returning from Majunga did have a certain pleasure although this was sometimes less than obvious. What was more, not every ground station appreciated the idiosyncrasies that were an integral part of the Shackleton Experience:

Homeward bound from Majunga, one started with an eight-hour leg to the beautiful city of Nairobi. Here in the capital of Kenya one could enjoy the cooler climate, having dragged the reluctant Shackleton up to the city's elevation of about five thousand feet, and one could sample again the pleasures of civilised society. The next day's journey started well with a flight past the majestic Mount Kenya. But over the next nine hours the scenery slowly changed as one crossed the deserts of Ethiopia and the Red Sea to land in the Saudi Arabian city of Jeddah. In this strict Islamic society one was wise to behave with decorum, and requests for alcohol were frowned upon by the hotel staff. This would not be a good place in which to go unserviceable.

The Saudis were efficient, but not tolerant or helpful to the crews of the antiquated Shackletons. At a civilian airport one should not start engines until one has clearance on the radio to do so. But the Shack's radios were effectively useless until electrical power was available from the generator of a running engine. At least one crew found themselves forced to shut down engines until they had permission to start, and they finally had to resort to sending a crew member to walk to the tower to request permission to start again. The Saudis were also adamant that clearance would be given to depart only if the aircraft would cross into Egyptian airspace at 15,000 ft. As this was at least three times higher than the laden Shackleton could hope to go with its high fuel load, crews resorted to agreeing to this demand, and then renegotiating a lower level with Cairo when they were safely on their way.

The flight up the Nile was always interesting, if a little unnerving in the days when the uneasy truce between the Egyptians and the Israelis had just expired. At Luxor one could see Mig fighters in their hardened pens as one flew over, and up the Nile strategic points were defended by SAM sites. Again it was a pleasure to get over the waters of the Mediterranean on the way to Malta and to reasonable stability.

It is perhaps not surprising that journeys that now could be done easily in two days took a week or more to complete. The Shackleton engines were not overly reliable. If a malfunction occurred in some out-of-the-way spot, there was often a delay of two or more weeks while diplomatic clearance to fly in a spare was negotiated. The knock-on effect was also huge, for diplomatic clearance to continue the journey after the repair had also to be re-negotiated, and if the delay was to an outbound aircraft, the clearance for the aircraft being relieved overseas would also have to be re-negotiated. Foreign Office staffs must have had nightmares about Shackleton transits.

The days of the epic voyages of Maritime Shackletons are now long gone, as are the days of the mighty four-piston engine operational aircraft with their origins in the Second World War. Crews of the modern Air Force jet along high above the weather, and see just a slight colour change below them, rather than the hostile grey and yellow wastes of seemingly endless desert. Their world is smaller too, and their opportunities to gather good 'war stories' are much reduced. Yet though those journeys were interesting and often exciting, I still remember the pleasure of seeing Ballykelly again, with a South Westerly gale lashing rain on to the sodden sides of Ben Twitch.

The Shackletons at Sharjah flew a specific role. Ian Tapster, who spent time at Sharjah in 1969 and 1970 as the wing commander in charge of administration, remembers the rotating detachment of Shackletons on MARDET. This maritime detachment took two or three aircraft at a time from Ballykelly or Kinloss. Each aircraft spent several weeks in the Gulf. Like many others in important ground roles, he became involved with the Shackleton detachment and its duties:

Their basic task was that of routine maritime surveillance although they took on others such as search and rescue if required. In the former role they regularly flew patrols (known as 'Bronze' and 'Double Bronze') in the Gulf and Indian Ocean.

In 1970 I flew on a 'Double Bronze' as supernumerary crew. My memories of that flight illustrate the job that the Shackleton crews did.

After an early morning take-off from Sharjah we had an RV with a Royal Navy submarine in the Straits of Hormuz where we spent some time exercising with her. We then headed out into the Indian Ocean and down the coast of Oman, making for the RAF staging post on Masirah Island. Flying low, we routinely checked any shipping we saw. Our task was to identify and report any vessels which might have been carrying illegal immigrants to the Gulf States. In addition, at this time the Sultan of Oman had a war on his hands in Dhofar so we were also looking for any vessels which might have been carrying insurgents. Moreover, the insurgency which had resulted in British withdrawal from Aden was still fresh in the memory so we were also alert for any possible seaborne activity in support of the self-styled Popular

Front for the Liberation of the Occupied Arabian Gulf (PFLOAG).

On this patrol we drew a blank as far as illegal immigrants or terrorists were concerned, but we did find one good prize. This was a Russian hydrographic survey ship which had not previously featured in the naval intelligence reports for the area. We flew some low level circuits with cameras whirring and took a good look at her aerial array in case she was also an eavesdropper.

Then on to land at Masirah where we had a welcome opportunity to stretch our legs, have a cold drink and have a spot of peace and quiet after several hours in the hot and noisy old Shack. After this we headed back to base, repeating the morning's maritime surveillance tasks until darkness fell. This was then the opportunity for the AEOs to get some practice in the area of the oil rigs which were just burgeoning in the Gulf and were to provide its later prosperity.

MARDET Shackletons took on Search and Rescue duties almost as a matter of course. They were usually the only aircraft immediately available that had the range, endurance and equipment to find ships in trouble. In March 1970 the *Nastran*, an Iranian vessel, capsized during a severe storm. She was found by a Shackleton of 210 Squadron on detachment to Sharjah and that aircraft guided two helicopters from 78 Squadron, also at Sharjah, to the scene. On 5 July 1970 the SS *Diffuri Maadu*, in transit through the Gulf, caught fire. Built by Hall Russell of Aberdeen, the 2,000-ton ship's distress calls scrambled a 204 Squadron Shackleton on detachment. WL758 located the ship and was able to guide rescue vessels to the scene. Of the crew of thirty-one on board, twenty-nine were rescued. The ship itself was beached two nautical miles off Dubai. No matter where they went, the Kipper Fleet was always available to help save lives.

In November 1970, with both defence spending and overseas locations under review, the MARDET rotational moves were abandoned in favour of basing some Shackletons at Sharjah on a more permanent basis. The five Mk2 aircraft took on the designation of 210 Squadron, their unit at Ballykelly. These operated until November 1971 when they gave up the task as British forces withdrew from the Gulf.

Number 204 Squadron became operational at RAF Honington on 1 April 1971 as a shipping surveillance and search and rescue unit. The first commanding officer of the squadron at Honington was David Leppard, who tells the story thus:

I was at Staff College in 1970 and was posted as OC Majunga Detachment Support Unit (MDSU) at Kinloss. The outfit was due to form on 1 April 1971 with four Mk2 and one in use reserve, five crews, ex-Ballykelly and ground crew, who were to become the first ground crew of 8 Squadron, due to form later that year. The reason for the MDSU in the first place was to continue with the Majunga Detachment/Beira Patrol upon the closure of Ballykelly as the Nimrod was unable to use Majunga. The runway was too short and there was nil technical support there.

I completed my varsity refresher at Manby on 12 February 1971 and was on leave when, on or about 15 February 1971, I was told to 'not pass go and not to collect £200' and proceed to Honington to become OC 204 Squadron. My kit was already on its way, courtesy of Pickfords to Kinloss!! When I got to Honington I was told that 204 Squadron was to be operational asap, and deploy two aircraft to Majunga. Over the next four weeks, some twelve crews and around 150 ground crew arrived on base. We also ferried nine Mk2 from Ballykelly (eight established and one in use reserve). I also collected the squadron standard from Ballykelly.

I was given a hangar, which had been vacated by a Navy Buccaneer Squadron, that was in something of a mess – no telephones, no ops communications, no furniture, nothing! I had to find accommodation for about 270 bodies and families, most of whom came from Ballykelly. We (the station was magnificent) found married quarters for most at Honington, Honington Rise, Watton and an ex-USAF missile base near Thetford.

The squadron was not exactly management top heavy. I was squadron commander, a squadron leader, OC Ops/QFI was Squadron Leader Ken Miles, who was specialist aircrew, and an administrative sergeant made up the squadron management. Engineering was commanded by Flight Lieutenant Walter Lynch, with a warrant officer in charge of first line servicing. We were fully autonomous and even did our own major servicing. This included on one occasion, a wing change! First line was commanded by a flight sergeant who operated from an old Valiant dispersal the other side of the runway.

The reason for the large squadron was because we had to take over SAR as well as the Majunga Detachment. The Nimrod Lindholme gear trials were going badly and the delay made it impractical for the Nimrod to take on the SAR task. As we were responsible for National SAR (no Normar and Soumar SAR standby) we had to keep one aircraft at one hour notice and one at three hours notice. During the lifetime of the squadron at Honington I recall that we launched the 1st SAR on forty-three occasions. Our average time from call out to airborne was thirteen minutes – not bad for those days. Ironically our largest incident was searching for a Honington Buccaneer, which crashed in the Irish Sea, the pilot being Squadron Leader Jock Gilroy. We never found him or the aircraft although we searched for three days.

We were declared operational about mid April and deployed two aircraft, crews and ground crew to Majunga on about 20 April. The public were told about us on 28 April, when we took the press airborne in a three-ship operation. Crews spent two months in Majunga. We rotated and resupplied by fortnightly Britannia flights. We rotated one aircraft every three months or so. I flew out two of them. Our routing was Honington, Gibraltar, Malta, Khormaksar, Nairobi, & Majunga.

We were nearly moved to Binbrook towards the end of 1971/early 1972 as the Navy wanted the hangar back because a Buccaneer squadron was coming ashore from a carrier. Although we fought it, in the end we accepted the use of an old Valiant Ops block adjacent to the dispersal we were using. We agreed with the Navy to keep half the hangar space to work on two Shacks simultaneously. The thought of moving the whole squadron again horrified us all. Needless to say it was the brainchild of some planner in MOD!! It's amazing how quickly you can get organized when you have to!

The Beira Patrol finished in April 1972 and the Detachment was withdrawn. The story of getting the last two aircraft out was quite a saga. By April 1971 some of the crews had disappeared off to Nimrod courses and only about eight or nine crews were left at the end. Many of the ground crew went up to the newly formed 8 Squadron (as indeed I did on 1 May 1972, to become the first Flight Commander Operations).

The squadron formally disbanded on 28 April 1972 and the standard was laid up in the Rotunda at Cranwell. We held the Final Guest Night on 28 April 1971 and our Guest of Honour was Air Chief Marshal Sir Christopher Courtney, formerly OC 4 Squadron RNAS, which of course became 204 Squadron RAF.

Shackleton aircrew never kept good fortune entirely to themselves. All that any male member of the ground staff anywhere on a unit need do to get a free flight in a Shackleton was to ask. It always helped if an official reason could be tagged on by the volunteer passenger. Andrew Morgan Clark takes up the story and, incidentally, reveals other aspects of how crews were always ready and willing to assist others:

From September 1969 to January 1972, I was the Station Accountant Officer at RAF Honington. When the runways were resurfaced in 1971 at Wyton, the aircraft of squadrons based there joined our Shackletons. The Officers' Mess was very crowded with over 200 officers living in Mess.

As the SAO I prepared imprests for the 204 Squadron crews heading out to Majunga and the Beira Patrol and therefore got to know most of them.

Flight Lieutenant Bob Parratt (I believe that's the correct spelling!), a Shackleton navigator and captain, invited me on a weekend trip to RAF Gibraltar as the imprest officer – out Friday, back Monday. I accepted the invitation and we flew into a sunny Gib on the Friday afternoon after experiencing Bob's description of the aircraft (a Mk2, phase III, tail dragger) as 40,000 rivets flying in loose formation. We never went above 3,000 feet and never flew over land after leaving the UK coast. As my father had served on Lancasters during the War this was an experience I relished.

On the Friday afternoon, SATCO at Gib asked Bob if they might use the Shack for fire drill on the Saturday, with Army squaddies as injured crew. Bob agreed but insisted that the flight deck be under the supervision of one of his crew. The second dicky 'volunteered'. All went well or so it appeared and we enjoyed a pleasant weekend viewing the Rock.

Come Monday, we are doing the pre-flight checks when the co-pilot discovered that the fire bottles in the port wing had all been discharged. Despite supervision, a squaddie had managed to raise the guard on the fire switches and depressed the port wing extinguisher switch; well, it was a fire drill! Needless to say we could not take off.

Of course there were no Shack fire bottles in store and of course BAC wouldn't touch the bottles with a barge pole, as they were dangerous cargo. I regret to say we had to sit in Gib until the Thursday when another Shack flew in with our bottles. We headed home late on Thursday.

It was dark when the flight engineer noted a slight oil leak on the starboard inner but the decision was taken to continue with it running. On short finals at Honington the co-pilot had the controls and we passed over the threshold at the correct height and speed (I was told later). We landed once, twice, and before the third landing the throttles were pushed through the gate and the senior pilot said, 'I have control'. We staggered around the circuit to execute a perfect landing on our second approach. As we walked away from the aircraft we looked at the starboard inner, completely covered in a sheen of oil. Bob observed that if he had realised the leak was that bad he would have ordered the engine shut down. I did not notice how subdued the crew were, being exhausted after the long flight.

Not having any part in the debriefing, I headed to the bar to get the beers in. As I was standing there, an air traffick officer walked in, having just finished his shift. He looked at me, asked whether I had been on the Shack that had just returned from Gib. When I said 'yes', he replied that in his opinion I was lucky to be there. When I asked why, he explained that he was about to hit the crash crew alarm button when we had opened the throttles and staggered into the air.

When the crew joined me in the bar I asked Bob about this. He calmly told me that if we had made the third landing we would have pushed the wheels through the wings!

Whilst at Honington, a Search and Rescue scramble never took more than twenty-four minutes, even at the dead of night. I can still remember the tannoy blaring 'Dinghy, dinghy, dinghy, Search and Rescue scramble'.

The first 205 Squadron Shackleton to leave Changi carried with it the wooden cross that had been erected by the grave of Flight Sergeant Dancy on Sin Cowe. When it arrived at St Mawgan, the station padre, Brian Lucas, took responsibility for the cross, which found a new resting place in St Eval church which was used as the Anglican place of worship for RAF St Mawgan.

The Shackleton, as the Air Staff had already decided, would be the interim solution to the need for an Airborne Early Warning System. There was a scheme in process by Boeing in the United States but that would not be available until 1976 at best. Development was a slow business. For British temporary purposes, it was clearly reasonable to marry the venerable Shackleton to the even more aged APS20. The combination only had to fill the gap for a few years so it made good sense to use the Shackletons with the lowest number of airframe hours.

This would normally have pressed the Mk3 into further use but that aeroplane showed distinct signs of airframe and mainspar wear, attributed to operations at very high weights. They needed Vipers to help them off the ground for the Mk3 operated at about 20,000 lbs more than the Mk2. A dozen low fatigue MR2 aircraft were accordingly converted to AEW2 standard with a further three as pilot trainers.

In the short time that remained for the maritime aircraft, they continued to do the work originally intended for them. From time to time, the Old Lady would show up the smart new Nimrods although this was often a case of a crew well knowledgeable of their aircraft against a collection of people learning the trade.

For many Shackleton crews, Andy Collins included, Sharjah and Majunga almost became second homes or, at the very least, holiday destinations with which they were only too familiar:

The Persian Gulf was usually comparatively peaceful. One could operate an aircraft without fear of being blown out of the sky by one of the many warring factions. Two Shackletons from Ballykelly were always detached to the state of Sharjah on the southern side of the Gulf.

There were normally three crews detached with the aircraft. The lucky ones got to fly the aircraft from UK to the Gulf; those less fortunate made the journey by the Britannias and Argosys of Transport Command. This option involved departing from Lyneham at the ungodly hour of dawn so beloved by Air Movements Staffs, to make the first leg of the journey to Cyprus where the Britannia was refuelled. The second leg of the journey was to Bahrain, where the heat hit you like a physical blow when the aircraft door was opened on the pan. A second later the distinctive smell of the mud flats crawled through the door and you knew that you were in the Gulf. The transit bar at Bahrain was always open, and it was inevitable that one should combat the heat and the odour with tins of Tennants Lager and of 'Charlie' or Carlsberg.

The last leg to Sharjah was accomplished by Argosy. As soon as the aircraft was airborne the pilot would feel a marked trim change as thirty passengers realised that they had to head for the toilets to dispose of the lager. By the time one arrived in Sharjah one was usually dehydrated, miserable and hating the heat. Acclimatisation did not generally take long, though there was always some macho idiot who believed that the way to acquire a tan was to lie in the blazing sun for an hour or so. Normally a short spell in hospital and careful nursing would have them back on their feet within a few days, although a slap on the back was not appreciated for a while afterwards.

Millennia of searing sunshine meant that Sharjah was a genuine desert station. The only vegetation was coarse scrub and the occasional palm tree. The roads of the camp were laid across open sand, and when the wind rose above about fifteen knots the sand would be whipped up and sting one's face and arms. As the wind speed rose higher a full-blown sandstorm would develop. The only thing to do then was to get under cover with plenty of fluids and wait till it was all over. In such a climate the accommodation had to be air conditioned; alas the machinery did not always function when sand got into its working parts, and there were long periods waiting for repair.

Experts stated that there were no scorpions in Sharjah. Scorpions did not know this, and found the ducts of inoperative air conditioning systems excellent places to settle down. When the air conditioning was restored, the wise man checked carefully beneath the grille and in his bedding to ensure that he had no unwelcome guests.

The Shackletons were in Sharjah to fulfil treaty obligations with the Gulf states. The main task was to patrol the waters of the Persian and Arabian Gulfs looking for illegal immigrants making their way on over-laden dhows to the shores of the southern Gulf. To get airborne with enough fuel to do a reasonable patrol the Shackletons had to take off at first light, before the relentless sun had raised the temperature to its normal inferno level. Even so, in the humid and sticky conditions the normal aircrew dress while flying was boots, underpants, flying suit and Mae West; the underpants were optional. It may not have been good flight safety, but it was the only way to avoid being poached in one's own sweat.

The air conditioning in the Shackleton was adjusted by having a window open or shut. The normal configuration was to have a window beside the pilot open and a look-out window at the back of the aircraft also open. That way a breeze – like that from a blast furnace – flowed from the back to the front of the fuselage. The aerodynamics of why it flowed that way were never clear, but we were all grateful for it.

Two islands in the Gulf, called Tunb and Abu Musa, were the subject of a territorial dispute between the Trucial States and Iran. The Shackletons were tasked occasionally to fly past the islands early in the morning to ensure that the flag of Sharjah still flew at the camp of the small army detachment. Not infrequently the first fly-past revealed a bare flagpole. It was then necessary to take a closer look and to ensure that the army personnel were properly awake to carry out the morning flag raising. The mighty roar of four Rolls-Royce Griffon engines passing about thirty yards above the sleeping accommodation always produced excellent results, and bodies could be seen tumbling from barrack blocks, and the flag was invariably fluttering in the light morning breeze by the time the aircraft made its next pass. Equally exciting were the coastal patrols flown along the beach in the Gulf of Arabia checking from 100 feet whether any dhows were beached and disgorging passengers.

At the end of a sortie that might have lasted nine or ten hours one was pleased to land and take a cool shower and a cold beer. There was plenty of entertainment available when one considers the remoteness of the station. There were several cinemas, and there was a film on in one or other of the Messes on most evenings. The very real risk of dehydration tended to discourage consumption of too much alcohol, but the barmen could mix an excellent non-alcoholic beverage called locally a 'Street Walker', which contained lemonade and bitters. The risk of dehydration was further reduced by taking salt tablets with every meal. These tablets were on each dining table, along with another small dish of anti-malarial tablets. Taking one of each as you started your meal became a way of life.

When one was not flying or at work, one could visit the local village of Sharjah. This was a typical Arab village with narrow streets and low flat roofed houses. The souk, or market, was a rabbit warren of open-fronted shops where you could buy almost anything. The most memorable was that of Sheikh Robbie. He was a goldsmith and jeweller, and his craftsmen could make lovely rings and bracelets at prices far below those available in the UK. Many servicemen took the work of Sheikh Robbie home to their wives or girlfriends, or sometimes to both.

And as for Majunga:

Of the regular detachments by Shackletons from Ballykelly, by far the most exotic was that to the airport at Majunga in the Malagasy Republic. The republic had previously been the Island of Madagascar, but had been renamed on acquiring its independence from France. The Shackletons were there on the island's north-west coast to fulfil their role in the Beira Patrol, ensuring that no oil was delivered to Rhodesia.

Majunga is about 15 degrees south of the equator and is a truly tropical location. There was, of course, no real RAF station, and the Shackletons operated out of the civilian airport where the servicing was done in the open and the ground crew worked out of large tents. Various buildings around the town had been rented to serve as the departments necessary for the running of any service establishment. Station Headquarters was in an office in the centre of town; the Officers' Mess was in a large flat about a mile from the centre of town; the Sergeants' Mess and the Airmen's Messes were in the countryside about two miles outside town.

The accommodation was fairly basic for everyone. The Officers' Mess had two air-conditioned bedrooms that slept two or three people. The rest of the officers slept in a room called the Barn, in which air conditioning was achieved by the simple expedient of having holes in the wall. The rest of the flat consisted of a large lounge cum dining room and a kitchen. For two months this was home to ten officers of the two detached crews. The two permanent staff officers had their own flat elsewhere in the town.

A flying day would start early for aircrew and ground crew alike. About half an hour before dawn a rickety old bus would appear outside the Maison Dessai, as the Officer's Mess was called. It would take five sleepy crew to collect the remaining crew members from the 'Maison du Maire', and then go on to the 'Campe Britannique' where the Airmen's Mess would have prepared breakfast. There the crew would eat on the veranda, listening to the dawn chorus of the cicadas, watching the spectacular tropical sunrise and sharing their breakfast with the mosquitoes.

After the meal, the bus would then take the crew the five miles or so to the airport. Here the navigators would file a flight plan while the pilots would go to receive Le Meteo, or the met brief. A met man who spoke little or no English would brief the pilots who spoke less French. Everyone would nod and smile, and the pilots would gaze at the synoptic chart and try to remember which way the wind blew round pressure patterns in the southern hemisphere. It made no difference anyway; it was always nice in the morning; there was a thunderstorm about 2 o'clock in the afternoon, and it was nice again in the evening as we came back to land. About half past seven the sortie would start, and the next ten hours would be spent in the sticky tropical heat, checking each radar contact.

'Unladen tanker northbound'. 'Laden tanker southbound.' These would be the reports from the look-outs as the contacts came over the horizon into the range of binoculars. Sometimes we would also have the pleasant task of dropping mail to the Royal Navy frigates of the Patrol. This would be the source of some light banter between the services. They were pleased to receive their mail, and we were pleased to do something different. And always after the mail drop would come 'Do you have time to do a fly-by? Our mast height is ninety-seven feet.'

While one crew was flying the other was on SAR standby, just in case anything went wrong. On those days one would wander down to the SHQ cum Ops building – 'Le Bureau' – and complete any administration tasks that needed to be done until lunchtime. Back in the Maison Dessai two Mess staff looked after the officers. We saw little of the cook, but the waiter, whose name was Georges, was a character. His main language was the pidgin French of the colonial days. Most of his charges spoke schoolboy French – badly – so conversation was just possible. However, Georges was also picking up English, and as he was picking it up from aircrew, it was, to say the least, of a colloquial nature. At a Battle of Britain cocktail party, which the Mess threw each year for the local dignitaries, Georges was handing round the canapés. A rather proper expatriate British Lady said, 'These canapés really are rather good, waiter.'

'Yes Missy,' replied Georges. 'I tell Cooky, shit hot.'

By the end of the detachment most people could speak a

ghastly mixture of English and French, known universally as Franglais. The local townspeople seemed to understand it, and if they did not, then one shouted a bit louder and waved the hands more violently until one's meaning became clear. 'Je will avoir un de those choses la' made perfect sense to customer and shopkeeper alike after a few weeks. The most horrid sentence produced was to the luckless Georges who was explaining to one tardy officer that he was too late for breakfast. 'Venez sur, Georges', said the hungry officer. 'Jouez le homme blanc.'

When one was neither flying nor working, the lifestyle was very relaxed. A ten-minute walk around the side of the town through the edge of the jungle would take one to the beach. The walk was sometimes enlivened by the sight of one of the huge, and probably poisonous, spiders, or of a snake who would wriggle furiously into the undergrowth to evade the intruding human. The local beach-bar – the Village Touristique – provided refreshment when the sun became too hot. Sometimes the ladies of the town would come to the beach to do their washing. They would settle a discreet distance down the beach, then unselfconsciously remove all their clothes and wash them in the sea. The visiting Brits would try to look unconcerned, as if this was just the sort of thing that happened at Bognor too.

Evening entertainment took several forms. On Saturdays an antiquated projector was set up in the Mess and a film was shown. Outside the window would be a large group of local children sitting watching the movie with rapt attention. Or one could visit one of the few local restaurants from which you were unlikely to contract food poisoning. Or one could go to Madame's!

Whenever anyone mentions Majunga, people naturally think of Madame's. It was unashamedly a brothel. The wise Brit went in a group of at least half a dozen and sat in the scruffy bar, drinking Trois Chevaux beer and watching the very attractive ladies seeking custom. The wise Brit also avoided becoming a customer, for it was said that the girls were cheap, but the subsequent treatment was painful and embarrassing.

It was hardly a wonder that some amusements were fraught, if not with danger, with difficulty:

At the end of one's evening, one could always return home in a 'pous-pous'. These rickshaw-like vehicles were usually pulled by the small Komorians, one of the main races of Madagascar. For a few centimes they would pull you from one end of town to the other. The Brits tended not to patronise these very much, except on Boxing Day. On that festive occasion after a strong lunch there was the annual pous-pous race between the airmen, the senior NCOs and the officers. The course was run over a distance of about a mile and a half, mostly down hill and it was a relay race with six members in each team. Each team would hail a pous-pous in a nonchalant manner, and too late the unfortunate owners would discover that they were expected to sit in their own vehicles while a number of less than sober Brits pulled them along at breakneck speed. There were, as I remember, no rules to the race, nor did it matter who won. After it was all over, the owners were showered with more money than they would normally earn in a month, given a drink to steady their nerves, and thanked profusely. The teams then probably celebrated their victory or defeat as appropriate, although to be honest, memory of events after the race is now a little hazy.

Majunga was a far-flung outpost, and most of the Royal Air Force knew nothing of our existence. One evening the Duty Officer was called to the Comcen to receive a signal that said 'Carry out Operation Cordwangle' or something similar. Having no idea what this meant he called out the Detachment Commander, who was equally in the dark. Three hours later, with every file in SHQ at their feet they admitted defeat and signalled back to the UK asking what it was all about. Next morning an apologetic signal came back saying 'Sorry; you should not have been on the distribution list, but we didn't know where you were, so we put you on just in case.' And early in January 1972 a signal came from HQ 18 Group that was framed and hung on the wall of the Officers' Mess. It read, 'Details of your snow plan have not yet been received at this HQ. They are to be signalled soonest.'

The two Shackletons at Majunga, supplied by 204 Squadron who were the last UK Shackleton Maritime Squadron, finally returned home. The Malagasy Republic in June 1971 asked for the air component of the Beira Patrol to end. The Royal Navy carried on but the whole affair ended in 1975. Mozambique gained independence from Portugal and assured the UN that no oil for Rhodesia would cross its territory. The entire blockade episode demonstrated how politicians pursue a failed objective irrespective of military reality.

Dave Leppard flew back one of the Shackletons. He had an uneventful journey although the companion aircraft had less in the way of good fortune. The Shackleton landed at Nouadihibou in Mauretania. It was apparently under the charge of a large colonel swathed with bandoliers who had a fondness for carrying a machine gun. As a rebel faction was threatening to overthrow the government that appointed him, he was intensely suspicious. The second Shackleton suffered a main wheel oleo collapse. The crew spent the next two weeks unable to go any-where while the Foreign Office suffered agonies as they attempted to arrange diplomatic clearance for an aircraft to take spare parts to Nouadihibou which does not feature in many holiday guides. There is little to see in the city and the peninsula on which it stands is nothing but sand.

The demise of the Shackleton's nautical commitments wound up the work of St Mawgan's Maritime Operations Training. In its place, 236 Operational Conversion Unit sprang back to life at Kinloss with the stated intention of converting aircrew on to the Nimrod MR1. Some pilots stayed with the Shackleton. Despite the Old Lady being called everything from a box of frogs to a worn-out and obsolete whelk, the Shackleton had won devoted admirers throughout her years of service. She would continue to do so even when reduced to being simply twelve aircraft in one single squadron.

Shackletons continued to carry passengers. Hugh Willmore, who retired as a colonel, was a young officer with the Staffordshire Regiment in Sharjah in 1971. He joined one flight, which gave him an abiding impression of how slowly the aircraft took off and the tedious boredom of the long flight. However, some good for his regiment came from the journey. He acquired the old inner tube that acted as a seat. He and his men subsequently used it as a Lilo in the sea.

David Greenway, in common with a number of maritime pilots who had flown the Shackleton, was sent to join 8 Squadron. As he recalls:

Number 8 (AEW) Squadron's role was to contribute to the Air Defence of Great Britain. To this end we were stationed at RAF Lossiemouth, on the Moray Firth in Scotland. We operated under the auspices of No 11 Group, the headquarters of which was down at Bentley Priory, in the old Fighter Command Headquarters in north London. They were primarily concerned with running the Air Defence set-up and had under command all the Sector Operations Centres (the ground-based radars) and all the UK fighter squadrons.

We were assigned to No 11 Group. This obviously came as something of a shock to them because they had no idea about large aircraft operations. All their thinking had been about fighters and thus, when we started out, because they were unable to get their heads round the Shackleton, we were directed to perform like their fighters. Thus we were asked to hold ridiculously short readiness states. It takes a minimum of about twenty minutes to get a Shackleton going from cold – you have to stoke the boilers and check the engines out before you get to the runway – and yet we were asked to hold readiness at five minutes and two minutes. To us this meant sitting on the end of the runway with the engines running while a fighter crew might still be in the crew room. Perhaps more to the point, the fighters may hold high readiness states, but they usually only flew for one or two hours as a maximum. We were expected to fly for anything up to twelve hours at a time so it was vital that we sent rested and refreshed chaps up into the ether. Keeping the boys at high readiness states simply tired them out to no avail.

Perhaps one of our problems was that we were simply too far away. Unbelievably, we used to get calls from 11 Group to say that we were short of night flying and would we kindly get organised and get some in. Invariably the response went something along the lines of, 'Short of night flying, eh?

When did you last visit Lossiemouth? It may surprise you to know that, in the middle of the summer, it doesn't get dark up here.' We seemed to be far away and very much on our own.

The alert state thing was eventually resolved to our satisfaction but there were many things working against us. Yes, we were in the far north, but the dear old Shack was designed to fly relatively slowly, so it took us a long time to get to an area of interest. Looking for Russian aircraft was a case in point. We didn't just lurk off in the hopes of meeting one. We worked in concert with the Sector Operations Centres who themselves were part of the NATO chain. Thus, information picked up by one operator would be passed on down the line so that everyone knew about it, from northern Norway right down to the south-east of England.

Russian Bear aircraft flew from northern Russia. They used to fly round North Cape (north of Norway) and then down past Iceland either to Cuba or to Conakry in West Africa. From time to time they would also probe the defences of the United Kingdom to see what reaction they got. Our job, therefore, was to show them that we were ready for them if they ever chose to come for real – the classic Mexican stand-off.

A Shackleton on its own is not really a great deal of use. Indeed, a ground radar station is only useful if it can pick up an incoming raid or aircraft. However, since radar essentially travels in straight lines, it is a relatively easy option for an enemy aircraft to come in, using the curvature of the Earth to avoid the searching beam. The ground station has practically no warning. Thus Shackletons were sent out to extend the radar coverage – to give Airborne Early Warning. But Russian Bears (the NATO designation of the 4-engined turboprop Tupolev Tu-95 strategic bomber), coming down from North Cape, posed a very different problem. They were way out of range of the UK radar stations and, as soon as they had rounded the Cape, they were out of everyone else's radar cover as well. Thus the trick was to try to position a Shackleton up north in an attempt to pick up the Bears (they usually operated as a pair) but this depended heavily on our being given sufficient warning of an impending Bear transit. To this end, in common with all the fighter squadrons, we held an aircraft and crew on QRA (Quick Reaction Alert) so that we could be off and away as soon as possible – as soon as we had warning of an impending incursion.

It took us about three hours to fly up to the area where we might pick up the Bears in transit. Thus it was vital that we had as much warning as possible. On the other hand, a Shackleton on its own could not intercept a Bear. We had to have fighters with us for this part of the operation so these were sent up for us to control on to the Russian aircraft. Because the fighters had limited fuel, we sometimes had an air-to-air refuelling tanker allocated to us as well so that they could top up the fighters' fuel. It was very much a combined operation.

As the Shackleton launched on QRA, there was often a period of extreme tension in the aircraft while the back end team tried to fire up the antiquated APS20 radar. More often than not, the boys got it going but there were many occasions over the years when we had to return because the 1940s-designed kit just would not play ball. At times it was very frustrating.

On the aircraft, the radar team were tuning their kit, the while sitting in front of minute seven-inch screens, usually surrounded by blackout material so that they could see any contacts which came up. It really was a terrible workstation, but somehow the team worked their wonders, picking out the diminutive aircraft returns from all the other distractions. In the centre of the cathode ray tube there was a great yellow blob caused by the radar signals being returned by the surface of the sea, so the rougher it was, the worse the radar picture was. Around the edges of the tube were returns from all the other things out there – ships, oil rigs, sea gulls, flotsam and jetsam and occasionally, a trifling contact from an aircraft. It was the radar team's job to resolve this mess and to make sense of everything.

Meanwhile, the navigators were trying to get the aircraft to the right place and, at the same time, passing position reports to the controlling authority while the pilots were not only driving the aircraft but monitoring just about everything else including the weather and the air traffic control frequencies. If all went well, as we got on task, the fighters turned up, ready to be sent out into the far reaches over the North Atlantic to intercept any interesting contacts we had on the radar. One of the radar team was allocated the task of looking after the fighters and, if we were lucky, the tanker aircraft as well. It was a team effort across the board with everyone working in harmony. The fighters could not intercept the Bears without the help of the Shack crew or that of the tanker. We weren't a lot of use on our own although the mere fact of reporting the incoming aircraft was part of the team effort across the NATO northern flank. Happily, we were not on our own because the Americans with their fighters and AWACS aircraft based in Iceland, were also watching the skies with us.

Having achieved a successful interception and, if necessary, a successful escort of the Bears out of harm's way, the fighters turned for base, landing within the hour. The Shackleton, of course, then had to flog the three hours or so back to Lossiemouth to get some well-earned rest. Is it any wonder that we relied heavily on getting decent food on board and, indeed, a couple of well-earned beers on our return? Intercepting Bears was always thirsty work.

CHAPTER FOURTEEN

The twelve Shackletons modified to undertake the Airborne Early Warning role were allocated the number of a disbanded squadron that had previously been at Bahrain and Khormaksar. Number 8 Squadron preferred to believe that it had been a fighter unit since the beginning of time although this was not precisely true. Even so, conversion from Hawker Hunters to big heavy aeroplanes and a complete change of role did not please many of its members. Mutterings that ties with the squadron badge were no longer suitable wear with civilian clothes and would be destroyed suggested a certain despondency at the planned new role. Aircraft descended from wartime heavy bombers were no steeds for jet-fighter pilots.

The squadron had good reason to pride itself on its history and prowess. As a Royal Flying Corps squadron, one pilot, Freddie West, had won the very first Victoria Cross awarded to an aviator. Throughout its life it had maintained a reputation for panache, a trait which had come to perfection during the time it spent in Aden.

General agreement maintained that Khormaksar was one of the grimmer postings in the civilised world. Legend has it that the squadron pilots felt they needed some relaxation from their daily duty of flying high performance single-seat aircraft. They founded a motor-racing club. All any participant needed was a

Fiat 500, a diminutive Italian car that was, when in the more intense state of dilapidation, markedly cheap, especially at tax-free prices. Many squadron members owned one. They had a race track which was, coincidentally, just outside the Officers' Mess which was itself a fraction inside the main entrance to the station. The Mess was proud of a shaded bar patio area that overlooked a traffic roundabout just inside the main gate. Substantial concrete troughs filled with colourful plants separated the bar patio from the road. There were gaps between the troughs which, astoundingly, were the tiniest touch wider than a Fiat 500.

Nobody claims the credit for driving the first Fiat to hurtle round the traffic island adjacent to the Mess bar, dash through one of the gaps to thus scatter drinkers, glasses, tables and chairs in all directions, escape through another gap and return to the roundabout. The patio furniture endured a fearsome toll although nobody was ever hurt.

These redoubtable fliers were less than happy when a new station commander decided to end the motor-racing ritual. With no warning, he simply arranged for a work party to concrete iron bollards in the gaps between the troughs. Dismay was total but fable claims the bollards were removed the very next night, the holes neatly filled in and an orderly ring of iron installed around the station commander's parking space outside his office before work the next morning. One particularly ardent Fiat racer was observed that day to be unusually tired and suffer from mysteriously blistered hands. Legends create their own history.

The arrangement of solving a pressing problem, even on a temporary basis, by marrying the 1950-vintage Shackleton Mk2 aircraft with a mid-1940 AN/APS20 radar set and expecting the result to be successful was a perfect example of political expediency and military achievement. That it worked could be considered a triumph of ingenuity over adversity. On 1 January 1972 the AEW2 began its service with Number 8 Squadron. The lash-up was a temporary affair until such time as the NATO countries agreed on a solution to their need for an AEW system. The pondering lasted too long for British political taste. In 1977 the Government gave the nod to proceeding with the Nimrod as an AEW platform, the Boeing development allegedly being tardier than anticipated. The Nimrod project appealed to Treasury thinking. Payments could be made in sterling whereas the Boeing project would swallow coveted dollars.

The authorities declared that the Shackleton would continue their AEW task until the Nimrod became ready for squadron service, an event ambitiously forecast for 1982. A little later, NATO made its decision. They would invest in eighteen spanking-new Boeing AWACS NE-3A, to be operated by multinational crews – which suggested that the operation could be an airborne version of the Tower of Babel.

The AEW specialist squadron proposal envisaged a joint RAF and RN unit. The front end, the pilots, the navigators and flight engineers would come from the RAF. The Royal Navy would provide a core of expertise for the radar teams. As a gesture of uniformity, squadron executive posts would be shared evenly. The two services would take it turn and turn about to provide the commanding officer. Predictably, the deal fell apart. This caused problems for the RAF which lost the expertise of the Navy's observers and radar technicians. Their hard-won knowledge of the quirks and foibles of the AN/APS20 vanished with them.

David Greenway joined the squadron on its inception at Kinloss. He tells stories of its early days which may seen a touch fantastical in this modern world but disputing what happened in 1972 is a little mean:

> Funny how these things happen, but it really is usually a cock-up. When No 8 Squadron Shackletons formed at Kinloss in 1972, we took over the squadron number, the squadron standard, the squadron silver and the squadron line books, and all the rest from the late, lamented former fighter squadron. Knowing no better, the aircraft were also painted with the same colour scheme as that worn by the Hunters in Aden – and very nice they looked too, particularly with the new, shiny acrylic paint job which must have given us at least a couple more knots.
>
> What was not realised at the time was that by using the same squadron markings and painting the squadron colours (yellow, blue and red) either side of the RAF roundel on the

side of the fuselage, we had, at a stroke, declared the AEW Shack to be a fighter aircraft. By tradition, only fighter squadrons are entitled to carry the so-called 'fighter flashes'. Thus, the only four-engined fighter aircraft in the world was born.

Amazingly, no one told us to take the colours down. No one even gave us a bollocking for such a heinous crime. We just went about our business in total ignorance, oblivious to any hurt feelings of the fighter fraternity. What was even more surprising was that we were in No 11 Group so they, at least, should have known. Perhaps it was not really their fault because they rarely visited us.

They did, however, get their own back by making us carry parachutes all over again. Actually, the one chap who really did visit us in later years was the lovely Ken Hayr, then AOC 11 Group, who himself had been a lead player on No 8 Squadron Hunters in Aden – and he wasn't going to blow the gaff on the colours. He wore the yellow blue and red cummerbund with pride.

As a further rider to the squadron colours saga, when No 8 Squadron moved over to its permanent home on the north side of the airfield at Lossiemouth, the next dispersal was occupied by the newly formed Jaguar OCU. Their QFIs were very taken with our smart look and so asked John Lumsden the OC of the Jaguar OCU if they could have some colours of their own. Since they were in Scotland, they thought that a tartan should be applied, so they asked John Lumsden to choose. Naturally, he chose the Lumsden tartan. So it was done. What was even better was that many years later, John went back to command RAF Lossiemouth. There were the same Jaguars, still flying his tartan on his station. So that's how it happens.

Shortly before I gave up command of No 8 Squadron on 16 May 1984, I did my last Gibex with the boys. Gibraltar is quite a haul from Lossiemouth (at least a three-steaks and four-breakfasts operation) so we had to leave in the wee small hours in order to get there before the airfield closed. Hindsight is wonderful, but it never occurred to me that something might be up. It was, however, a filthy night, so I was grateful when my co-pilot offered to do the external checks on the aircraft while I lurked in the relative warmth of the aircraft and did the internal checks. Off we staggered and blundered down the airways before heading for the open sea and the south. It was only when the dawn came up that I saw what Ray Donovan and the boys had done. As a special treat, they had painted the spinners yellow, blue and red in honour of the occasion! A very nice touch and, to my knowledge, the only time it was ever done – unless you know differently.

Just to complete the squadron colours story, when No 8 Squadron Shackletons disbanded, the squadron standard, the silver and all the memorabilia was handed over to No 8 Squadron at Waddington with their new E-3D AWACS. Happily, the tradition of painting the squadron colours either side of the roundel has been carried on, albeit in toned-down shade, so we now have the only four-jet-engined fighter in the world. Who knows, there may be others to come, but we'll never have another four-engined contra-rotating propeller-driven fighter.

With their Shackletons wearing fighter squadron markings, 8 Squadron revived another old RAF habit. They named their aircraft. Unlike the air forces of some other nations who apparently had an eye for the propaganda value and named the aircraft after gallant national heroes, the Shackletons gathered in the identities of PC Knapweed for WL741, Sage for WL745, and Florence for WL747. WL754 took on the name Paul while WL756 became Mr Rusty. Brian became the name for WL757. Mr McHenry was the first name for WL790 but it later took the identity of Zebedee when the original holder suffered misfortune. WL793 became Ermintrude while WL795 took the role of Rosalie. WR960 was honoured with the name Dougal, WR963 collected Parsley and WR965 began as Dill (but later became Rosalie). The original Zebedee was WR967.

It was absolutely reasonable that the trustworthy Shackletons, hard-working and no longer young, should perpetuate the characters in a much loved children's television programme. Its five-minute episodes broadcast in the slot just before the early evening news ensured *The Magic Roundabout* had millions of viewers. Originally a French creation especially for children, the British version became an intricate affair aimed at adults as well, with an eclectic selection of characters.

Zebedee, or WR967, had the misfortune to one day suffer a flying accident. No casualties resulted but the affair put paid to the wings. With no possibility of repair, the squadron made the most of the fuselage. This turned into a ground classroom, an AEW training simulator, and the name changed accordingly. Zebedee became Dodo, for even wingless birds deserve respect.

The twelve Shackletons had an important job to do. Communist regimes seemed to be hell-bent on dominating the world. Every minor independence movement since the end of the Second World War appeared to adopt that creed. Not unreasonably, Western reaction was often fierce and brutal. Worse was the undisguised hostility of existing states governed by 'left wing dictatorial dogma', the most powerful being Soviet Russia. British politicians had no doubt that world, or at least European, domination was the main aim of the men in the Kremlin. It followed that Communist rulers should be left in no doubt that other countries would fight to the bitter end to retain their freedom.

Although the supply of pilots was no real problem, nor indeed was the provision of radar navigators, slight concerns were felt in the RAF about the supply of flight engineers. As piston engines on aeroplanes became quaintly old-fashioned, there were fewer entrants into the service who understood them to the level of expertise required of a flight engineer. Because the requirement was so small for the skill, it was hardly worth the effort of setting up a special training school. Faced with the problem, the administrators took the obvious course. They simply recalled to flying duties former flight engineers who were happily spending time on the ground in undemanding tasks from running unit motor transport to watching recruits march back and forth.

Once again, the Shackleton Song could be heard echoing round the station, the tune well familiar to anybody who had served in the Forces. Originally written in 1917, allegedly by a member of the Royal Naval Air Service, 'Bless 'Em All' flourished as the unofficial trooping song of the newly founded Royal Air Force. The tune acquired a huge quantity of new lyrics over the years and it shot to fame during the Second World War. It became a tremendous hit but remained always associated with the Royal Air Force. The music continued to do its duty in a series of unofficial versions:

> Shackletons don't bother me!
> Shackletons don't bother me!
> Clapped out abortions with flaps on their wings,
> Damn their propellers and their piston rings,
> For we're saying goodbye to them all,
> Three fifths of five eighths of f*ck all,
> You'll get no promotion flying over the ocean,
> So cheer up my lads f*ck em all.

> Now they say that the Shack is a mighty fine kite,
> This we no longer doubt,
> When you're in the air with a Mig on your tail,
> This is the way to get out,
> Da, da, da, da, daaar (Sung while holding the arms
>   outstretched as wings and jinking furiously. As if.)
> Just keep cool just keep calm keep sedate, mate
> Don't let your British blood boil!
> Don't hesitate shove 'em straight through the gate,
> And smother the bastards in oil!

Somebody considered that the recalled should manage a refresher course on the Shackleton to remind them how the aeroplane actually worked. In practice, this came down to an academic element to which some flying was added at Lossiemouth. A good number of the returnees were warrant officer aircrew, the rank distinguished by the name of Master Aircrew. This also gave them, as it gave all warrant officers, exactly the same uniform as commissioned officers. A warrant officer's rank badge is a reproduction of the Royal Arms. This tells all that the wearer holds the Queen's Warrant. It was known casually as 'the fighting cats'. Master Aircrew had a special version. A metal eagle that looked golden in any light appeared under the lion and unicorn. The whole was surrounded by leaves of laurel. Holders of this distinction sometimes claimed that Master Aircrew were never worse the wear from drinking alcohol; should this mischance happen, they asserted that they never fell over as a result. If they should fall over, they always contrived to collapse with their arms beneath the body so that passers-by would assume it was just another drunken flight lieutenant.

Flight engineers in particular, enjoyed the reputation of possessing prodigious appetites, sometimes confessing to being a touch peckish. They were supreme professionals. Master Engineer Roy Paige gained his warrant on Lancaster bombers in 1945, eventually holding the unofficial title of the Senior NCO in the Royal Air Force. As a contemporary remembers:

Roy Paige was outstanding. He was a man of immense presence; if you can imagine the Emperor Augustus, crossed with Napoleon Bonaparte, with just a dash of Louis XIV, you sort of get the idea.

He was also merciless with those who fell short through carelessness or idleness. On one occasion we had an aircraft returning to Lossiemouth from Malta, commanded by a guy who really didn't like being away on detachment and who tended to let this cloud his judgement. Normally the route home was over the Massif Central in France, which entailed taking the aircraft up to 15,000 feet if the weather was bad. On the climb-out from Malta, one of the engines had given an unusual twitch in its RPM and power readings, and wouldn't develop full power. Not being confident of making it 'over the top', the captain opted to fly back via Gibraltar, which meant he could stay at low level all the way home, although it was going to take him two days rather than one. When he landed at Gibraltar he sent a message back to base explaining why they had not attempted any diagnosis of the engine problem, either while airborne or after landing, but had discovered that the RPM and power settings still didn't look right during the post-landing engine runs. When the message arrived, Roy scanned it quickly, went red in the face with rage, roared at the top of his voice 'THIS WAS NEARLY ANOTHER INDIAN OCEAN' – a reference to the incident in 1967 when a Shackleton en route to Singapore crashed, killing all but one on board. Roy stamped off to beard the squadron commander in his lair to tell him to stop the crew in Gibraltar trying to get airborne again. Sure enough, on inspection it was found that the engine control system was shot and they had been very lucky not to have already had an overspeed. The strip that Roy tore off the errant captain, and his flight engineer, when they finally got back to base was awesome. Even the squadron commander was impressed, and he gave Olympic-standard bollockings.

One initial irritation with the dictates from Bentley Priory concerned total immersion suits, immediately named 'goon suits' by Shackleton crewmen. These were identical to divers' dry suits and, indeed, made by the same company. More than one Shackleton crewman suffered mild panic when he saw the maker's label inside them for they were made by the Frankenstein Company, albeit from Birkenhead. The firm was not new to RAF orders for they had made suits for Hurricane pilots on the Murmansk convoys during the Second World War. Orders to fighter pilots to wear the suits on long flights over the sea had continued in force. Frankenstein also produced pressurised suits for aircrew in high-flying aircraft and heat-resistant clothing for firefighters. As a sideline, they also came up with the space suits for the film *2001: A Space Odyssey*, a corollary of their work for the Apollo missions.

Bentley Priory were reluctant to differentiate between fast jet pilots on short flights and Shackleton crews on lengthier trips. The suits had indeed proved their value in the past, although a number of Shackleton aircrew were certain that their usefulness would be minimal if they had to bale out or the Shackleton crashed in the sea. Their chance of survival was remote, as previous accidents had shown. The suits had not been a requirement in Coastal Command. 11 Group did not apparently appreciate that fighter crewmen stay strapped in their ejection seats. Ventilation outfits maintain their bodies at a level temperature even under the goon suit. Shackleton crew had no such luxury. They had to manoeuvre around the aircraft in an atmosphere in which they either roasted or froze if conditions were against them.

In general terms, the suits were worn when sea temperatures

fell below 10 degrees centigrade. Putting them on was an obstacle course. The suit had close fitting rubber seals around the neck and wrists. Entry into the suit was via a diagonal waterproof zip which ran from the lower left hip to the upper right shoulder. The suit allowed some ease of movement by release of a back zip that ran horizontally across the back of the waist.

The goon suit was not the only necessary clothing for the well-dressed Shackleton AEW flier. Underneath the immersion kit was a one-piece fleecy green outfit known as the 'bunny suit' although this could be replaced by a white fleece two-piece affair with a T-shirt under that. Thick socks completed the ensemble. Once the crewman managed all of that, the final piece of icing was the life jacket, known throughout the service as the Mae West as it gave useful curves in the right places. Attending to often essential bodily functions in flight was a time-consuming business. It is sufficient to say that the wearer really needed to go before he went aft to fight the appalling Elsan.

Mandatory survival drills, particularly in winter, proved less than welcome. Crews were taken out in the Moray Firth on a launch – for some reason the Treasury objected to a genuine Shackleton crashing into the raw-cold water simply for crew practice. Despite the goon and bunny suit, the crews felt the cold attack their bodies. They usually had about twenty yards or more to swim to their dinghy, which had, naturally, been turned upside down by the instructors. After righting the craft, the crew had to climb in, inflate it, bail out the water and follow the remaining laborious rescue procedure before receiving the nod of approval that brought the whole experience to an end.

Overall, most Shackleton crew decided that it was better to be safe than sorry. If the suit helped survival, it was worthwhile. They certainly kept out draughts.

It was not the first time that the Royal Air Force had experimented with airborne early warning. Their first attempts had been with the Neptune aircraft that came from the United States. For various reasons, although the aircraft was suitable, the equipment did not perform as well as the air marshals thought it should so they discontinued the trials. Now there was no choice, AEW Shackletons had to work in a vital role. Kevin Byron, a navigator, joined 8 Squadron in its earlier days:

My initial acquaintance with the Shackleton was at one remove. When I went through navigation training at Finningley, the school itself was going through a phase of an unusual number of Kipper Fleet navigators as instructors. I never understood this phenomenon. Finningley would have waves of truckies (transport navigators from Hercules, Britannias, Belfasts, Andovers and VC10s), bomber navs (from Canberras, Buccaneers, Vulcans and Victors), helicopters and Air Defenders (ex-Phantoms and/or Javelins) and, of course, Kipper Fleet. These waves tended to replicate themselves thereby restocking their old squadrons, although it wasn't quite as straightforward as that.

The thing about former Shackleton navigators was their outlook on life. The old cliché, 'fight hard, play hard' could have been coined for them. They were absolutely brilliant at their jobs, having wrestled with the problems of navigating the Shackleton in all corners of the Earth, in all kinds of weather (usually foul) with totally obsolete navigation equipment. Their experiences made them a great deal more tolerant of student mistakes than some of their colleagues from the shinier end of the spectrum as they had made most of the mistakes themselves. Because of this, they salvaged the career of many struggling students and turned them into really quite good navigators in their own right.

On the other hand, they knew how to party and they almost all appeared to have married either like-minded or long-suffering wives. I have lost count of the number of times a bunch of fairly inebriated students and Kipper Fleet instructors would descend upon some poor lady, late at night after an extended happy hour, demanding egg and bacon sandwiches, which were always produced most hospitably, although I daresay the guilty husband dined on hot tongue and cold shoulder for a day or two afterwards!

Anyway, when it came close to the end of my course my Course Commander, Dickie Robson, late of 205 Squadron Shackletons in Singapore, called me in to discuss my future. He had me firmly pencilled in for Vulcans as an attack navigator, since I had shown high aptitude for radar interpretation but at this stage they were also recruiting for the fairly new

256

Airborne Early Warning (AEW) role. This interested me as a chance to get in on the ground floor of a new specialisation – I was still moderately ambitious in those days. Dickie had doubts but agreed to put me forward and, since most people would have paid good money to avoid Shackletons, any volunteer was snapped up (having undergone the necessary sanity checks).

Still, as I was assured when I joined the squadron in April 1974 'You've arrived at just the right time to transfer to the AWACS when we take delivery in 1976'. I duly completed my course despite suffering from dreadful airsickness caused by a combination of the abominable stench of years of stale sweat that pervaded the aircraft and sitting sideways at the radar scope – a notoriously bad position for inner ear function, and graduated as the lowest form of animal life on the squadron – an AEW operator.

At the beginning, both the front and back end crews were a mixture of RAF and RN. The RAF had sent some first-tour navigators to the RN to fly the Gannets. They, together with some RN observers seconded to us, were the actual core of the back end. We also inherited a couple of former Gannet pilots, and bloody good they were too. One of them, Lieutenant Dave Moojen, held the record for the longest sortie with the radar running. He flew for slightly over fifteen hours during which the radar went for almost fourteen. This really upset some old Kipper Fleet pilots!

It was during my spell as the junior AEW operator on my crew that I acquired my nickname. To this day you could mention to someone from Shacks that you know Kevin Byron and they would probably look at you blankly but mention that you know 'Scrote' and the light will dawn. The problem was that as junior operator one had to load up the crew coach with everybody's kit, plus the safety equipment, plus the in-flight rations plus the crew box containing the collection of herbs, spices and pet cooking pots and utensils. On one particular morning I took a shade longer than normal. As a result, I was late for pre-flight briefing. I tried to sneak in at the back unnoticed but to no avail. To a man they turned and glared at this piece of navel lint that had dared to interrupt

proceedings. So, to lighten the moment I did my imperson-
ation of a *Goon Show* character, an ancient butler figure,
which put in rare appearances in the show. 'Enter Scrotum,' I
croaked, 'the wrinkled family retainer'. Collapse of stout parties all round; me stuck with the nickname for life (thirty-four
years later my closest friends still call me Scrote).

So, once I stopped throwing up how did I find the old
beast? Well, it was unbelievably noisy. It has been described as
being like a flying Nissen hut that had several hundred people
apparently beating seven shades out of the outside with large
hammers.

It was, as I've already mentioned, terribly smelly. Now I
thought that this had accumulated over the previous twenty-
odd years of operations given the lovely leather-upholstered
seats, which are notorious for getting smelly if not saddle-
soaped regularly and the cotton covers of our Mae West life
jackets which were rarely if ever laundered added their five
penn'orth to the general miasma. In fact, when we took our
last five Shacks down to Woodford in 1989 to celebrate the
old girl's fortieth anniversary, we had the very first Shack
Squadron CO on board as guest – Air Vice Marshal Peter
Farr. He paused at the door, took a deep appreciative sniff and
said, 'Do you know, they smelt exactly like that when they
were brand new!!'

Temperature control was indifferent to say the least. You
either froze or sweltered.

One radar problem was the instability of the electrical
supply. To enable the Shack to provide the sparks, the alter-
nating current generators had to run at their slowest possible
speed. This coincided with the highest possible continuous
speed at which Griffons could run, even with gearing up.
Consequently, power supplies were uneven which resulted in
an erratic and noisy radar signal. Over the years some money
was spent and some slight improvements made. The most
noticeable came, according to gossip, when we acquired a
bunch of 'new' radar screens from a scrap merchant in the
States. He was about to crush them when he heard on the
grapevine that the RAF was prepared to pay cash money for
such obsolete rubbish. He had a screen crated up, hopped on

the first plane to London and presented himself and crate at Whitehall. He apparently sold us all his APS20 spares for serious money.

The instability of the electrical supply meant that we tended to go through a fair number of fuses. Most of these were low voltage and low current. One could pluck them out of their holders using just leather flying gloves as protection and give them to the flight engineer for testing. One of our more colourful RN TACOs tried this one day inside the main radar power panel – twenty amp fuses – without switching off the generators. He was delving away when there was a bang and a blue flash and he went flying backwards down the aircraft. Picking himself up and shaking his smoking gloved hand he said, 'I think that one's OK.'

The Shackleton in its new role often proved itself a match for the rest of NATO's Air Forces. As Geoff Cooper remembers it, there were times when the RAF's AEW system caused embarrassment to rivals who enjoyed greater financial largesse from their government:

We used to go up to the US Keflavik base in Iceland on a regular basis to operate with the US AEW outfits that rotated through there. In the early days it was the Lockheed EC-121 Warning Star, developed from the 1049 Super Constellation four-engined airliner. This was equipped with the same APS20 radar as the Shack plus it had a AN/APS-45 height-finder radar.

The 'Connie' was operated by the Air Force Reserve. We quickly formed a strong bond of kinship with our fellow four-piston operators. I well remember the final Connie detachment to Lossie that ended up in the Bothy Bar till late into the night. It was no hardship to fly the Connie too as we were able to operate their equipment with virtually no need for supervision. They were fun people to be with. When the Connie was finally withdrawn with the entry of the E-3 into USAF service, it truly was the end of an era in many ways.

The E-3 was manned by the regular USAF and they belonged to Tactical Air Command (TAC). The first E-3 I saw up there was roped off in a hangar with an unsmiling armed guard. I managed to get on board for a look around. Not only was the floor carpeted but the top of the consoles were as well. The carpet quality was better than that found in many houses. The crews were different types too. The wild old hard drinking Connie piston guys had been replaced by clean cut career men – conformists to a man – who all turned up to meet us in their immaculate flight suits and silk scarves. I think they thought we were an anachronism (they weren't wrong!) but every now and again a well handled Shack showed them that we were well capable of holding a couple of Bears on the APS20 when they in their hi-tech E-3 had contrived to lose contact due to zero doppler.

We regularly took part in an exercise in Iceland called Fan Angel. For part of the exercise we were tasked to act as a low slow target for the resident Black Knights F4 squadron. This called for us to fly an eastbound track to the south of Iceland at some 7,000 feet at warp factor 160 kts. We picked up an F4 taking off from Keflavik to come out to intercept us and I started flicking through the radio frequencies used by Drainage (the ground radar air defence unit) to see if I could find the frequency that it was going to be controlled on. Bingo! I identified the voice of a young USAF lieutenant at Drainage known privately as 'Peppermint Patty'. She was talking to the F4, I listened for a minute or two while she checked in with the fighter.

I waited until there was a gap in the transmissions and came up on the frequency announcing myself as the new controller. I kept up a steady stream of information to the F4s not allowing them time to think of authenticating me. I started giving the F4 target information about a low slow target heading east at 7,000 feet, 160 kts except the position I passed to him was a further 10-15 miles east of our present position, ie, ahead of us. I vectored the F4 for a 120 degree intercept and then turned him in front of us on to the easterly heading.

I paused.

The F4's radio clicked on:

'Where's my target?'.

I replied, 'Check six', (that is, 'the target's behind you.)

There was a short pause while the penny dropped and he realised he'd been had. Then, without further ado, he plugged in his burners and disappeared back to Keflavik in high dudgeon. When we landed a few hours later, we walked across to the Whiff bar, home of the 57th FIS 'Black Knights' to have a beer with (or off) our chum. We were saddened to hear that he had stormed back to his room complaining that he'd been shot down by a 'goddam World War 2 bomber' and he wouldn't come out of his room.

Allied co-operation occasionally did strain at the seams.

CHAPTER FIFTEEN

One manning problem that haunted the new Shackleton squadron was the supply of radar operators. Replacements appeared eventually from new entrant RAF navigators into the RAF, 'volunteers' who had eschewed the idea of sitting in a fast jet.

Applicants found that there was usually an alarming lack of information at navigation school about what the job actually entailed. No instructors seemed to know very much about the role or that the Shackleton continued in service. With the demise of Coastal Command, many assumed that maritime reconnaissance and anti-submarine warfare had ceased to exist. Purists even maintained that crew working an AEW Shackleton were different to those who had served the Kipper Fleet for the previous twenty years.

Success in the RAF tests to select suitable people for aircrew training produced the occasional strange result. Some successful candidates could be described as ideal for treatment by qualified mental specialists. One young radar operator turned up in the Officers' Mess one evening proudly wearing an emerald green suit. The President of the Mess Committee, a senior officer, told him through gritted teeth never to wear it again. The next evening, the offender appeared in a canary-yellow suit only to receive a somewhat terser injunction from the PMC. The third night, he took the advice of the President never to wear either suit. He paired the green jacket with the yellow trousers to produce an appealing sartorial blend. The PMC gave up which was possibly the wisest course of action. The mixture could have got worse.

Geoff Cooper was one of the navigators who gritted his teeth and chased a posting to the last Shackleton squadron. He originally believed that his ideal first tour would be with the Hercules fleet. He never quite saw the appeal of fast jet flying. This was, in some eyes, enough to guarantee his consignment to the worst of all worlds. Those instructors who had been members of the fast jet fraternity generally had the feeling that anybody who looked elsewhere for employment clearly did not have the right stuff.

The idea that a successful student would prefer extensive foreign travel at the Queen's expense as opposed to sitting on an ejection seat while scuttling through thick grey cloud over the North Sea was alien indeed. One thing led to another. Geoff ended up at Lossiemouth where 8 Squadron managed its affairs. The initial impact was of a rapid introduction to the Cold War. One of Lossiemouth's station commanders had ensured that the bleak admonition that the task of the station in peace was to train for war and that should never be forgotten. The statement had a prominent position in the operations room.

The Cold War did indeed dominate both Western and Russian political thinking. Belief in private enterprise and personal obligation pitted itself against Communist belief in state control in every facet of life. Whether much intrinsic difference existed between the Western politician who rode around Whitehall or Washington in a large car driven by an obsequious chauffeur and the Soviet apparatchik who reclined in the back seat of the latest Zil armoured saloon controlled by a police driver is a matter more for philosophers than historians. For many years, it seemed as if the dispute would be resolved only by a war. Both sides had large military budgets.

Geoff Cooper recalls his days with 8 Squadron:

I well remember the first time I stepped into the Squadron hangar at Lossie and confronted the Grey Lady for the first time. Most aircraft have at least one viewing position that shows off their lines to best effect. Most that is, bar the Shack. The Mk2 Shack with its bulbous radar excrescence under its jowls would never – let's be honest – have won a beauty contest. Some cynics said that it was best seen in one's rear-view mirror.

In the 1970s, it was difficult to feel much pride at all in flying a 1950s airframe updated with the addition of an already obsolete 1940s radar. At the same time, relative youngsters like me and others had been posted there straight from nav school. My heart sank even further when I realised that I wouldn't even be navigating. I was to be an AEW operator in the mission crew.

It took me two years to settle down and get my teeth into the job. I then flew with Brian Hill as my Tactical Co-ordinator (TACO), an experienced and positive AEO who had been where I was sat and understood full well what I was going through. He achieved the impossible and fired my enthusiasm for flying in the Shack. As a result I started climbing the ladder within the crew hierarchy.

AEW flying did produce a remarkably different squadron. The Royal Air Force itself was changing from a service that had happily employed senior NCOs in flying jobs to one in which all aircrew were commissioned officers. Geoff describes a typical training sortie:

After briefing and kitting out, a crew bus will drop you and the rest of the crew by the aircraft about thirty minutes before take-off. The smiling crew chief and his merry men are waiting in front of the beast. The crew comprises two pilots, a flight engineer, a nav plotter and a radio nav, and the radar team – a TACO, a controller and usually one to two operators. The radar team was generally composed of navigators with a sprinkling of AEOs. In my day, only the flight engineer was an NCO.

Walking around to the entrance door at the rear of the starboard side, there's generally a fairly uncoordinated milling about exercise as parachute bags, cameras, crew boxes and other impedimenta are passed up the ladder into the dark interior. The Shack's lineage with the Lancaster is evident from the first step as the ladder is a simple yellow painted device that hooks over the rear door entrance. While everyone else is chewing the fat outside, we'll climb aboard and take a quick tour.

The first thing you'll notice in the beam area is the unique and indescribable smell that is peculiar to the Shackleton – an all-pervading assault on the nostrils composed of Avgas, oil, Racasan, leather, hydraulic fluid, cigarettes and the accumulated pungent odours of thirty years of aviation. The crudity of the internal finish is plain to see as the inside walls of the fuselage are bare and all the ribs and stringers are clearly visible. There are two electrical power packs with ancient wiring looms hanging off them and both the port and starboard beam windows are equipped with a comfortable-looking leather armchair. As someone once remarked (just before his lobotomy): 'It's a real gentleman's aeroplane – sitting in a soft leather armchair being propelled through the skies by 4 Rolls-Royce supercharged V12s.' Quite.

Looking aft, there's a dark tunnel beyond the magnificently odiferous Elsan that leads under the elevators to a small tail look-out position. Coming forward and uphill again, we step into the tiny but well-appointed galley complete with two rest bunks that no one in my experience ever used. The concept of resting or sleeping in an airborne Shackleton was obviously dreamt up by someone who had yet to fly in one.

Moving forward again, you'll open a small door that leads into the confines of the radar team's area. The first things you notice are the three radar screens and the mass of equipment and black boxes that line the port wall. If you like switches, this is Switch Heaven! Breaking up the space are two massive main spars which cross the fuselage up to a height of about three feet. There's a seat for one operator to the rear of the aft main spar while the other two operators sit snugly between the forward and aft main spars. Clambering over the spars, you'll next see the plexiglass astrodome in the roof that offers a superb all-round view.

Further forward still brings you to the nav table and the

radio nav position – both on the port side. Level with the radio nav position but on the starboard side is the flight engineer's panel upon which a mass of dials, switches and controls for the aircraft systems were mounted. It takes 3,284 gallons (these figures remain indelibly etched in my mind) of Avgas to fully fuel a Shack and, depending on diversions and RPM settings, this should be enough to enable it to stay airborne for between twelve and fourteen hours. Don't ask me how I know. The relatively short endurance (compared to the maritime Shacks) was as a result of running the Griffons at 2175 RPM – which was necessary to keep the AC generators on line to power the radar.

A central walkway leads to the flight deck. This is first-generation stuff – no powered flying controls or glass cockpits or head up displays here. Any Second World War bomber pilot could step straight in and feel at home in seconds. Looking sideways out of the windows there is an excellent view of the four supercharged V12 Rolls-Royce Griffons, each of around thirty-five litres, with their contra-rotating propellers. This product from Rolls-Royce was the ultimate in piston engines at one time and each produces approximately 2,500 hp at fairly low RPM.

Ducking down beneath the instrument panel brings you into the relatively spacious nose area. Here, there are two crew positions; a prone bomb-aiming position that allows a crew member to stretch out on a leather-covered foam mattress and, above that, the plexiglass nose look-out position which offers arguably the best view in the house. Two 20 mm Hispano cannon used to be situated in the nose and they were operated from the upper seat here. When things were quiet, I'd take a break and this was my favourite place for a rest. I'd sit up in the nose, with all the hullabaloo of the radios behind me, contemplating the meaning of life with a coffee and a Hamlet cigar for company.

Starting the four engines had modified slightly over the years of Shackleton service. The Griffon, for all its power output, was capable of going into an unremitting sulk. This more often than not came out on starting. The starter motor would jam. The generally accepted cure of taking off a panel and hitting the offending item with a high quality hammer fell into slight disfavour. The crew inside the aircraft plug their headsets into the intercom while the crew chief outside plugs into an external socket. Once air traffic control approved Engine Start, the procedure went, as Geoff Cooper recalls, along the lines of:

'Clear start 3, Chief?'

Crew chief's muffled response. 'Clear start 3 sir!'

'Switches 3.'

'Contact 3.'

'Turning 3.'

At this point you can feel the pulsing as No 3 engine turns over on the starter. And remember, each cylinder is approximately three litres! There's the sudden roar as the engine fires and the revs rise before being brought under control and reduced to (I think) about 1200 RPM.

'Oil Pressure 3.'

'Charge temp hot.'

'3's on the throttle.'

'Fire light out 3.'

'Clear bomb doors, Chief?'

'Clear bomb doors sir.'

'Travelling.'

'Closed.'

'Clear 4, Chief ?' etc., etc.

Before long, all four Griffons are running and have settled down into a steady rumble. Once taxi clearance has been obtained, the engines are throttled back further to allow the chocks to be removed and then the aircraft inches forward dipping its nose as the pneumatic brakes are checked with a hiss. After conducting checks on all engines for mag drops, we whip through the take-off checks, turning our seats to face forward, tightening our harnesses and ensuring that there are no loose articles.

Once lined up on the runway and with ATC giving the nod for take-off, the Griffons change from their rumbling when the Shackleton is in taxi mode to a vigorous deafening roar. The flight deck releases the brakes and the aircraft rolls forward. At 60 knots, the tail comes up. The aircraft goes on, gently bouncing on its main wheels as it thunders down the runway. As the Shackleton rises into the air, the pilots call 'Safely airborne', followed by 'brakes on, off, undercarriage up, please'. It is always good practice to stop the wheels whirling before retracting the undercarriage. The Shackleton mounts gently towards its intended altitude. The flaps come in and the aircraft is cleaned up for cruising. A call to air traffic tells them that the Shackleton is on its way to its designated area. Geoff Cooper continues the story:

With the engines steady at cruising RPM, we switch on the 200v AC generators and apply start-up power to the radar to warm up the innumerable valves. Meanwhile, the galley slave (aka the spare operator) is preparing the first round of drinks while the oven heats up in preparation for cooking the breakfast. People take advantage of the transit to select what they want to eat at lunchtime and to pick a bar of chocolate (inexplicably known as nutty) to eat with their hot drink. The flight engineer responds to various calls for heat around the aeroplane and lights the petrol-fired heaters. Cigarettes, cigars and pipes are lit and soon the atmosphere is quite snug. The mission crew study the sortie brief again to make sure that all are happy with the content and their part in the plan.

As we reach Peterhead, I check in with Buchan, the Air Defence unit, and confirm our mission details and note any changes. At the same time, the radar has finished its warm-up sequence and can be commanded to 'Transmit'. The black curtain is pulled around us so there can be no witnesses! Soon all three seven-inch radar screens are alive with yellow radar returns from the land, the sea, weather, ships and, occasionally, aircraft. I make an assessment of the picture and confirm with the crew captain that the picture is good enough to control fighters. We contact the Air Defence unit on an already agreed frequency and establish good communications with the fighter marshal there.

At the appointed time, a pair of F4s come up crisply on the radio and we search for them on the screens. Soon, the screens are a mass of chinagraph dots as the team manually track and form the radar picture.

A few words on detecting and tracking targets using the AN/APS20: we had 2 tools to enable us to track aircraft – a white chinagraph and a rag. Every last radar contact in the area of interest would be quickly marked with a chinagraph dot. The vast majority of the radar returns were either random noise, weather clutter or sea return. Random noise, by definition, occurred in a different place on the screen with each sweep of the antenna. Weather clutter was generally not a problem for the operator. The extent of the sea return, however, depended upon the sea state (and the surface wind) and the operating altitude. The greater the altitude, the greater the extent of the sea return but the further the radar horizon. Another major factor at our usual operating altitudes was inversions (when the outside air temperature (OAT) did not lapse at the standard rate of —2 degrees Celsius for each 1,000ft of altitude climbed. A temperature climb to plot the OAT and thus reveal the presence or otherwise of inversions was usually carried out at the start of each sortie. If an inversion was detected, we then had to choose which side of it to sit.

Optimising the radar picture was always a compromise between the many seemingly conflicting elements (task, radar performance, communications, weather, sea state, alert states, etc. etc.) and the ability to do this quickly, without fuss and almost instinctively was the hallmark of a radar team on top of their game. The whole thing was a dynamic process though and somewhat akin to trying to nail a jelly to the wall. The radar would constantly be tweaked, the pilots would be asked to climb another 500 feet while the nav would be asked to move the barrier centre point 30nautical miles to the south-west.

A genuine air target should start to form something that looked like a trail and generally the operator needed a minimum of three hits to be able to declare a new track. Needless to say, before too long the screen became hopelessly covered with chinagraph dots, which was where the rag came in handy. All non-essential chinagraph would be wiped before starting the process over again. And again. The operator would make an estimation of any contact's track and ground speed by a combination of the trained Mark One eyeball, mental dead reckoning or experience and we became surprisingly adept at this. A fully worked up three-man team with a good radar, could detect and manually track almost twenty aircraft at any one time and subsequently report them by voice (no encrypted radio or high speed date links!) to either a ground radar unit or to a naval task force.

Back to our F4s. Once identified, we take control of them and run whatever exercise is called for. Someone once observed that controlling a fighter using the Shack radar was 90 per cent dead reckoning and 10 per cent bulls★★★. Or it may have been the other way around.

All too soon, it's time to say goodbye to our fighters. We depart the area to conduct further crew training as required. This could involve dropping the Lindholme Search and Rescue gear, assisting Buccaneers in their maritime attack role, practising ship homings and photography at low level (100 feet), reporting air tracks or the surface plot to the Air Defence unit and/or naval units, firing flares, conducting practice diversions for pilot training or setting up a navex especially for the nav's benefit out to somewhere like Rockall. Finally, we'd polish our emergency drills, especially if we had a 'standards' ride imminent.

After all the training is finished, we close down on the radios with the Air Defence unit and head for home. We tidy up the aircraft and ensure that any classified material is accounted for. Soon we are in good two-way with base and I give the squadron a quick call on our 'company' frequency to give our ETA for them to pass to the ground crew on the line. The pre-landing checks are rattled through and we are all ready for landing.

Over the intercom, you'll hear the occasional muttered curse from the pilots as the aircraft often seems to have a mind of its own if there's a significant crosswind. The pilots' heavy breathing is clearly audible as the ground approaches and the power is gradually reduced. On a good day, the aircraft settles into a slightly nose-high attitude and sinks gently on to the runway with a yowp of rubber and stays there. On a bad day, we could balloon back up into the evening sky and, losing airspeed fast, drop like a piano back on to the runway with a sickening impact. Luckily, the Shack was built like a brick outhouse and its undercarriage can withstand much abuse.

Clearing the runway, we turn on to the taxiway and run through the after-landing checks and head for the bright lights of our dispersal area where we can see the ground crew and the crew bus waiting for us. The cheery voice of the crew chief welcomes us back as he plugs in. We quickly run through the shutdown checks (aka the noise abatement checks). Finally, there's only No 4 engine left running, as this is the engine that powers the hydraulics. The bomb doors are opened and when the indicator doll's eye is white, the pilots finally cut the engine and the sudden silence after nine hours or so of brain-numbing noise is very welcome. ('Only nine hours . . . ?' I hear the ex-Shack maritime readers exclaim!)

We tidy up our own stations, clean off the displays, carefully stowing all the leads and leaving the ground crew with as little to do as possible.

Sitting on the crew bus, I see the fatigue of nine hours of Shack flying etched deep into grey faces as the crew board the dimly lit bus. It's back to the squadron for a quick, frank and effective de-brief before changing out of flying kit back into uniform and heading to the Bothy Bar in the Mess for a few beers.

The Bothy was something of an institution. It was a real crossroads where sooner or later you would meet an old mate from training or another squadron. Run on an honesty basis, it was a self-service aircrew bar made from two Mess bedrooms that had been knocked together. It was where you could ignore most Mess rules and drink in your uniform or flying suit after the seven pm witching hour before lurching off home. This was where the real one-on-one debriefs took place and what was said in the Bothy stayed there. It goes without saying that non-fliers were jealous of it and were constantly trying to close the place down as the boys were obviously having too much fun in there.

For the first hour or so after landing, our heads would still be ringing after exposure to four Griffons and multiple radios for nine hours and so it seemed like a good idea not to go home until our heads had cleared. Well, that's one explanation anyway.

Readers will not be astonished to learn that the mooted 1976 Boeing AWACS purchase was cancelled by the then Labour Government because, it was alleged, the over water performance of its radar was poor. The Shackleton carried on. A new contender took the place of the Boeing. Once again, the Nimrod was touted as being an ideal AEW aircraft. The Shackleton had only to manage for a few more years. The interested can find many sources that detail the unmitigated disaster of the Nimrod AEW3 project.

A converted Nimrod MR1 first flew with prototype AEW equipment on 16 July 1980. Work immediately went ahead but the Ministry of Defence imposed new and more rigid provisions for the radar. Phil Burton took over 8 Squadron, as he explains, shortly before experts claimed it would be supplanted by the Nimrod.

Bringing the Shackleton into service was a stroke of classically British brilliance. The RAF was entering the new era of Airborne Early Warning and Control (AEW&C) with a 1950s design airframe 'updated' by inserting a radar designed to counter the kamikaze threat in 1945. To add lustre to this decision by the top brass, the rationalisation revolved around the concept that the AEW Shackleton would only be in service for a few years before the all-singing, all-dancing Nimrod AEW 3 would enter service. This was, of course, an update of the six Nimrods that were bought to keep the politically important Woodford aircraft factory in business some years previously and which the RAF had not actually ordered at the time that the order was announced in the House of Commons.

I was told by the AOC in C Strike Command before I joined 8 Squadron in 1978 that I would be the last Shackleton CO; my successor in 1980 would be the new Nimrod AEW CO!

The good news was that the crews on 8 Squadron were

really good. The only problem was that everyone in the upper echelons kept telling them that they weren't that good (because all the really clever guys were selected for fast jets) and that the aircraft was a joke, an aged relic that was a not very good stopgap. Hence we were exempt all kinds of checks and tests, notably the Strike Command Taceval (Tactical Evaluation), and we had a very relaxed scramble time of two hours to bring in a crew and fire up a Shackleton to find the Soviet Naval Air Force Bear D and Bear F incursions into the UK Air Defence Region (UK ADR). The old MR Shackletons had usually scrambled in well under one hour for Search and Rescue.

So we changed all that. The air defence Quick Reaction Alert (QRA) team that was usually a pair of F4 Phantoms or Lightning Interceptor plus a Victor Tanker was soon joined by a Shackleton from Lossiemouth that was airborne in under an hour. Because the trade was normally coming from the north that meant that we were often passing Cape Wrath ahead of the jets and well before the Russians appeared.

The Kipper Fleet tradition was to fly the Shack for maximum range at fairly low speeds to conserve fuel and cover the greatest area while looking for submarines. This thinking was still in place in our Standard Operating Procedures (SOPs), and made worse by the tactic that the AEW Shack was simply an airborne radar aerial that would sit on one of the pre-ordained patrol points scattered round the UK ADR at around 8,000 feet, possibly flying at endurance speeds, which were even lower. To add lunacy to the tactic, it was ordained that main communication would be on the short range UHF radios, so the patrol points were all in line of sight to the main ground-based radars and Control and Reporting Centres. The furthest north was at Saxa Vord in the Shetlands.

I decided that none of that made sense. The object of the exercise was to detect the low-flying Bears as soon as possible as they approached the Iceland/UK gap. This took them further out into mid Atlantic, their hunting ground for the US Naval Task Forces, particularly the Carrier Groups, or to try to detect the British ballistic missile submarines as they left their home port at Faslane.

273

Accordingly, we simply went pretty close to flat out on a QRA scramble. We burned much fuel but made a lot of progress north and we abandoned the fixed AEW patrol points. The first reaction of the senior members of the hierarchy was horror that I was getting the squadron to break the rules, but the much earlier detection of the opposition soon changed all that.

We then changed further. The APS20F radar in the Shack effectively gave us a doughnut-shaped detection area on aircraft targets, with a good maximum range (well over 100 nautical miles) but a horrible lack of discrimination between aircraft and returns from waves and general 'surface clutter' that gave us a huge blind area over a significant distance from the Shackleton. The most skilled AEW radar operators could fine-tune the radar to hang on to a target, but, once lost, it was really hard to detect again. Generally we accepted that once the operator was getting down to one detection every six sweeps of the radar because of ground clutter we'd lost it.

So, by holding a steady position geographically, targets would fly into our doughnut-shaped detection area, move swiftly through it and then enter this huge blind area in which we only detected clutter. Some time later, the target could be re-acquired as it came out of the central clutter and into the detection doughnut. So we decided that we could improve our contact with the opposition by taking up a parallel or similar track, keeping the targets positioned in our good radar area for much longer. We called this 'running with the raid' and it was a huge success.

The then Head of the Central Tactics and Trials Organisation, Air Commodore Johnnie Walker (later Air Marshal Sir John) thought so too. He asked me to submit the new AEW tactics to him for evaluation, and we were awarded the Battle of Britain Memorial Trophy Sword for the best improvement in RAF tactics in 1980.

As we started to hone the tactics and drive the dear old Shack AEW2c as hard as was safe, 8 Squadron's morale and belief in itself rose exponentially. It was a huge squadron, with over 100 officers and around 200 ground crew, by far the biggest in the RAF at that time: as CO, I had more officers on the squadron than Binbrook had as a fighter base. Accordingly, we started going in for sports competitions not only against other squadrons but also other 11 Group fighter bases, and won most of them.

We managed then to get ourselves admitted to Taceval by the Strike Command Taceval Team. This was a fearsome process, with a call to operations in the run-up to a simulated war usually being at some awful hour, either in the early hours of the day or at the end of a normal working day.

We had to prepare immediately the maximum number of aircraft for operations and scramble one aircraft for QRA. The Taceval team used co-operating forces to generate targets for us and to fly fighter intercepts, as well as getting hard nut troops (usually Marine Commandos or Special Forces) to infiltrate the base and attack the squadron and our aircraft on the ground.

Sadly for the Taceval team on our first test they were working to the old rules, so we had to launch one aircraft in two hours, and the next in six hours to meet our goals. Nor were they ready for the aggressiveness of the squadron.

When the Taceval started we launched the first aircraft in thirty minutes, complete not only with its crew but also a set of ground crew under a Crew Chief with tools and simple spares that would keep the aircraft running away from base for a week or more. The Taceval team leader looked on surprised, but approvingly. An hour later we launched another aircraft into the dark, and half an hour later, another. All the while the ground crew under their leader, Squadron Leader Fred Pike, were busy preparing yet more aircraft and the aircrew were steadily being called in to fly. We ended up launching six aircraft pretty rapidly.

The Taceval team leader looked at his notes: this was not in the Taceval plan. He asked where these aircraft were going and what they were doing. I explained that, as RAF Lossiemouth held the only RAF squadron of AEW aircraft, it would be an early target for enemy attack. I was therefore dispersing aircraft away from Lossie to other bases. The crew captains had all the authority of Detachment Commanders to find accommodation and shelter and maintain their aircraft away from Lossiemouth and await further orders.

There was a flurry of phone calls in the night to and from the Taceval leader. They couldn't find, nor had they access to, the highly secret war plans for 11 Group and Strike Command which would give details of these measures. I knew them intimately because my tour of duty before coming to 8 Squadron had been as writer of these plans at HQ Strike Command. Our Shackletons and their crews simply started to disappear from Lossie. And I wouldn't tell them where, because they were not on my 'need to know' list.

I suggested that the leader should call Air Commodore Johnnie Walker for guidance from CTTO. Of course, Johnnie was in the loop and confirmed that this was what we should do, but of course he personally didn't know where the dispersed bases were.

To make matters worse, Johnnie Walker had helped us in one other way. Part of my war and contingency plans job had me working very closely with Special Forces, so I knew their capabilities well. I also knew that Johnnie had several pairs of state of the art heat-detecting monoculars on trial: I'd borrowed one set a few weeks previously and it was now stationed on top of one of our hangars. As the 'enemy' crept through the dunes behind the hangars we saw them and guided RAF Regiment teams to ambush positions. By dawn all the 'enemy' were safely locked up inside our most secure hangar while the Taceval team looked at their watches and waited for the panic to start.

Never again were the aircraft, officers and men of Shackleton 8 underrated by the hierarchy in the Headquarters.

As time went on in this glorious coming of age of RAF AEW&C, we had loads more fun. On QRA scrambles, often running at several a week, we started to encounter major Soviet exercises or deployment to Cuba. Instead of one or two Bears, we started to get waves of aircraft, both Bear D and Bear F and sometimes much modified Coot transports acting as electronic intelligence gatherers, or Badgers simulating missile attacks on carrier task groups.

The role of the fighters was usually to intercept every intruder and take close up photographs for our own intelligence purposes. But in these large Soviet operations we started to run out of fighters. I flew an early QRA trip on which this happened. The pair of Phantoms from Leuchars was chasing down three pairs of Bears. As the fourth pair of Bears appeared on the APS20F radar we asked the Victor Tanker pilot if he would mind positioning to identify these new intruders. He was delighted to do so and set off accordingly: we now had a four-engined jet fighter.

By the time we got to the sixth pair the Victor/fighter combination was running out of fuel to do any more. There was only one option, so we turned towards the last pair. The final run at Vne (Velocity Never Exceed speed) towards the estimated position of the Bears (they were well within our ground clutter) was a thrill, but we emerged from cloud just as a Bear F emerged from a nearby cloud. There was a distinct twitch to the controls of the first Bear as they sighted a nose-down Shack bearing down on them for the visual ID! Thereafter it became the goal of every crew to try to get a visual ID on a target from a Shack.

By 1979 the disaster of the Nimrod AEW3 was becoming all too apparent. 8 Squadron Shackletons were flying on safety watch over the Nimrod trials because the Nimrod AEW kit was performing so badly. We had officers from the Squadron actually engaged in the trials on the Nimrod AEW and their news confirmed what we saw in the air. I detached a few key people to do parallel work looking at what we really needed in the new generation AEW&C role.

Fortunately we had a good relationship with the USAF AEW aircraft detached to Iceland. Initially these were the EC 121, a modified Constellation, but they were then replaced with the Boeing E3 AWACS. We had to get on board these aircraft and see what they could do. As with all new bits of kit in the military, and particularly the USAF and USN, security was very tight and no one wanted to speak to us, let alone give us a ride in the aircraft such as we had enjoyed with the EC 121s. But we soon got the opening we needed.

On a QRA scramble a few days after the first AWACS of the 552nd AWAC Wing was deployed to Keflavik I was in the Shack hunting down two pairs of Bears east of Iceland.

We found them and vectored in our F4s from Leuchars for the visual ID. The radar team under our TACCO (Tactical Controller, the AEW team leader on the radar) also noted a large contact circling south-east of Iceland and two smaller faster aircraft that could only be the F4s of the Keflavik-based 57th Fighter Interceptor Squadron. The Bears went past them, quite close, but the fighters and AWACS just stayed where they were.

On return to Lossie, I went on the secure line to Keflavik Ops. I welcomed the AWACS to the North Atlantic and asked if everything was OK. I was reassured that all was 'A-OK'. I mentioned that we had a good ID and pictures from our Phantoms of four Bear F aircraft. There was a bit of a pause on the end of the line. We ended by agreeing that a Shackleton would pay a friendly visit to Keflavik.

We were treated to a friendly reception and repaired to the Snake Pit, the fairly unofficial bar in the BOQs, still in our flying suits. Late in the evening the hooter went off and the AWACS was scrambled. There was a rush for the aircraft and, somehow, some of us ended up on the AWACS as it launched after the trade. Once on station it wasn't long before we spotted the familiar gang of RAF fighters, Victor Tanker and Shackleton heading north from Scotland, but there was no sign of the Russians. An hour or so later, we could see our fighters starting to head west and then south-west, as did the Shackleton. This had a familiar ring to it, so I was given our Squadron chat frequency from the AWACS and called up our QRA crew.

They were a bit surprised, but we went through the simple procedure to authenticate who we were and then we got the shock. The APS20F had the Russians but the AWACS did not.

With a bit of rearrangement, we then had the Shack crew pass the bearings and range on the two Bears to the AWACS and the AWACS crew passed this to the USAF F4s. So the first intercept from an AWACS over the North Atlantic was done with the Shackleton Radar. So started a very close co-operation between the 552nd AWAC Wing and 8 Squadron which lasted for many years.

It seemed a strange pairing between the old and the newest technologies, but it brought together the skills and experience of the RAF and RN and the technology of the USAF. Our USAF exchange officer on 8 Squadron summarised it neatly: 'This squadron does more, with less, than any other flying unit that I know'. In a way, it was a fitting accolade for the aircraft too. The Shackleton AEW aircraft went out with head held high, and flown proudly by her crews right to the end.

Phil Burton was deservedly awarded the Air Force Cross for his work with 8 Squadron. He does insist that the decoration belongs to the squadron and not himself. No matter how much he protests, there is little doubt that Phil Burton lived up to the traditions of the service as a talented commander with principles. Like many pilots, indeed any aircrew, he constantly reminded himself of the immemorial maxim that probably dated back to the first accident in the Royal Flying Corps. In short, accidents come along when least expected. As he describes it:

I had the old adage about flying accidents proved to me as a commander of Number 8 Squadron. We were returning from an excellent long weekend in Gibraltar that had included an unscheduled eight-hour exercise with HMS *Fearless* the previous day. We got up at 0500 and by 0630 were getting a poor met forecast for the route home – lots of cumulonimbus and a steady 15 to 20 knots headwind. For a Shackleton, that's 10 per cent of true airspeed and it meant an eleven-hour sortie to Lossiemouth.

The start-up went slightly awry but we fixed the minor unserviceabilities. We took off only thirty minutes behind our plan. However, by the time we rounded the south-west tip of Portugal we already had more problems. Two of the RPM gauges were fluctuating – a normal Shackleton symptom that is usually the indicator but, of course, could be the engine. A third engine had low oil pressure – only just over the minimum, but again it was just serviceable. The fourth engine had a nasty oil leak from between the contra-rotating propellers. Again, that was a normal Shackleton problem but one that could necessitate shutting down the engine if it got too bad.

Individually, none of the problems was serious and the aircraft was still serviceable, but we crept up the Portuguese coast keeping a very close eye on our diversions. Off the northern coast of Spain we assessed our options, noted that nothing had got worse and set course for St Mawgan.

With a sigh of relief we saw the Scillies hove into sight although we were still dodging cumulonimbus. Our landfall was marked by a sudden increase in cheeriness among the crew. As we passed St Mawgan on the way to join airways at Brecon, all the nav kit failed. Panels came off and were put back on, Flight reference cards and fuse lists flicked and flapped and slowly we got the nav gear back, just in time to join at Brecon with sufficient gear to fly airways quite legally to Perth.

It soon became apparent that our best aid, the TACAN, was unreliable in bearing, and the flight up the airways was a real struggle as we sorted out when the bearing was good and when we had to ignore it. Added to which we were in continuous cloud with heavy rain, moderate icing and a fair bit of turbulence.

Then, as we left Perth at FL85, the miracle happened. We burst out of cloud into a beautiful Scottish night. Sitting in the right-hand pilot's seat, I could see the lights of Aberdeen gleaming brightly sixty miles away. To the left we could see Inverness and ahead of us were the welcoming lights of Elgin and Forres. Approach came up loud and clear on VHF confirming a light wind, unlimited visibility and no low cloud at base. Fifteen hours after getting up all was well for the first time.

We gleefully requested descent with radar vectors, confirming that we were VMC and that we were in visual contact with the ground below us. Successively we received VFR clearance to FL65, then 5,000 feet and 4,000 feet. We started on the pre-joining checks and the crew brief for an approach with radar vectors to a visual approach to land. The lengthy checks were interrupted by further clearances, first to 3,000 feet and then to 2,000 feet. It crossed my mind that the young lass in Approach was a bit harassed with the number of aircraft making approaches – including two 'foreigners' who didn't quite understand all that they were told and had poor VHF communications. We helped out by re-transmitting messages, interrupting our checks to do so.

The aircraft was now being flown by the regular crew captain, 'Beery' Weir, from the left-hand seat, and I was sitting in the right hand seat doing my usual 'competent co-pilot' act for a squadron commander's check. The joining checks flowed on as something strange caught my eye. I looked up at the beautiful night outside. What was wrong? Nothing really – just those anti-collision lights winking brightly from the Atlantic aircraft some distance away.

But there was something wrong. The town lights just short of the airfield were the wrong shape. The checks rattled on 'Bomb Doors – closed MI Black' as I puzzled at the phenomenon. There was no doubt about it now – there was a big black bite into the bottom right-hand corner of the town's street lights. Cloud? No – a hill – a BIG HILL. 'CLIMB LEFT!' I shouted at the captain, ramming up the RPM levers and the throttles, 'Hill ahead!' I glanced automatically at the altimeter – 2,300 feet – as we pulled up. Magically, the town lights reappeared and resumed their proper geometry. A very shaken crew resumed their approach checks and we landed without further incident ten minutes later.

Afterwards on the ground the back-plot told the horrifying story. As we pulled up we had been heading for the left side of a hill 2,800 feet high. At the pull-up we were about one mile from the nearest ground on track at our height. Even in a Shackleton, that's only twenty seconds' flying time. In clear VMC, with a fully serviceable aircraft with two Master Green pilots with over 16,000 hrs flying time between them we had been twenty seconds from disaster. Why?

Well, yes, we had been up a long time. Yes, we were tired. Yes, we had 'heard' our VMC descent clearance when the tapes revealed a VFR descent clearance with terrain avoidance our responsibility. Yes, the young lass in Approach was inexperienced. Yes, the R/T was busy, and the situation was complicated by the foreign visitors so she just hadn't noticed that our height checks were far too low for our radar positions.

But most of all, we had relaxed too much as a crew. We simply didn't expect something as basic as being too low. We had been unaware of the dangers of returning to our own base. I wonder how many unexplained accidents have happened that way?

Phil Burton, long retired from Shackletons, but still flying his own aeroplane, has never let it happen to him again. He hopes, as everyone in aviation hopes, that it never happens to somebody else either.

CHAPTER SIXTEEN

Another Nimrod AEW prototype flew on 9 March 1982. The technical specification had changed yet again — several times over. Attempts to discontinue the Nimrod AEW project were not uncommon. The airframe was much smaller than that of the Boeing AWACS. This resulted in the available equipment being crammed into cupboards the size of filing cabinets, a process that gave precious little room for operation. Doubts arose as to whether the apparatus could manage the proposed task. Despite strenuous efforts by the industry, this proved to sadly be the case.

The Royal Air Force did finally receive a Nimrod AEW aircraft for joint trials with the industry in 1984 on a date that coincided with a full review of the AEW requirement. To cut a long and dismal story exceptionally short, a review in September 1986 eventually decided to end the Nimrod AEW project and selected the Boeing E3 as the most suitable aircraft. The Nimrod AEW3 programme was a total, hideously expensive shambles, its deficiencies underlined by the Falklands War. Ships were lost and brave men died for the lack of AEW cover. Matters had not improved with the decision of John Nott, Margaret Thatcher's Conservative Minister of Defence in 1981, to halve the strength of 8 Squadron. Six Shackletons went to the junk yard.

The final six Shackletons in service were Florence, Mr Rusty, Brian, Mr MacHenry, Ermintrude and Rosalie.

During its Shackleton times, 8 Squadron was home to some fine eccentrics. Amongst them was Bill Houldsworth who had been involved with the Christmas Island flights. He made the 24 hour 36 minute flight in a Mk3 Shackleton and also claimed the record for flying at the lowest height, namely zero feet, when he served with 204 Squadron. His aircraft bounced off the sea, losing the belly antenna but otherwise surviving. Kevin Byron met him at Lossiemouth:

My first captain on Shackletons was a gnarled little dwarf with bandy legs called Bill Houldsworth, God rest him. He was a nice enough old buffer except that he had one overriding ambition in life – to be the pilot with the most flying hours on the Shackleton. His rival for the title was a chap named John Elias who had amassed a total of about 12,000 hours on type, and then been posted to maritime patrol Nimrods, and was currently based at the other end of the country at RAF St Mawgan.

Every time we visited St Mawgan Bill used to trap John in the bar and enquire whether there was any chance that he would be posted back to Shackletons. To this, John always replied that he'd love to be posted back but he had been told that he would finish his flying career on Nimrods. Bill used to drive us mad, punching holes in the sky for no other reason than to accumulate flying hours. On one occasion we were engaged in a NATO exercise as the most northerly of three Shackletons strung out down the North Sea. We formed, we believed, a radar barrier to attacks from Continental Europe, and, as such, we were closest to base. After about ten hours on task the end of the exercise was declared. Instead of turning north-west for home, Bill turned south-east. We watched on our radar as the other two Shackletons flew past us and around the corner towards base before we turned back and followed them. We were airborne two hours longer than was necessary. At this point, Bill really lost any sympathy that the crew had with him and a deputation of the more senior crew members went to see our squadron commander to tell him that if Bill didn't stop this nonsense, nobody would fly with him. Shortly afterward, Bill achieved his record, beating John

Elias' total by about 200 hours. He arranged a final ground tour for himself in station operations at RAF Coningsby in Lincolnshire. You can imagine our hilarity when, about two months later, John Elias was posted from Nimrods to our squadron. He went on to amass an amazing total way above Bill's – and a career total of 17,000hrs.

The main documents show John Elias clocked 12,297 hours in all on the Shackleton in a career which saw him fly in every variant of the Growler.

The disagreement in the South Atlantic about the sovereignty of the Falkland Islands required Shackleton services in the AEW role. They simply could not get there, particularly as the transit was by way of Buenos Aires. The Falkland Islands also lacked Avgas supplies so the British response lacked vital equipment. The conflict began in 1982 and the bitter words outside the public domain between politicians, admirals and air marshals are better left undisturbed. Sufficient to say that, despite fine sentences from Downing Street, many of the military felt that, as usual, they had been expected to do a vital job with the wrong equipment – and even if it had been the right gear there was too little of it. As the armed forces had become well accustomed to functioning with less than the ideal, the final result was duly greeted with cheers and approbation.

Geoff Cooper also ended up in an aircraft flown by John Elias, in a slightly nerve-wracking encounter:

I was scheduled to fly WR963 on a routine air test with Squadron Leader John Elias on 9 September 1980. John was reputed to have around 18,000hrs in his log book and was believed to be the RAF's top hours man.

The crew consisted of two pilots, a flight engineer, a navigator and a scopey (me). The plan was, after wheels up, to carry out a V2 climb up to one thousand feet, then depart Lossiemouth for the Moray Firth for the rest of the sortie.

Following a short brief, we took the bus out to the aircraft and started up in accordance with SOPs. Following this we called Lossie ATC to request taxy clearance. I was in the astrodome as a look-out while the nav went through the pre-take-off checks on intercom. After running up the engines in pairs to check the magnetos – an absolutely deafening operation for whoever was up in the 'dome – the pilots reduced the RPM to a more civilised level before continuing to the active runway threshold. Once the checks were complete and all confirmed they were strapped in, we turned on to Runway 23.

At around 60 kts, the tail came up. After a few exploratory bounces on the massive single tyred mainwheels, we were airborne.

'Brakes on – off, undercarriage up, please.' John pulled back on the column to instigate the V2 climb. At one thousand feet, he pushed the stick forward to level off as per the brief and at this point things began to go wrong. The nose started to rise again so he automatically wound in some nose-down trim. The nose continued to rise so he wound in some more nose-down trim and immediately felt a further increase in the force required to keep things level. He started keeping a closer eye on the airspeed which by now was starting to decay. He asked the co-pilot to assist him with holding the nose down as the required stick forces were becoming fairly significant.

From my position in the rear, I naturally started taking a more than keen interest in this dialogue and at the same time could feel the onset of the familiar wallow and sound of the airflow around the aeroplane as it approached the stall. Suddenly, one thousand feet up in a Shack didn't seem such a good place to be.

The captain came up on intercom and told the crew to put out a Mayday 'as we were going to crash.' This order removed all remaining doubt from my mind. If John Elias thought we were going to crash then we were going to crash. The nav transmitted a Mayday on Guard and I transmitted a belt and braces Mayday on our squadron company frequency (straight through to our Ops desk). I received the standard response of 'Pan Zero, transport booked' from some clown (I was never able to find out who) who clearly didn't have his entire mind on the job.

Meanwhile, back in the air – fortunately Kinloss Runway

286

26 was almost dead ahead. Those few short miles to Kinloss seemed interminable as we staggered through the air just above the stall with both pilots working manfully to keep the nose from rearing up. I looked out of the side window to see cars beetling from Duffus towards Elgin completely unaware that, just a few hundred feet above them, we were engaged in a life or death struggle. It was the longest few minutes of my life.

Suddenly we were over the threshold of Runway 26 at Kinloss. We landed with the usual yowp of rubber, took the first exit off the runway, stopped and shut down. I opened the rear door, put the ladder out and I'll never forget the feel of terra firma under my feet. As the rest of the crew jumped out, I noticed that they all had the same grey, bloodless faces. I remember feeling the wind cooling the sweat on the back of my neck as we stood to one side and had a quick fag.

John said that he thought he knew what the cause of the problem was – that the elevator trim had been connected in the wrong sense, so that winding in nose-down trim had the opposite effect to that desired, i.e. the nose came up more – but 1,000 feet up on the edge of the stall was not the place to test his theory.

Later engineering investigation proved that this was indeed the case.

Time airborne? Five minutes.

The handful of Shackletons in service with 8 Squadron had flown for more than two decades without a fatal accident marring their service. As the time for their replacement in the AEW role came ever closer, the thought that 8 Squadron would reach the end of its Shackleton operations with no fatal accident against it became ever stronger. A good number of its flight deck crew were former Kipper Fleet men who had absorbed every facet of Shackleton flying. The accident of 30 April 1990 when WR965 crashed in the Outer Hebrides distressed every squadron member.

Charlie Montgomery takes up the story:

Coastal Command had adopted protective measures to avoid Controlled Flight Into Terrain. Although the number of

Shackleton aircraft in service was much diminished, knowledge gained from previous disasters had been applied. Protective measures for the safe conduct of low-level flight had developed before all the sophisticated kit in current use became available. It was quite simple. Operations were classed as Offshore or Inshore. Offshore, by definition, meant that there was no land within 50 nautical miles of the operating area. In Offshore Ops, the crew could descend to the Minimum Operating Altitude (MOA) normally 100 feet Above Sea Level (ASL) with the radar off, or in a tactical mode such as side sector scan.

In Inshore Ops, the aircraft had to work in Visual Meteorological Conditions (VMC) to allow descent below Safety Altitude. Safety Altitude is the height of the highest ground in the area, plus 1,000 feet supplemented by an extra 10 per cent. Thus if the highest ground is 3,000 feet, the Safety Altitude is 3,000 plus 1,000 to a total of 4,000 with the supplementary 10 per cent which gives a working height of 4,400 feet. If the aircraft is on a published approach to an airfield, the appropriate minima for the approach must be applied. If the aircraft is to be flown in conditions of less than VMC, it must be above Safety Altitude, or the radar must be in all-round scan. Simple; if you go into cloud or mist Inshore, you must either climb to Safety Altitude or call the radar to all-round scan.

On Monday 30 April 1990, Wing Commander Steve Roncoroni, now the commanding officer of Number 8 Squadron, was the captain of an AEW Shackleton tasked for a training exercise off the west coast of Scotland. Having carried out the first part of the exercise, they were approached by a Tornado F3 fighter for photography. In accordance with Standard Procedure, the radar was switched off whilst another aircraft was in close proximity.

The next part of the training was to fly an instrument approach to the civil airport at Benbecula. The crew reported their position and air traffic gave them clearance for the approach. Witnesses, including RAF personnel, heard the unmistakable sound of a Shackleton above them. They were familiar with the distinctive roar of four Rolls-Royce

Griffons, as it was quite different from the other aircraft that frequented Benbecula. Then, abruptly, the noise stopped. The Shackleton had flown into a hill, a mere thirty feet from the summit; all the crew were killed instantly. Subsequent investigation showed that the position the Shack reported to ATC was fifteen miles in error. Realising that they were not on the correct track for the approach, the pilots had started a climb. However, the engines were at cruise power. Had they selected a higher RPM setting for the approach (2,600 or Max RPM) much more thrust would have been available for the climb.

Thirty feet! What a tragedy.

Now for the spooky bit. By fluke of circumstance, Steve Roncoroni cheated death in a Shackleton crash in the Scottish Highlands in December 1967. He then perished in a crash, on the same type of aircraft, which by then was almost obsolete, twenty-two years later, just seventy-two miles from where his original crew died.

Who knows what the Fates have in store?

Kevin Byron supplies a postscript to the story that simply shows that seriousness has its place and that humour arrives on the most unlikely occasions.

Apart from our usual duties of Airborne Early Warning (AEW) and Search and Rescue (SAR), we used to pick up all sorts of strange little tasks, one of which was dropping people's ashes (usually those of ex-RAF members or, occasionally, their family's). This was a task that was fraught with potential problems.

The last drop we did was particularly sad because it was for one of our own squadron members who had been killed, along with the rest of the crew, in a collision with a hilltop hidden in cloud, back in 1990. Anyway, young Graham had been a keen hill walker and had always asked to have his ashes scattered along the Pennine Way, a famous route for hill walkers down the spine of northern England. His family asked if they could be on board to carry out the drop themselves so, determined that we were not going to have a cock-up, our engineers constructed a wonderful piece of equipment, which looked rather like a bazooka. It consisted of a steel pipe, which exactly fitted the diameter of the flare chute.

Handles were fitted to ease carrying it and to stop the pipe slipping down the chute and being lost. Finally, it had a cunning arrangement of two lids at top and bottom. These were joined by a long rod with a spring which ran through the top lid, but opened the bottom lid when the knob at the top of the rod was pressed. This released the ashes. Until then, they were securely confined between the two lids. Young Graham's ashes would be loaded into this device.

His family were to be picked up at Manchester Airport, about ninety minutes flight south from our base. We decided, just to be on the safe side, that we would make a trial run en route, using some ashes from a wood burning stove. These were duly loaded into the tube on the ground. As we arrived at the aircraft, we were met by the young padre who was to officiate. 'That's an impressive-looking piece of kit,' he opined. 'How does it work?' On having it explained to him he, in all innocence, pushed the handle. The wood ashes fell in a pile on the dispersal. The ground crew didn't know about the trial drop and thought that the ashes were Graham. There was a look of horror followed by frantic activity as my mate who was carrying the gizmo said, 'Well, don't just stand there. Get something to sweep him up before we lose him!' They were not too amused when we let them into the secret later on.

You will be pleased to hear, however, that the trial was fine. We refilled the tube with Graham on the journey and his family carried out the drop by all putting their hands on the knob and pressing together.

It passed off faultlessly.

For those who perhaps think that the Royal Air Force has lost such compassion, a short note suffices. Scrote's own ashes were dropped over the Moray Firth on 27 June 2009 from a Sea King HAR3 from 'D' Flight, 202 Squadron SAR Flight based at Kinloss.

The Shackleton spent longer in the employment of the country than any of the men who flew her. She was an unsung heroine of the Cold War, unfashionable even when new. She spent forty years in an unglamorous, largely unseen duty, fulfilling a necessary task against an enemy who waited outside the gate.

She and her crews found themselves not only at the extremities of the UK but also in the furthest reaches of the world. When she finally finished her time of wearing blue, white and red roundels, her passing went largely unmourned except by those who had flown and maintained her.

History is fashioned from remembrance. As long as the aircrew and ground crew live, the morning sun will rise each dawn on the bulk of a faded Shackleton. As long as those who sat in her, flew her or prepared her for flight, continue to breathe, the aeroplane will stay alive. The dew inside the cockpit windows will fade away. The hulk will creak as the sun warms it while the voices of the hundreds who served the aeroplane will sound again in the minds of men who remember.

When all have gone, gone to join the knights who fought at Agincourt, the sailors who faced the Armada, the British infantry who waited for German grenadiers and all the others who have marked our little British world, their words will remain to pay homage to the Shackleton. Their anecdotes will become a segment of tapestry, connecting earlier times and being bound by those who come after. History does not stand still.

The last Shackletons to fly in the Royal Air Force left the Service in July 1991. *The Magic Roundabout* ground to a halt. Florence, or WL747, took the record for the longest active service at nineteen years and three months. She finished her days as a derelict wreck at Paphos in Cyprus. Ermintrude, also known as WR963, clocked up the greatest number of flying hours for any Shackleton, finishing her career with 15,431 total hours. She fared rather better and lives at Coventry Airport, the property of the Shackleton Preservation Trust. Mr McHenry, wearing the US registration NW790WL in tribute to its service identity of WL790, made the final Shackleton flight to Tucson Arizona from Texas on 9 December 2007 to go on static display.

The Newark Air Museum at Winthorpe has WR977 and Gatwick Aviation Museum displays WR982 whose engines are fired up on Open Days. Manchester's Museum of Science and Industry exhibits Shackleton WR960, described as ' the most complete and best-preserved extant example'.

Static display aircraft are akin to stuffed specimens of extinct wildlife. Aeroplanes should be seen in their natural element, the air. For the men who flew her, for those who serviced her, the Shackleton took a special place in their affections. She was certainly noisy and shook as if she suffered from ague. Her crews became accustomed to shivering with cold in the front and suffering heat stroke in the back. The Griffons leaked oil around the globe but the whole mixture never lost the faith of those who served. She killed more men than any other RAF aircraft in the piping days of peace but they never stopped admiring her. She was a reminder of a vanished age. Forty years of service was no bad accomplishment for a front-line piston-engined aircraft in an era of jet aeroplanes. Even when new, she acted as a stark reminder of an earlier time. She nudged memories, emphasised the power of the air. She was the last of the breed with four piston engines and nothing after her looked remotely the same.

1991 was a most appropriate year for the Old Grey Lady to finally leave the Royal Air Force. That same year, the first female navigator and pilot joined active RAF squadrons. Die-hards firmly believed that the aeroplane welcomed a man's firm handling.

Three of those who served her give their opinions, not of the aeroplane, but of the spirit that she inspired.

From Trevor Dobson:

On reflection they were two interesting and happy years working with a good bunch of men where discipline was relaxed as far as dress for work was concerned, wearing only shorts and shoes for work during the summer months but no slacking where aircraft were concerned as aircrew lives could be put at risk.

From Douglas Wilson:

It must never be forgotten that lives were lost in Shackletons during the Cold War although none were due to combat action. Remember the aircraft by all means but let's not forget the crews and the ground crews. the ops staff, air traffic, the medical section, the fire section, the safety equipment workers, the MT section and the in-flight caterers. They all had a part to play in getting an aircraft airborne. You work as a member of a crew, as a member of a squadron, as a member of a wing, as a member of a station and as a member of a Group and Command within the overall function of the Royal Air Force. The team counts.

From Tom Holland:

I must mention 'B' Flight, the people who keep us in the air. The flight commander was a general duties officer like me, Squadron Leader Stott. Jim Stott, a navigator, for most of the time I was there but he was not posted as a navigator but commanded the ground crew. He had a specialist engineer warrant officer. Warrant Officer Taylor was absolutely first class. He was a very, very good engineer but, more important in his position, he was very good at organising the servicing of the aircraft.

He was backed up by some really excellent senior NCOs and airmen but of course not only did we have to train but they had to train, so when we were operating funny hours, they were operating funny hours, so it was a typical squadron. It just happened to be a Shackleton squadron. It would be done on any squadron but those fellows were experts on all Shackleton equipment and I found them totally reliable. I can't think of any incident at all when I would have found one of the servicing crew at fault and it was a real pleasure to have people like that working with you. I don't say 'for you' – they were providing aeroplanes for us but they were working very much with us.

There is no Shackleton still flying. Hopes remain that a survivor may one day growl overhead again. Until that happens, if ever, given that her Griffons need impressive quantities of increasingly rare and more expensive high-octane aviation fuel, the venerable aeroplane who served so well for so many years can be seen in the air only on film.

The Old Grey Lady, like other long gone stars, continues to charm.

ALPHABETICAL INDEX

Service ranks and other titles are not given in this index. Many listed below are quoted directly while others have given extremely helpful information.

A few peripheral individual references, which do not relate directly to the life and work of the Shackleton, are omitted from this index.

Robson, Dickie 256
Roe, Alliott Verdon 1, 2, 3, 58
Rogers, Mike 90,107
Rolls, C S 12
Roncoroni, Steve 197, 199, 288, 289
Royce, F H 12, 13

S
Salta 163
Scampton 39, 40, 42
Scott, Lionel Derek 158, 159
Seletar 141, 151, 191
Sharjah 109, 110, 154, 223, 224, 227, 228, 234, 235, 236, 241
Shackleton
  VP254 21, 114, 115
  VP258 78
  VP259 56, 99
  VP261 40, 41, 42, 49
  VP263 22
  VP268 21
  VP281 21
  VP283 25
  VP286 48
  VP294 22, 141
  WB818 141
  WB828 94
  WB833 199
  WB835 113
  WG511 38
  WG531 65, 66
  WG533 146
  WL739 144
  WL741 250
  WL743 65, 67
  WL745 50
  WL746 61
  WL747 250, 291
  WL749 55
  WL751 91
  WL752 91
  WL753 91
  WL754 250

  WL756 250
  WL757 161, 250
  WL758 91, 173, 228
  WL786 190
  WL789 59
  WL790 250, 291
  WL792 95
  WL793 250
  WL794 63
  WL795 250
  WL800 112, 213
  WR955 212
  WR957 109
  WR959 109
  WR960 250, 291
  WR961 109
  WR963 250, 285, 291
  WR965 250, 287
  WR967 250, 251
  WR968 141
  WR969 109
  WR970 73, 82, 84
  WR973 175
  WR976 193
  WR977 184, 291
  WR982 291
  WR988 125
  XF702 196
  XF710 165
Shackleton Song 251, 252
St Athan 28
St Eval 15, 30, 38, 39, 44, 48, 57, 62, 65, 72, 73, 90, 109, 112, 233
St Mawgan 16, 31, 59, 67, 70, 71, 77, 86, 103, 108, 112, 113, 121, 130, 136, 146, 150, 157, 159, 162, 176, 178, 194, 206, 208, 233, 280, 284
Silent Enemy, The (film) 77
Singapore 57, 113, 114, 152, 190, 191, 192, 202, 253, 256
Smith, Ian 180, 181, 185,
Smith, Mike 207–210